Nathalie Dupree Cooks for Family and Friends

Nathalie Dupree Cooks for Family and Friends

WILLIAM MORROW AND COMPANY, INC.
NEW YORK

With thanks to
Kay Calvert, Sue Hunter,
and Ray Overton.

Copyright © 1991 by Nathalie Dupree

Illustrations by Christine A. Richie

It is the policy of William Morrow and Company, Inc., and its imprints and affiliates, recognizing the importance of preserving what has been written, to print the books we publish on acid-free paper, and we exert our best efforts to that end.

Library of Congress Cataloging-in-Publication Data has been ordered.
Dupree, Nathalie.
NATHALIE DUPREE COOKS FOR FAMILY AND FRIENDS
ISBN 0-688-09767-7

90-28857
CIP

Printed in the United States of America

First Edition

1 2 3 4 5 6 7 8 9 10

BOOK DESIGN BY TASHA HALL

Acknowledgments

Recipes are not created in a vacuum. They are the result of the many people whom I've learned from, lived with, taught to, cooked for—family and friends as well as all those cookbook authors who pass through Atlanta each year and whose books I have used and enjoyed and been inspired by. Their influence is gratefully acknowledged: Annie Audsley, Bill Baker, Cynthia's Uncle Ben, Rose Beranbaum, Guiliano Bugialli, Elizabeth Burris, Kay Calvert, Robert Carrier, Forsythia Chang, Julia Child, Bernard Clayton, Dudley Clendinen, Betty Collins, Evelyn Cook, Bob Coram, Shirley Corriher, Judy Davis, Will Deller, Ecole de Gastronomie Française Ritz-Escoffier, Merle Ellis, Mariella Fante, Cliff Graubart, Bert Greene, Randy Harris, George Heery, Sue Hunter, Cynthia Jubera, Ann Kay, Richard Lands, Carey LeGrange, London Cordon Bleu, Veronica Love, Bob Lynn, Abby Mandel, John Markham, Lillian Marshall, Julia Martin, Vickie Mooney, Barbara Morgan, Jeff and Jinx Morgan, Joan Nathan, Dave Norman, Ray Overton, Russ Parsons, Jacques Pépin, Paul Prudhomme, Gayle Robbins, Barbara Robinson, Barbara St. Amand, Roberta Salma, Candy Sheehan, Philip Schultz, Denice Skrepcinski, Jeff Smith, Cynthia Stevens, Marion Sullivan, Margaret Ann Surber, Audrey and Pierre-Henri Thiault, Henri Thiault, Jozette Thiault, Terry Thompson, Elizabeth Tilden, Gregory Usher, Chef Thomas Valenti, Jean Van den Berg, Julius Walker, Gail Wescott, Anne Willan, and Martin Yan.

Evie Righter contributed a great deal in her copyediting of this book.

And thanks again to the friends pictured on the cover: Kay Calvert, Dudley Clendinen, Whitney Clendinen, Evelyn Cook, Will Deller, Mimi Hails, Sue Hunter, Richard Lands, Nigel Levine, Beverly Molander, Cynthia Stevens, and Marion Sullivan.

Contents

Nathalie Dupree Cooks for Family and Friends

Introduction

Nathalie Dupree Cooks for Family and Friends is meant for real life, for people who cook at home, on boats or at campfires, with interruptions, children, dogs, cats, telephones, doorbells, neighbors, friends, bosses, car pools, jobs, deadlines, funerals, weddings, bad days and good days. It is meant to accommodate them, to make the cooking and serving of food a joyous pleasure whenever possible, bringing with each meal a sense of nurturing and warmth.

Some of my favorite times are when my friends have me to their homes for casual meals, sometimes fashionably smart and a bit upscale, and other times for everyday baked beans. And who would give up those special, ritzy moments? The wedding supper for a best friend's daughter, the celebration of a promotion, and the family Christmas Eve dinner of bouillabaisse are all times when we put forth our best effort.

My mother says I "never knew a stranger." I can meet people and feel within minutes I've known them my whole life.

In my early twenties, I lived briefly in a small walk-up flat in New York. I spread newspapers on the floor of the postage-stamp-sized living room, and there, sitting in front of the curtainless windows reflecting the lights of the Village, four of us ate shrimp, clams, and lobsters, dabbed our mouths with paper napkins, and tossed the residue on the newspapers where we sat. We laughed and cried as we recalled our Virginia home and days growing up, peeling shrimp, and digging out clams.

Now, my home is Atlanta, Georgia, where I can eat outdoors nine months of the year, spreading newspapers on the tables on my deck, celebrating my friend Alma's birthday the same way I did as an impoverished copy editor.

The food hasn't changed much, nor the conviviality—only the walls containing the laughter. Both times the meals were incredibly cheap due to a bountiful harvest in nearby waters, bringing one of America's magical feasts within reach. The food could have been anything that was slightly messy, eaten with the fingers—mussels or crabs or clams in a bucket, lobsters or shrimp or even fried chicken. It was the vehicle for shared memories, for touching each other's lives, for expressing support and affection in good times and bad.

Designed for the individual who uses the ingredients at hand to produce the best possible food in the time allotted, this book notes what may be frozen, and if a dish is quick and easy. It doesn't strive to duplicate restaurant food that needs special equipment. It does provide occasional challenges, but no last minute duress to ruin the pleasure of the moment.

I do not picture my readers surrounded by staff and imagine they perhaps don't even have a helping hand in the kitchen. So, much of the food may be fixed ahead of serving time, like the cassoulet in stages, able to be reheated or perhaps frozen.

Everything used is available at my local grocery store, with the exception of Parmigiano Reggiano, which I special order. I use real food—no manufactured sugar or fat substitutes, whips, and dips. The recipes are geared towards a balanced diet, and the way that my viewers tell me they eat today.

The book is arranged according to the way I think people divide their cooking experiences and their lives. Each chapter provides the core courses for a type of meal, with each chapter being a little more upscale than the previous one. The book follows a natural progression from the basics—home food plain and simple, to fancier home fare, and then on to elegant entertaining. It rounds off with a note of "sweet inspirations" as does a full-service well-planned meal.

The courses in each chapter are arranged progressively from standup food and appetizers to soups, entrees, and brunch. "Everyday Fare" is just that, the core for the casual gourmet—a range of the meals the home cook, single, married, eating alone or with others, can choose from for everyday fare. It is by and large familiar food, sometimes spicy, sometimes cheap, sometimes a little challenging. Some recipes may play a roving part in the meal, from starter to main course.

A dish from one chapter will work very well with menu items from other chapters. You can mix and match—mix for variety and match for compatibility.

These menus were designed for family and friends, but remember —your ritziest friends would welcome an everyday meal; your family, who are your most important friends and associates, would welcome a fancy dinner done just for them.

All the recipes in the television series, *Food for Family and Friends*, to air in fall 1991 on over 240 public television stations, can be found in this companion book.

Everyday

Fare

Everyday meals are important meals. They form the nucleus of the memories of life. Who does not remember the soup their mother brought them when they were ill or the moussaka or spaghetti served every week as much—or more—than formal dinners when everyone in the family was on their best behavior for a visiting personage. Or the cookie served after school, dipped in milk to soften slightly?

It is from everyday meals we pull when we remember our favorite meals—spaghetti, meatloaf, moussaka, for instance. And it is everyday meals that are the hardest. Whether feeding oneself or a family, it is the daily repetition that is hard, the possibility of few compliments—combined with the pressures of rushing home after work, meeting or car pools and having to cook on a near empty stomach. So everyday meals need to be meals that can be easily prepared by the harrassed and harried as well as those who have time to spare and can afford to work leisurely—if any such still exist!

My idea of an everyday meal is not something that comes out of a box or the grocery store freezer case. But it should not be an onerous chore to prepare an everyday meal. I don't try to make everything from scratch every day. I operate a lot out of the freezer and refrigerator, combining a leftover of last night's with a casserole from the freezer. In fact, I might be reheating something from the freezer while browning meat for tomorrow's meal, doing two things at one time, one for today, or for tomorrow, when I know I'll have no time.

There are three babies in my daily life, so there is a high chair in the corner of the living room, and a playpen junks up the stairwell. One is the son of my TV producer, Cynthia, and her husband, Cliff. I introduced them and was their matron of honor when they were married in Italy. The second baby, Nigel, the son of my former roommate Beverly and her husband, Blair, seems to have a greater affection for the cat food in crawling distance than he does my food, while the third, Elizabeth's Ryan, came into Elizabeth and Bob's life when she was doing the publicity for my television show.

When these babies and their parents come to supper, it is quite a different occasion from a smart dinner party. That doesn't mean everything is mundane, however, as I might whip my most gorgeous cake out of the freezer, after serving a casserole that can be reheated and eaten in spurts between picking up Cheerios thrown on the floor. I'd rather have a baby in the house than an immaculate carpet.

And so we'll all remember the day this baby walked, or that baby talked, by what we ate together that night. Just another everyday dinner.

Appetizers and Soups

Yogurt Cheese

MAKES 1 CUP OR 3/4 POUND

This is a lower-calorie substitute for cream cheese. One cup of low-fat yogurt has 140 calories; one cup of cream cheese has 790 calories. I like this with crackers. For herb cheese, add 3 to 4 tablespoons chopped fresh basil, thyme, or other herbs. For a sweet spread, add cinnamon.

1 (16-ounce) container plain
    yogurt

Empty the yogurt into a piece of cheesecloth. Tie it well, then suspend it over a dish, and let drain overnight in the refrigerator. Remove the yogurt cheese to a covered container. Keeps, covered, 1 week or so in the refrigerator.

Tangy Yogurt Cheese Ball

MAKES A 1½-POUND CHEESE BALL

This pretty, multicolor-flecked cheese ball is not really low-cal, but it is certainly lower in calories than many others. It's usual for me now to make up a batch of yogurt cheese to keep on hand for this appetizer.

2 cups Yogurt Cheese (recipe precedes)
½ cup shredded or chopped Cheddar cheese
¼ cup shredded or chopped Mozzarella cheese
¼ cup shredded or chopped Monterey Jack cheese
½ cup chopped cooked ham
¼ cup fresh bread crumbs
1 tablespoon Dijon mustard

½ to 1 teaspoon cayenne pepper
1 heaping tablespoon finely chopped fresh basil
1 heaping teaspoon finely chopped fresh oregano
1 heaping teaspoon finely chopped fresh Italian parsley
Salt
Freshly ground black pepper
1 cup chopped pecans

In large bowl, combine the yogurt cheese, Cheddar, Mozzarella, Monterey Jack, ham, bread crumbs, Dijon mustard, cayenne, basil, oregano, Italian parsley, and salt and pepper to taste. Form the mixture into a ball and wrap it in a double layer of cheesecloth, then in plastic wrap. Refrigerate at least 6 hours to allow the flavors to mellow. Remove from refrigerator and unwrap. Roll the cheese ball in the chopped pecans.

The cheese ball freezes well and thaws in the refrigerator in only a few hours.

Grilled French Sandwiches

SERVES 6

This open-faced sandwich of bubbly cheese, flecked with red pepper and black olives, gives you many options. Use as an appetizer; or, serve it for lunch, as a snack, or, as an accompaniment to a soup supper. And add 6 slices of fried bacon, crumbled if you desire meat.

¼ cup butter, softened
½ cup freshly grated imported
    Parmesan cheese
1 cup black olives or Niçoise
    olives, pitted and chopped
1 roasted red pepper, peeled
    and chopped (page 99)
2 heaping tablespoons finely
    chopped fresh herbs, such as
    basil, oregano, rosemary, or
    Italian parsley
3 small loaves French or
    sourdough bread, halved
    lengthwise

1 cup assorted cheeses:
    (1½ ounces per slice)
    Crumbled Yogurt Cheese
      (recipe follows)
    Crushed Brie cheese
    Grated smoked Gouda
      cheese
    Grated Cheddar cheese
    Crumbled Montrachet
      cheese
    Crumbled Mozzarella cheese

Preheat the broiler. Combine the butter, ⅓ cup of the Parmesan, the olives, red pepper, and herbs until well mixed. Spread on the bread halves. Top with your choice of cheeses. Sprinkle on the remaining Parmesan. Broil 3 inches from the heat, 1 to 2 minutes, until golden and bubbly.

Broiled Cheese Fingers

MAKES 8 STRIPS

Ordinary bread and cheese is instantly transformed into a tasty spicy treat to serve hot or at room temperature. I serve this when I need a quick appetizer for last-minute casual company or as a pick-me-up for family. Everything can be done ahead, except the final broiling, and the recipe can be multiplied easily to serve more.

2 slices bread
½ cup grated Cheddar cheese
2 teaspoons butter
1 garlic clove, chopped
2 teaspoons chopped white
   onion

½ teaspoon ground cumin seed
Dash Tabasco sauce
Freshly ground black pepper

Toast the bread on one side. Mix together the Cheddar, butter, garlic, onion, cumin, and Tabasco. When ready to serve, spread over the untoasted side of the bread. Broil until bubbly and kissed with brown. Season with pepper. Slice into finger strips and serve immediately.

Easy Liver Pâté

MAKES 2 TO 3 CUPS

This tasty traditional pâté is simple to make in the food processor. I freeze chicken and duck livers and when I have enough I make pâté. Using chicken or duck fat increases the flavor (see page 171). For a coarser texture, chop the livers instead of puréeing them.

½ cup butter or rendered
   chicken or duck fat
2 medium onions, chopped
2 garlic cloves, chopped
1 pound chicken or duck livers
3 tablespoons sherry (optional)
½ cup heavy cream (optional)
3 heaping tablespoons finely
   chopped fresh thyme

Salt
Freshly ground black pepper
Melba Toast (page 363), white
   or rye toast points, or toasted
   pita bread, brushed with
   butter and garlic

In a large frying pan, heat half the butter. Add the onions and garlic and cook until soft. Turn up the heat and add more fat if necessary. Add the livers and sear them, browning the exteriors quickly, leaving the insides pink. Add the sherry if desired and let nearly evaporate. Scrape the mixture into a food processor or blender and purée. Add the cream if using. Taste for seasoning and add the thyme, salt, and pepper. Scrape the pâté into a serving dish. Pour any leftover butter on top. Cover well. Serve with the melba toast, toast points, or pita bread. The pâté will keep in the refrigerator several days or it may be frozen..

Dilly Dip

MAKES 1½ CUPS

In the late summer or early fall, fresh dill is abundant. This dip is perfect with crudités for a T.V. snack or for a large party.

1 cup plain yogurt
1 cup sour cream
½ cup mayonnaise
1 lemon, juiced

5 heaping tablespoons finely
   chopped fresh dill
Salt
Freshly ground black pepper

Place the yogurt, sour cream, mayonnaise, lemon juice, and dill in a food processor or blender. Purée until smooth. Season with salt and pepper to taste. Refrigerate, covered, until ready to serve.

Yogurt Honey Mustard Dip

MAKES 1³/₄ CUPS

It's hard to know what taste in this I enjoy the most: the tart yogurt, mustard, and honey are so enhanced by the herbs and sour cream. Serve with grilled fish or poultry or raw vegetables.

1 cup plain yogurt
3 tablespoons sour cream
2 green onions or scallions, white and green parts, finely chopped
1½ tablespoons Dijon mustard

⅓ cup honey
2 tablespoons lemon juice
¼ cup finely chopped fresh basil, thyme, or parsley
Salt
Freshly ground black pepper

Combine the yogurt, sour cream, onions, mustard, honey, lemon juice, and herbs. Season to taste with salt and pepper. Refrigerate, covered, 2 hours.

Quick Thighs

SERVES 2

The herbs, mustard, and garlic give these easy-to-fix chicken thighs a lot of dash and verve, hardly looking like the last-minute treat they are!

2 heaping tablespoons finely chopped fresh rosemary
2 heaping tablespoons finely chopped fresh basil

3 tablespoons Dijon mustard
2 garlic cloves, chopped
Freshly ground black pepper
6 chicken thighs

Combine the rosemary, basil, mustard, garlic, and pepper. Spread on the chicken thighs. Broil (or grill), skin side down, until brown and crisp. Turn and brown the other side. Repeat, if necessary, until chicken reaches 170 degrees on a meat thermometer. Serve hot.

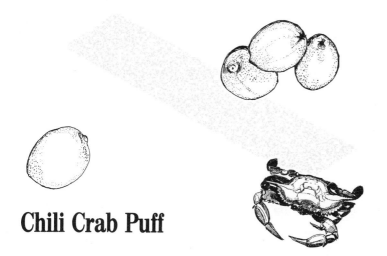

Chili Crab Puff

SERVES 4

Easy, hot, and tasty. You can use the canned Spanish-style tomato sauce in this puffy casserole and no one will know! Good for a simple lunch or supper to be served with a salad or as an appetizer with crackers for a crowd.

1 pound Monterey Jack cheese, grated	4 eggs
1 cup crab meat	½ cup flour
2 (4-ounce) cans diced green chilies	1 cup Marinara Sauce (page 38) or prepared tomato sauce
1⅓ cups half-and-half	

Preheat oven to 400 degrees.

Grease a deep 1½- to 2-quart baking dish. Set aside ½ cup of the cheese for the top. Place ⅓ of the cheese on the bottom of the baking dish. Add ⅓ of the crab and ⅓ of the chilies. Repeat, making 3 layers of each. Whisk the half-and-half with the eggs and flour, and slowly pour into the baking dish. Top with the marinara sauce and sprinkle with the reserved cheese. Bake, uncovered, for 1 hour, or until hot and set in the center.

Broiled Shrimp

SERVES 4 TO 6 AS AN APPETIZER
OR 2 AS A MAIN COURSE

This dish appeals to those who love spicy food, which is why I like it so! It calls for shrimp with the tails left on so they can be picked up and eaten with fingers! Do not overcook these!

¼ cup butter
1 teaspoon curry powder
1 teaspoon ground cumin seed
1 teaspoon ground coriander
    seed
1 teaspoon ground fennel seed

1 lemon, juiced
Salt
Freshly ground black pepper
1 pound large shrimp, peeled,
    with tails intact

Preheat the broiler.

Melt the butter in a small pan. Add the curry powder, cumin, coriander, fennel, and lemon juice. Add salt and pepper to taste. Place the shrimp side by side on a baking sheet or pan. Brush them with the butter. Broil 2 to 3 minutes, until light brown. Turn. Repeat on second side if necessary. Serve as an hors d'oeuvre, holding the shrimp by the tails, or serve them with toothpicks.

Sassy Crab Spread

MAKES SPREAD FOR 30 TO 40 CRACKERS

This looks like a giant mound of fresh crab, sprinkled with parsley. It's a delight to dig in and find the zesty spread inside under the slathers of cheese. Whether for a large party or a quick visit with friends just stopping by, this is a quick and easy appetizer. It's easy to keep in the freezer or refrigerator, ready to be topped at the last minute. It doubles easily.

8 ounces cream cheese,
  softened
1 tablespoon lemon juice
2 tablespoons mayonnaise
2 tablespoons Worcestershire
  sauce

1 small onion, finely chopped
½ to 1 cup bottled chili sauce
½ pound fresh crab meat
4 tablespoons finely chopped
  fresh parsley
Crackers

Combine the cream cheese, lemon juice, mayonnaise, Worcestershire, and onion and shape into a mound. May be made ahead to this point several days and be refrigerated or frozen, tightly wrapped.

When ready to serve, cover with the chili sauce and top with the crab meat and parsley. Serve with crackers.

Babybobs

MAKES 24 KEBOBS

These bite-sized kebabs are popular at stand-up parties, which I frequently give outdoors on my deck. The ingredients are marinated before being cooked on large skewers. Toothpicks are used for serving; hence the name.

1 pound pork tenderloin or
  boned chicken
2 large yellow or red bell
  peppers, cored and seeded
3 tablespoons soy sauce

4 tablespoons red wine vinegar
1½ teaspoons brown sugar
1 garlic clove, finely chopped
1 tablespoon oil for the grill

Cut the meat in twenty-four ½-inch pieces. Cut the peppers into 48 squarish pieces. Mix together the soy sauce, vinegar, brown sugar, and garlic. Add the meat and marinate, covered, for 1 hour, or overnight in the refrigerator.

Thread the meat and peppers onto large metal or wooden skewers. (If using wooden skewers, soak in water before threading ingredients onto them to prevent the skewers from burning on the grill.) Brush ingredients with oil and grill on all sides until done, 10 to 12 minutes. Remove from skewers. Cool slightly. Thread on toothpicks, sandwiching 1 piece of the meat between 22 peppers. Serve hot or refrigerate, covered, and serve chilled. May be made several days in advance.

Crudités

SERVES 12

I think every cocktail party should have crudités (raw vegetables) just for the drama they give to the table. I use a huge black platter to set off the brilliant colors. Crudités are also handy for picnics and tailgating. If desired, the vegetables may also be used for a cooked vegetable platter. The color of the broccoli will be lighter, and the vegetables softer but still crisp. And the cooked version keeps equally long. If you want to get real fancy, make carrot flowers. Cut 5 equally spaced "V"-shaped notches down the length of each carrot, then cut the carrot into slices, making "flowers." It really isn't hard. Serve with a dip.

1 large head broccoli
8 carrots, peeled and cut into
    finger-length strips
⅓ cup red wine vinegar
⅓ cup lemon juice
6 tablespoons oil

4 garlic cloves, chopped
Salt
Freshly ground black pepper
¼ cup finely chopped fresh
    oregano or parsley

Cut bite-sized florets off the broccoli, saving the stalks for another use. Set the florets aside in a bowl. Set the carrots in another bowl.

Combine the vinegar, lemon juice, oil, garlic, salt, pepper, and oregano. Pour half the dressing over each vegetable. Cover and refrigerate overnight. May be prepared 5 days in advance. To serve, drain the vegetables. Pile the broccoli in the center of a platter and surround it with the carrots. Serve cold. For a cooked vegetable platter, place the vegetables separately into pots of boiling water. Boil 3 to 5 minutes. Drain. Refresh with cold water and dry with paper towels. Dress as described above.

Chicken Soup

SERVES 4

Good and good for you! This is super comfort food. I love chicken soup on a cold day. If you have time to cook a whole chicken first by placing it in simmering stock and/or water with some vegetables and herbs, then removing the meat from the bones, and straining and degreasing the broth, you'll have a fantastic dish!

3 cups cooked chicken, fresh, frozen, or canned
8 cups chicken broth or stock, fresh or canned
1 onion, sliced
3 leeks, white part and some of green, sliced (optional)

1 pound carrots, sliced
1 small bay leaf
½ cup combined long-grain and wild rice

Combine the chicken, broth, onion, leeks, carrots, bay leaf, and rice in a large pot. Bring to the boil, reduce heat, and simmer until the vegetables are crisp-tender, 20 to 30 minutes.

The soup freezes well in an airtight container.

American-Oriental Chicken Soup

SERVES 6 TO 8

This striking soup, beautiful in its simplicity, is a grand mix of flavors—the chicken broth enhanced by the soy sauce and hoisin sauce.

Barbara St. Amand, a former assistant of mine from Rich's Cooking School, has now turned international expert and lives in Washington, D.C. She made this recipe up from leftovers in the cabinet when she came to visit me one Christmas and it was cold outside and we craved a simple pretty soup. To give additional color, add 2 carrots (1 cup), thinly sliced on the diagonal, with the ginger, green onions, and celery.

6 cups chicken broth or stock, fresh or canned
1 (2-inch) slice fresh ginger, cut into julienne strips
2 bunches green onions, sliced on the diagonal into ½-inch pieces
2 stalks celery, cut into thin diagonal slices

2 cups cooked chicken, slivered or torn into bite-size pieces
2 tablespoons soy sauce
1 teaspoon hoisin sauce
1 (8-ounce) can sliced water chestnuts
Salt
Freshly ground black pepper

Put the chicken broth in a soup pot. Add the ginger, green onions, and celery. Bring to the boil over high heat, reduce heat, and simmer 10 minutes. Add the chicken, soy sauce, and hoisin sauce and simmer 5 minutes. Add the water chestnuts. Taste for seasoning and add salt, if necessary, and pepper. Canned broth usually does not need any salt. Serve hot. May be made ahead a day.

The soup freezes fine for a leftover, but not for making an impression.

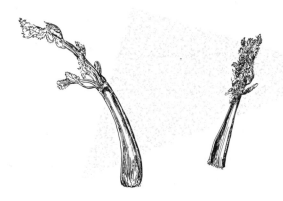

Bits and Pieces Soup

SERVES 6 TO 8

Some days I make a fabulous rich soup from all the bits and pieces in my refrigerator, and I discover new combinations I like. The raw vegetables are so gently cooked they are still crunchy. Perfect for a fall lunch or dinner, or any time you need a quick, satisfying meal. For a lighter version, cut the white sauce by half. The soup is also good cold.

3½ cups chicken broth or stock, fresh or canned
½ medium onion, chopped
1 stalk celery, sliced (no leaves)
1 medium carrot, shredded
2 cups broccoli florets and sliced stems
2 garlic cloves, chopped

3 tablespoons butter
3 tablespoons flour
2 cups milk
1 cup (4 ounces) shredded sharp Cheddar cheese
Freshly ground black pepper
½ to 1 teaspoon hot sauce (optional)

Bring the broth, onion, celery, carrot, broccoli, and garlic to the boil; reduce heat and simmer 10 minutes. Meanwhile, melt the butter in a heavy saucepan, stir in the flour, then the milk. Bring to the boil, stirring, and add the cheese. Pour the cheese mixture into the simmering vegetable mixture, stirring. Taste and season with salt, pepper, and optional hot sauce. The soup can be made ahead several days and reheated over low heat.

Country Soup with Potatoes, Green Beans, and Garlic

SERVES 6

Ever since I spent several months in Spain, I've loved her tasty peasant dishes. My friend Betty Collins, who also lived there, loved this soup, too, which was served in a small Majorcan restaurant located on a hillside out in the middle of nowhere. Sausages hung from the ceilings, and this soup was served in large brown pottery bowls with a slab of hearty bread alongside. Basque in origin, the combination was originally made with water rather than chicken stock, but it is surprisingly flavorful either way. I think it's better made ahead, and I don't add the garlic and olive oil until ready to serve.

1½ pounds potatoes, peeled and cut into 1-inch chunks
6 cups chicken broth or stock, fresh or canned
1 pound green beans, tipped and tailed

4 tablespoons olive oil
6 large garlic cloves, thinly sliced
Salt
Freshly ground black pepper

Place the potatoes and the chicken broth in a large pan. Bring to the boil over high heat, cover, and reduce heat. Simmer gently until the potatoes are nearly cooked through, but not mushy, about 15 minutes. Add the green beans, and cook, uncovered, until tender, about 15 minutes. Meanwhile, heat the olive oil in a small saucepan. Add the sliced garlic, and cook, stirring, until golden brown, about 5 to 8 minutes. May be made ahead to this point several days. When ready to serve, bring the soup base back to the boil, add the garlic and olive oil, and stir. Season to taste with salt and pepper.

The soup freezes well in an airtight container.

Ham Bone and Bean Soup

SERVES 10

This is a very hearty winter soup, perfect with a sandwich, or with a giant salad (particularly Bob Lynn's Bread Salad, page 200). Try to chop the ham bone at the joint, as a chopped bone adds more flavor and body. I freeze the scraps and ham after a Christmas party or "big do" and make the stock a few months later. I also save the rind of imported Parmesan cheese and add it to the soup with the beans. The rind softens and adds flavor and creaminess. Really nice!

Often dried beans have packets of artificial flavoring added. Use them if you wish. This is not a rigid recipe; if you have other leftovers you want to add, do so.

10 ounces (½ package) 15-bean soup beans or other "ham" beans
1 pound ham, with 1½ cups ham scraps or fat, divided
1 ham bone chopped (optional)
1 turkey carcass (optional)
1 stalk celery, sliced
½ carrot, sliced
½ bay leaf, crumbled
2½ to 3 quarts water
1 onion, chopped
2 garlic cloves, chopped
Salt
Freshly ground black pepper
Tabasco sauce (optional)
Finely chopped fresh herbs (optional)

Cover the beans with water and soak overnight, or place in a pan, cover, and bring to the boil. Remove from heat and let sit 1 hour. Drain. Make a stock of 1 cup of the ham scraps and/or ham bone and optional turkey carcass, celery, carrot, bay leaf, and water by bringing the combination to the boil, reducing heat, and simmering a couple of hours. Degrease and strain. This may be done ahead and frozen.

When ready to finish, add the beans, onion, and garlic to the base, bring to the boil, and reduce heat. Simmer until done, about 45 minutes to 1 hour. Season to taste with salt and pepper and optional Tabasco. Add herbs if desired. Remove from the heat. May be made 1 to 2 days ahead. Add remaining ham 30 minutes before serving. Bring back to the boil, reduce heat, and simmer, covered.

The soup freezes in an airtight container.

Leftovers' Soup

SERVES 8 TO 10

This is a tasty clean-out-the-refrigerator soup. If I don't have one of the ingredients, I substitute another. And I make no apologies if the rendition is not always fantastic. After all, I've been virtuous!

2 tablespoons butter
1 onion, sliced
2 garlic cloves, chopped
1½ cups cooked butter beans or baby limas, with juices
1½ cups cooked lady peas or other peas, with juices
2 cups chicken broth or stock, fresh or canned
1 (28-ounce) can tomatoes, chopped, with juice
¼ cup rice
½ cup heavy cream
Salt
Freshly ground black pepper

Melt the butter in a heavy saucepan. Add the onion and garlic and cook until soft. Add the butter beans, peas, broth, tomatoes, and rice. Bring to the boil, reduce heat, and simmer until the rice is tender, about 15 minutes. Remove from the heat, and stir in the cream. Season to taste with salt and pepper. Serve with cornbread or other fresh hot bread.

Pork and Cabbage (or Greens) Soup

SERVES 6 TO 8

Fresh tomatoes and fresh pesto add the blush of summer and color to this winter soup. However, rather than use a non-ripe tomato or pesto made with dried basil, omit them. The soup will still be tasty. Good as a starter or for dinner on a chilly evening and great as a light meal on a late fall afternoon.

1 tablespoon dark Oriental
    sesame oil
½ pound lean pork, chopped,
    ground, or shredded
2 tablespoons chopped fresh
    ginger
6 cups chicken broth or stock,
    fresh or canned, boiling
1 tablespoon soy sauce
½ pound Chinese cabbage,
    veined, or fresh spinach
    leaves, stemmed, sliced
    thinly or shredded

2 tablespoons Pesto Sauce
    (page 58, optional)
Salt
Freshly ground black pepper
Sugar
Dash Tabasco sauce

Garnish
2 fresh ripe tomatoes, roughly
    chopped (optional)

Heat the oil in a large pan. Add the pork and ginger and stir-fry briefly until the pork is white. Add the boiling broth and soy sauce. Reduce to medium heat and simmer, covered, 15 minutes. Add the cabbage or spinach and simmer until wilted, 3 or 4 minutes. Stir in the optional pesto sauce. Taste and add salt, pepper, sugar, and Tabasco. To serve, garnish with the fresh tomatoes. May be made ahead a couple of days and reheated.

Root Vegetable Soup

SERVES 6 TO 8

With its whole garlic cloves, this marvelously flavorful soup is best served with bread. Sometimes I put a slice of crusty French bread in a bowl and ladle the soup over it; at other times I nibble on toast rubbed with garlic. Incidentally, I don't always use the Parmesan, particularly for a home supper.

- **Consider other breads, such as Basil Crescent Rolls, (page 353), Curried Wreath Bread (page 344), or Barbara Robinson's Cheddar Muffins (page 359), as an accompaniment.**

4 to 6 tablespoons butter
4 medium onions, sliced
1 large head garlic (2 ounces)
4 (9 ounces) large carrots, cut diagonally into ½-inch slices
¾ pound potatoes, peeled and cut into 2-inch chunks
3 (14½-ounce each) cans chicken or beef broth

10 to 12 thyme stalks tied in a bunch with string (optional)
Salt
Freshly ground black pepper
½ cup freshly grated imported Parmesan cheese (optional)

Melt the butter in a heavy pan. Add the onions. Place the head of garlic in the microwave and cook 1 to 1½ minutes, until tender; peel. Or break up the head, add the unpeeled cloves to boiling water to cover, and cook for 30 minutes. Let cool enough to peel. Add the peeled garlic to the pan with the onions, heat, and cook until golden brown.

Meanwhile, in another pan combine the carrots, potatoes, and broth and heat until hot. When the garlic and onions are golden, add the broth-vegetable mixture and bring to the boil. Add the thyme. Cover. Cook 30 minutes, or until the potatoes are cooked and the carrots are crisp-cooked. Taste for seasoning and add salt and pepper. Serve hot with the Parmesan if desired. May be made 2 to 3 days in advance and reheated. The soup freezes in an airtight container.

Shellfish Chowder

SERVES 4 TO 6

I believe chowder means a luscious rich milk-based stew with potatoes and salt pork, regardless of whether the chowder features clams, oysters, scallops, or even corn. And there are some people who call a tomato-based stew a chowder, which is their business, but I can't bring myself to do it! Fresh or canned clams and oysters are recommended. Serve this chowder as a main course with salad and good bread for a light dinner. Leftovers freeze adequately but not optimally.

¼ cup cubed salt pork or bacon
1 small onion, chopped
½ cup chicken broth or stock,
    fresh or canned
4 medium potatoes, cut into
    1-inch cubes
2 cups clams, oysters, or
    scallops, shelled, reserving
    juice

2 teaspoons chopped fresh
    thyme
1½ to 2 cups milk
½ cup cream
Salt
Freshly ground black pepper

Garnish
Fresh thyme sprigs
Paprika

Fry the salt pork or bacon in a heavy casserole until crisp. Remove and set aside. Add the onion and cook until soft. Add the broth and potatoes, cover, and bring to the boil. Reduce heat and simmer until the potatoes are done. Add the shellfish and their juices, the thyme, milk, and cream. Return the pork to the casserole. Bring to the boil, reduce heat, and simmer until the shellfish are plump and heated through, about 1 to 3 minutes. Add salt and pepper to taste. Garnish with the thyme sprigs or paprika.

From the Sea

Grilled Honey-Ginger Fish Steaks

SERVES 4

There is such a wide variety of exciting fish now available, I love experimenting with it in combination with Oriental flavors.

2 tablespoons finely chopped
    ginger
4 tablespoons finely chopped
    whole green onion or
    scallion
1 cup soy sauce
2 tablespoons peanut oil

2 tablespoons honey
2 tablespoons Ginger Sherry
    (recipe follows, optional)
4 (½-pound each) amberjack,
    swordfish, or tuna steaks or
    fillets, 1 to 1½ inches thick

Combine the ginger, green onion, soy sauce, oil, honey, and ginger sherry. Pour over the fish. Cover and let marinate in refrigerator 2 to 6 hours. Preheat and oil the grill (or broiler). Drain the fish, reserving the marinade. Cook 5 to 7 minutes per side (a total of 10 minutes per inch of thickness). To serve, bring the marinade to the boil and pour over the fish.

Ginger Sherry

¼ pound ginger, cut up
½ cup dry sherry

Steep the ginger in the sherry. Let marinate, covered, for 2 weeks. Use ginger and sherry as needed.

Whole Steamed Trout

SERVES 4

Dramatic, glamorous, very easy, and particularly nice for company. This is essentially a warm salad. Plan on one whole trout per person for presentation or prepare fillets in the same manner, but cut the cooking time approximately in half.

4 whole rainbow trout
(about ½ to ¾ pound each),
cleaned (page 163)

Marinade
6 tablespoons dry sherry
½ teaspoon Chinese five spice
    powder

Sauce
Scallion tops
8 slices fresh ginger
6 tablespoons red wine vinegar
½ cup olive oil
3 tablespoons dry sherry

3 tablespoons light soy
1½ teaspoons hoisin sauce
1 tablespoon finely chopped
    fresh ginger

Garnish
1 head Chinese cabbage,
    shredded
2 cups cooked rice, still warm

4 scallions, thinly sliced on the
    diagonal

Combine the sherry and five spice powder and marinate the fish for 15 to 30 minutes. Remove from the marinade and discard the marinade.

Put water in a steamer or wok, taking care it does not come to the level of the rack. Place the fish on the rack, cover the steamer, and steam fish over high heat 10 to 12 minutes.

Meanwhile, mix the sauce ingredients together. Prepare a bed of shredded Chinese cabbage on a serving plate. Top with the cooked rice, ½ cup per person. For a lovely presentation, skin the trout, leaving the head and tail intact. Lay the fish on top and pour the sauce over all. Serve warm. Reheats nicely in the microwave and is delicious cold.

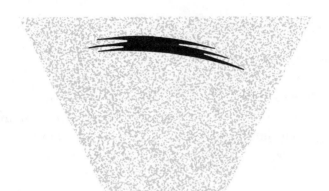

Poultry and Meats

Carey LeGrange's Chicken and Smoked Sausage Gumbo

SERVES 6 AS A MAIN COURSE;
10 TO 12 AS AN APPETIZER

Once I was asked by Paul Prudhomme to judge a gumbo contest in Lafayette, Louisiana. It was a dreary day, damp and chilly with patches of rain. The cooks were of good cheer, calling to each other from booth to booth, and the bubbling caldrons of gumbo added tantalizing aromas and a sense of well-being and joy. The judges met inside the church. As I was tasting one of the gumbos, another judge remarked that we were sitting and eating on the table usually used to hold caskets during wakes. It was a sobering thought. It was quite a fête with several dozen gumbos served outdoors amid much laughter, and children playing, with a Cajun band, and dancing inside.

Carey LeGrange organized the contest, and this was the recipe he served the judges. I've adapted it.

A Note on Roux

- **You can make the *roux* in advance and then add it to the chicken particles. Some of the flavor may be lost, but it will work. *Roux* can also be made in large quantities and stored in the refrigerator. Use as needed to thicken sauces.**

1 teaspoon salt
1 teaspoon garlic powder
1 teaspoon to 1 tablespoon
  Tabasco sauce
1 (2- to 3-pound) chicken, cut
  into pieces
1¼ cups all-purpose flour
Vegetable oil
5 garlic cloves, finely chopped
2 medium onions, finely
  chopped
1 to 2 stalks celery, finely
  chopped

1 to 2 green bell peppers,
  seeded and finely chopped
7 cups chicken broth or stock
  (preferably double strength)
½ pound smoked pork sausage,
  such as Cajun *andouille* or
  Polish *kielbasa*, skinned and
  cut into small cubes
4 cups cooked rice, still warm
  (page 262)

Sprinkle the salt, garlic powder, and 1 to 2 teaspoons of the Tabasco on both sides of the chicken pieces. If possible, marinate the chicken 30 minutes at room temperature. Set aside ½ cup of the flour. Add the chicken to the remaining flour and turn until well coated.

Heat enough oil to come half way up the sides of a large frying pan to 360 degrees. Place the chicken in the pan, skin side down, brown and turn. Reduce the heat, and finish cooking the chicken, uncovered, about 8 minutes. Remove, drain on paper towels, and carefully pour the hot oil off into a container, leaving the browned chicken particles in the pan. Scrape the pan to loosen the particles, then return ½ cup of the hot oil to the pan. Place the pan over high heat. Gradually stir in the ½ cup reserved flour. Stir constantly, and cook until the *roux* is dark red-brown, about 4 minutes. Remove from the heat to stop the cooking. Add the garlic, onions, celery, bell peppers, and 1 teaspoon of the Tabasco, stirring until the *roux* stops getting darker. Return the pan to low heat; and cook about 5 minutes, stirring constantly and scraping the bottom well.

Bring the chicken stock to the boil and add to the *roux*, stirring. Bring the stock mixture back to the boil, stirring constantly. Reduce

the heat to a simmer, and add the smoked sausage. Simmer, uncovered, for 45 minutes, until the liquid is reduced by half and is
very thick; stir frequently to prevent scorching. May be made ahead
to this point and reheated.

Meanwhile, remove the chicken from the bone and cut into bite-
sized pieces. When the gumbo is done, stir in the chicken pieces.
Serve over the cooked rice.

Chicken and Sausage

SERVES 4 TO 6

When I get a craving for Italian-type home cooking, I start the sausage, then get on the phone and call a few friends. By the time the
chicken is cooked, the table is set and my friends have gathered, all
in less than an hour.

½ pound hot Italian sausage
1 (2½-pound) chicken, cut up
½ pound fresh mushrooms,
    sliced
1 large red bell pepper, cored,
    seeded, and cut into thin
    strips
2 garlic cloves, chopped
½ cup dry white wine or non-
    alcoholic white wine

Salt
¼ teaspoon ground cayenne
    pepper
Freshly ground black pepper
¼ cup finely chopped fresh
    oregano
1 pound pasta, cooked

Garnish
⅓ cup finely chopped fresh
    parsley

Prick the sausages all over with a fork. Heat a large skillet. Add the
sausages, and brown on all sides. Drain on paper towels, and slice
into 1-inch pieces. Set aside. Add the chicken to the skillet, skin side
down. Brown, turn, and brown on the other side. Remove. Add the
mushrooms, and sauté briefly. Return the chicken and sausages to

the skillet and add the bell pepper, garlic, wine, salt, ground peppers, and oregano. Bring to the boil. Reduce the heat; and simmer, covered, 20 minutes, until the chicken and sausages are cooked through. Serve over the pasta, and sprinkle with the parsley. May be made ahead. Refrigerate up to 2 days.

The dish freezes up to 3 months: defrost and reheat.

Chicken Marinara

SERVES 4

This classic Mediterranean-style dish is quick to make, pretty to look at, and delicious to eat.

3 tablespoons olive oil
8 to 10 chicken thighs with skin
    or 1 (3-pound) chicken,
    cut up
2 tablespoons red wine vinegar
½ cup chicken broth or stock,
    fresh or canned
Salt

Freshly ground black pepper
1½ cups Marinara Sauce (recipe
    follows)
8 ounces black olives, pitted
2 heaping tablespoons finely
    chopped fresh oregano or
    basil

Heat the oil in a large heavy skillet until sizzling. Add the chicken pieces, skin side down. Brown, turn, and brown the other side. Add the vinegar, and boil briefly to reduce. Add the broth, salt, and pepper. Cover, and simmer until the chicken is cooked, about 30 minutes. Stir in the marinara sauce, olives, and oregano; and cook together 2 to 3 minutes. Can be made ahead and refrigerated. Reheat over moderate heat.

The chicken freezes well.

Marinara Sauce

MAKES 4 CUPS

This garlic and herb-enriched tomato sauce is fabulous over fish, pork, poultry, or pasta. I frequently substitute it for plain tomato sauce over spaghetti.

½ cup olive oil
2 large garlic cloves, chopped
2 pounds fresh ripe tomatoes, or
    2 pounds canned tomatoes,
    preferably Italian, drained
5 tablespoons chopped fresh
    basil or parsley

1 teaspoon fennel seed
    (optional)
Salt
Freshly ground black pepper

Heat the oil in a heavy pan over medium heat until warm. Add the garlic and cook until soft. If using fresh tomatoes, cut them into 1-inch pieces. Add fresh or canned tomatoes, basil, and optional fennel seed to the pan and cook for 25 minutes, stirring often. Pour into a blender or food processor and purée. Return the sauce to the pan, season with salt and pepper, and simmer over medium heat for 10 minutes to reduce slightly.

    The sauce freezes well.

Chicken and Yellow Rice

SERVES 6

This is a beautiful dish that adds stunning color to the table with the yellow of the rice, the green of the bell pepper, and the red of the pimiento strips.

⅓ cup olive oil
1 (3½-pound) chicken, cut into
    8 pieces
1 onion, finely chopped
½ medium green bell pepper,
    finely chopped
1 large ripe tomato, peeled,
    quartered, seeded, and
    finely chopped
2 garlic cloves, chopped
¾ cup lemon juice or dry white
    wine, divided
1 bay leaf, crumbled

1 tablespoon salt
¼ teaspoon hot sauce
Pinch saffron (optional)
1 cup chicken broth or stock,
    fresh or canned, boiling
1 heaping tablespoon finely
    chopped fresh parsley
2 cups long-grain rice
2¼ cups chicken broth or stock,
    fresh or canned
1¼ cups cooked peas
1 pimiento, cut into strips
Chopped parsley

Preheat oven to 325 degrees.

Heat the oil in a large skillet. Add the chicken pieces, skin side down, and cook until just pale golden in color. Turn and brown. Remove. Add the onion and green pepper to the skillet. Cook until transparent. Add the tomato, garlic, ¼ cup of the lemon juice, the bay leaf, salt, and hot sauce. Mix well and cook until mushy.

Dissolve the optional saffron in the 1 cup hot chicken broth and combine with ¼ cup lemon juice. Pour into the skillet, add the parsley, and stir well. Arrange the chicken in a heatproof casserole and pour the vegetable mixture over it. Cover and cook over medium heat until the chicken is tender, about 15 minutes. Add the rice and stir to distribute it evenly in the casserole. Add the 2¼ cups chicken broth and stir once carefully. Bring to the boil and cover. Bake for only 20 minutes. Remove from the oven. Garnish with peas, pimiento strips, and parsley. Sprinkle generously with the remaining ¼ cup lemon juice diluted to taste with water. Cover and allow to stand 15 minutes before serving.

Quick Chicken Taj Mahal

SERVES 4

When you are in a hurry, this wonderful, spice-laden chicken is a special treat for company. The saffron flavor is enhanced by soaking in lemon juice. If you can't find saffron in your grocery store, try an Indian market and ask at the cash register. Saffron is so expensive it is frequently kept locked up. Fenugreek is also hard to find, so I omit it when necessary.

One pound boned and trimmed lamb pieces may be substituted for the chicken.

1 tablespoon vegetable oil
1 (1-pound) chicken breast, skinned and boned, cut into 1-inch pieces
1 medium onion, chopped
1½ to 2 cups chicken broth or stock, fresh or canned
1 cup raisins or currants
⅓ cup dried apricots or peaches, cut into 1-inch cubes
1 teaspoon saffron threads, soaked in the juice of ½ lemon (optional)

1 teaspoon ground turmeric
1 teaspoon ground fenugreek (optional)
½ teaspoon cinnamon
½ teaspoon cayenne pepper
½ teaspoon ground coriander seed
Salt
Freshly ground black pepper

Garnish
⅓ cup blanched slivered almonds, toasted

Heat the oil in a large pan. Add the chicken and the onion and stir-fry 10 minutes, until the chicken is well browned on all sides and the onion is soft. Stir in 1½ cups of the chicken broth, the raisins, dried fruit, saffron-lemon juice mixture, turmeric, fenugreek, cinnamon, cayenne, and coriander seed. Bring to the boil. Reduce heat

40

and simmer, covered, 5 to 10 minutes, until chicken is cooked through and flavors are married. Add salt and pepper to taste. Garnish with the almonds.

Indiana Cubed Steak

SERVES 6

This steak is great made with beef, but even better with venison! Cynthia Jubera says this is the kind of recipe her mother regularly served to the farm hands on her farm in Indiana.

About Cubed Meat
* **"Cubed" meat has been mechanically tenderized. You can get cubed steak at the store, usually round steak about ¼ to ½ inch thick that has been run through the "cuber." You can achieve the same effect yourself by pounding the steak with the edge of a plate or with the toothed side of a meat mallet.**

3 tablespoons butter, divided
3 tablespoons vegetable oil, divided
1 cup flour
1 teaspoon salt
1 teaspoon freshly ground black pepper

2 pounds cubed venison or beef steak
2 onions, chopped
2 cups milk

Melt 1½ tablespoons of the butter and 1½ tablespoons of the oil in a large heavy frying pan. Meanwhile, season the flour with the salt and pepper. Place the steak in the seasoned flour and turn, coating each side. Add to the hot fat, brown, turn, and brown the other side. Remove the steak to a warm serving platter. Add more butter and oil to the pan if needed. Add the onions and cook until translucent and soft. Add 4 tablespoons of the seasoned flour and stir until medium brown, without burning the onions. Heat the milk in a saucepan. Add to the flour and bring to the boil, stirring constantly. Pour the gravy over the meat. Serve at once.

Chicken Fried Steak

SERVES 6 TO 8

About Beef
- **Round and chuck are very flavorful pieces of meat, but can also be tough. Pounding tenderizes them. Slicing the meat thin across the grain helps mask any toughness as well.**

Television personality butcher Merle Ellis is a real "meat and potatoes" man. This recipe of his is perfect for a cold night; serve with lumpy mashed potatoes, homemade biscuits or cornbread, and a green vegetable.

⅔ cup flour
1 teaspoon salt
Freshly ground black pepper
2 pounds top round or chuck
    steak, cut ¼ to ½ inch thick
2 eggs
2 tablespoons cream
½ cup vegetable oil
2 cups saltine cracker crumbs,
    rolled fine

1 onion, sliced
½ cup cream
About 2 cups chicken broth or
    stock, fresh or canned
Dash Worcestershire sauce
    (optional)
Dash hot sauce (optional)

Mix ½ cup of the flour, the salt, and pepper together. Pound the mixture into both sides of the meat with the edge of a heavy plate or mallet. Cut the meat into serving pieces.

Beat the eggs together with the cream. Heat the oil in a heavy cast iron skillet over moderately high heat. Reserve 3 tablespoons of the flour. Dredge the steaks in the remainder of the flour, dip in the egg mixture, and then into the cracker crumbs. Put the steaks in the hot oil and brown well. Turn and brown the other side. Reduce heat to medium, cover the skillet, and cook for 15 to 20 minutes, turning occasionally, until the steaks are cooked through and tender. (Chicken fried steak should be well done, but not dry.) Remove the steaks from the skillet, and drain on brown paper bags. Keep warm.

Add the onion slices to the skillet and sauté quickly. Pour off all but 3 tablespoons of the fat in the skillet and stir in the 3 tablespoons reserved flour. Stir to incorporate any particles on the bottom of the pan and cook for 1 to 2 minutes. Stir in the cream, then the chicken broth. Season the gravy with Worcestershire and hot sauce. Slice the meat across the grain and top with the gravy.

Easy Reuben Casserole

SERVES 4

Now you can buy pre-corned beef and cook it yourself. Unless you live in New York or New England, it's much better than buying pre-cooked, storebought corned beef! As a plus, it fills the house with lovely aromas. The rye bread crumbs are critical: What's a Reuben without rye?

3 cups sauerkraut, drained
9 (¼-inch-thick) slices cooked
   corned beef (3 pounds)
1½ cups grated Swiss cheese

⅓ cup chicken broth or stock,
   fresh or canned
1½ to 2 cups rye bread crumbs
¼ cup butter

Preheat oven to 350 degrees.

Place 1 cup of the sauerkraut in a 9- × 12-inch casserole or 2-quart ovenproof dish. Place 3 slices of corned beef on top. Sprinkle with ½ cup of the grated cheese. Repeat this layer 2 more times. Pour the chicken broth over the top. Cover and bake for 30 minutes. Uncover, top with the rye bread crumbs, dot with the butter, and bake for 15 minutes, until the crumbs are toasted. May be made ahead several days and frozen.

Bert Greene's Roast Beef Hash

SERVES 6 TO 8

Hash is an inglorious name for a glorious all-in-one dish—an enticing, robust meal for family or good friends. I cook hash in a paella pan rather than a deep casserole to prevent it from turning into a stew. I've fooled around with this recipe of Bert's so much over the years it now bears only a vague resemblance to the original. But every time I cook it I remember my dear friend and his grand appetite for good home fare. In this the meat must be well done.

1 (4- to 5-pound) 4-inch-thick chuck roast or rolled roast of beef
¼ cup butter
6 medium potatoes, boiled for 10 minutes
2 garlic cloves, chopped
6 medium onions, cut into ½-inch cubes
3 green bell peppers, cut into ½-inch cubes

1 (28-ounce) can Italian plum tomatoes, broken up
1 tablespoon Worcestershire sauce
1 teaspoon sugar (optional)
1 tablespoon red wine vinegar
Salt
Freshly ground black pepper

Preheat oven to 375 degrees.

Place the beef in a large skillet or paella pan and roast for 1 hour, until brown on the outside, still rare inside. Remove the skillet from the oven and cut the meat into 2-inch squares or chunks, reserving the juices. Add the butter to the skillet. Chop the potatoes into 2-inch chunks and add them to the skillet. Add the garlic, onions, peppers, tomatoes and their juice, Worcestershire, sugar, and vinegar. Return the meat and its juices to the pan. Bake for 1 to 1¼ hours, until the meat is tender and potatoes are cooked through. Add salt and pepper to taste. May be made in advance and reheated.

My Chili

SERVES 12 TO 16

I top my chili with tortilla chips, grated Cheddar or Monterey Jack cheese, and/or sour cream.

¼ cup vegetable oil
4 medium onions, chopped
3 garlic cloves, chopped
3 pounds lean ground chuck
6 cups (2 28-ounce cans) tomatoes, chopped, reserving juice
3 pounds home-cooked kidney beans or 3 (16-ounce each) cans, drained and juice reserved
½ cup red wine vinegar

8 tablespoons chili powder
1 tablespoon ground cumin seed
1 tablespoon chopped fresh or dried oregano
1 to 2 teaspoons cayenne pepper
2 to 4 ounces canned green chilies, chopped
Salt
Freshly ground black pepper
Additional herbs to taste

Heat the oil in a large Dutch oven and in it sauté the onions and garlic until soft. Remove the onions and garlic with a slotted spoon, and set aside. Add the meat to the hot pan, and brown over high heat. Drain off excess fat. Reduce heat, return the onions and garlic to the pan, and stir in the tomatoes and their juices, beans, red wine vinegar, chili powder, cumin seed, oregano, cayenne, and chilies. Add bean juices if necessary. Bring to the boil, reduce heat, and simmer, stirring occasionally for 30 minutes. Season to taste with salt, pepper, and additional herbs. Refrigerate and remove fat if time allows.

The chili freezes well.

Sautéed Calf's Liver and Onions

SERVES 3 OR 4

There are those who love liver and those who don't. I'm one who does. I crave it regularly, in fact. If I feel weepy I eat some liver and onions and feel better, somehow! I like my liver pink inside. The brown butter puts this over the top.

The type of vinegar called for here is very much "to taste." Cider vinegar would be fine; white wine vinegar, a bit more refined; sherry vinegar, subtler; Balsamic vinegar, richer and more complex; red wine vinegar, fuller flavored.

¼ cup butter, divided into tablespoons
5 onions, thinly sliced
1 tablespoon oil
Salt
Freshly ground black pepper

4 tablespoons all-purpose flour
4 slices calf's liver, each about ¼ inch thick (about 1 pound)
¼ cup red wine vinegar or other vinegar

Heat 1 tablespoon of the butter in a skillet. Add the onions. Cook over low heat until they are very soft and lightly colored, about 20 to 30 minutes.

Heat another tablespoon of the butter and the oil in another skillet. Add a little salt and pepper to the flour. Lightly dredge the liver slices in the flour, add to the hot pan, and cook 2 to 3 minutes on each side for medium-rare. Cooking time will vary depending on the thickness of the meat. Remove the cooked liver to a plate. Avoid crowding the skillet. Pour off the excess grease. Add the vinegar to the skillet, bring to the boil, and deglaze the skillet, stirring any juices into the vinegar. Pour over the onions.

Melt the remaining 2 tablespoons butter and let it turn brown. Arrange the liver on a platter, pile on the onions, and drizzle them with the browned butter.

Lamb Meatballs in Sour Cream Sauce

SERVES 6

Great served over rice as a main course, accompanied by a cucumber or other green salad, or as an appetizer in a chafing dish.

2 medium potatoes, peeled
3 tablespoons butter
¼ cup heavy cream
2 pounds ground lamb
4 garlic cloves, chopped fine
1 large onion, chopped
1 cup bread crumbs
1 tablespoon Dijon mustard
1 tablespoon Worcestershire sauce
½ teaspoon Tabasco sauce

1 heaping tablespoon finely chopped fresh mint
1 tablespoon finely chopped fresh or dried rosemary
⅛ teaspoon ground ginger
Salt
Freshly ground black pepper
2 tablespoons olive oil
2 cups beef broth or stock, fresh or canned
¾ cup sour cream

In a large saucepan boil the potatoes. Drain. In another pan melt the butter, add the cream, and then mash into the potatoes. While still hot, add the lamb, garlic, onion, bread crumbs, mustard, Worcestershire, Tabasco, mint, rosemary, ground ginger, salt, and pepper and combine very well. Form into 1-inch meatballs. In a heavy skillet, heat the olive oil. Add the meatballs, brown, turn, and brown on all sides. Lower the heat, add the broth, and cover with a tight lid. Cook about 20 minutes, until done. Remove the meatballs and keep warm. Bring the broth to the boil, and boil to reduce by half. Add the sour cream and heat through, but do not let boil. Pour the sauce over the meatballs.

May be made ahead and refrigerated. Reheat carefully without bringing to a boil.

The meatballs, without the sauce, freeze well. Defrost and prepare the sauce before serving.

Out-of-This-World Skillet Moussaka

SERVES 4 TO 6

Moussaka is traditionally a layered casserole of chopped meat and vegetables. I like this interpretation, which came to me via a Greek student, because it is easy and fast and you don't have the casserole to wash!

1 medium eggplant
4 tablespoons flour
1 pound ground lamb (or lamb and ground beef combined)
½ cup chopped onion
1 garlic clove, crushed
1 (8-ounce) can tomato sauce
½ heaping teaspoon finely chopped fresh or dried oregano leaves
¼ to ½ teaspoon cinnamon

Salt
Freshly ground black pepper
2 tablespoons butter
1 cup milk
1 egg yolk
1 cup grated imported Greek Kefalotiri cheese (or Parmesan cheese, or Parmesan and Swiss cheeses combined)

Garnish
3 heaping tablespoons finely chopped fresh rosemary or oregano (optional)

Peel the eggplant and cut the flesh into ½-inch pieces. Toss to coat with 2 tablespoons of the flour and set aside. Place the lamb, onion, and garlic in a heavy skillet. Cook over medium heat, stirring to crumble the meat. When the meat is browned, drain, and then return the meat mixture to the skillet. Add the eggplant, and cook 6 to 8 minutes, or until tender. Stir in the tomato sauce, oregano, cinnamon, salt, and pepper and simmer for 5 minutes.

Melt the butter in a saucepan. Stir in the remaining 2 tablespoons flour; cook, stirring, 2 minutes. Add the milk, and bring to the boil. Pour a portion into the egg yolk, whisk together, and then return the yolk mixture to the pan. Combine well. Pour the sauce over the meat mixture and top with the cheese. Cover and cook over medium heat until the cheese melts. Garnish with the fresh rosemary or oregano if desired. Reheats in microwave or oven.

The moussaka freezes in an airtight container.

All-in-One Sausage and Zucchini Casserole

SERVES 6 TO 8

This is a tasty one-pot family meal, but also so nice for neighbors and good friends. And, oh, yes, church suppers.

2 to 3 tablespoons olive oil
1½ pounds ground chuck
1 pound hot or mild Italian
    sausage, sliced
3 zucchini (1½ pounds), cut
    into ½-inch cubes
4 garlic cloves, chopped
1 onion, sliced
1 cup long-grain rice
1 (14½-ounce) can whole
    tomatoes, chopped
2 teaspoons fennel seed

½ teaspoon red pepper flakes
1 heaping tablespoon finely
    chopped fresh basil
1 heaping tablespoon finely
    chopped fresh rosemary or
    oregano
Salt
Freshly ground black pepper
3 cups chicken broth or stock,
    fresh or canned, boiling
1 cup freshly grated imported
    Parmesan cheese

Preheat oven to 375 degrees.

Heat the oil in a large 5-quart Dutch oven. Add the ground chuck and sausage. Brown. Drain and set aside. In the Dutch oven in the oil, sauté the zucchini, garlic, and onion until soft and translucent. Add the rice and cook until opaque, about 2 minutes. Add the tomatoes, fennel, red pepper flakes, basil, rosemary, salt, pepper, and chicken broth. Heat through until just to the boil. Stir in the meat. Transfer to a rectangular baking dish. Top with the Parmesan and bake 1 hour. Top with additional Parmesan if desired, when served. May be made 1 to 2 days ahead.

The casserole freezes. Defrost and reheat.

German Pork Chops with Sauerkraut and Apples

SERVES 4

I've always loved the zestiness of pork chops and sauerkraut. My Russian friends, like Drew Jubera's family in Pittsburgh, Pennsylvania, would love this.

You may also substitute half a large head of cabbage, grated or julienned, for the sauerkraut. Stir-fry it until crisp but cooked.

4 (1-inch-thick) pork chops
Freshly ground black pepper
3 tablespoons vegetable oil
1 to 2 cups apple cider vinegar
½ cup apple cider or apple brandy
½ cup chicken broth or stock, fresh or canned
1 tablespoon Dijon mustard

½ cup heavy cream
Salt
⅓ pound bacon, cut into ¼-inch slices
3 cups sauerkraut, drained
1 Granny Smith apple, peeled, cored, and cut into wedges or grated

Season the pork chops with the pepper. Heat the oil to very hot in a heavy frying pan. Add the chops and brown on both sides, leaving them slightly pink inside, about 160 degrees. Remove the chops to a plate. Combine the vinegar and cider or brandy in a bowl. Add ⅓ cup of the combined liquid to the hot pan to deglaze, stirring to get all the goodness from the bottom and sides. Bring to the boil and boil until reduced by half. Remove excess fat. Add the chicken broth, bring back to the boil, and boil until reduced by half. Whisk in the mustard and cream and season to taste with salt and pepper. Pour into a sauceboat.

Meanwhile, in another pan, cook the bacon until crisp and let drain on paper towels. Remove all but 2 tablespoons of the bacon fat and deglaze with the remaining vinegar mixture. Bring to the boil, stirring, and boil until reduced by half. Add the sauerkraut and apple and toss over high heat for 2 minutes. Remove to a platter. Season the sauerkraut with salt and pepper to taste. Crumble the bacon and sprinkle over the chops. To serve, place the chops on the sauerkraut and apples and coat them lightly with the sauce. Pass the remaining sauce.

Rum-Glazed Ribs

SERVES 6

Many of us fantasize about running a restaurant on a remote tropical island, with a view of the ocean, a pool, cool evenings and hot days, and flowers and fresh home-grown vegetables. Jinx and Jeff Morgan have done just this at the Sugar Mill Inn on Tortola, in the British Virgin Islands. This recipe is adapted from their *The Sugar Mill Hotel Cookbook* (1987).

6 pounds pork spareribs
2 (8-ounce) cans tomato sauce
1 cup dark rum
1 cup honey
¼ cup red wine vinegar

1 medium onion, chopped
2 garlic cloves, finely chopped
1 teaspoon Worcestershire sauce
Salt
Freshly ground black pepper

Cut the ribs into sections of several ribs suitable for serving. Place them in a pan and cover with cold water. Bring to the boil, reduce heat, and simmer, uncovered, for 20 minutes. Drain, discarding the liquid or saving it for stock. This may be done in advance. If the ribs cool (or are refrigerated), let them come back to room temperature before cooking.

Combine the tomato sauce, rum, honey, red wine vinegar, onion, garlic, and Worcestershire, and season with salt and pepper. Bring to the boil, reduce heat, cover, and simmer for 15 minutes, being careful not to let the sauce burn. Preheat the broiler or prepare the barbecue grill. Grill the parboiled ribs slowly, 5 to 6 inches from the heat, turning and basting often with the rum sauce until brown and glazed, about 20 minutes, turning once.

Stir-Fried Pork in Wrappers

SERVES 4 TO 6

This dish is fun for a family dinner or as a spontaneous dinner party for good friends. The stir-fry may also be wrapped in Phyllo pastry (page 153), baked as directed below, and served as a snack or as a main course.

3 tablespoons oil
2 garlic cloves, chopped
1 slice ginger, chopped
½ pound boneless lean pork, cut into very thin strips
1 carrot, grated or julienned
¼ cabbage, shredded
¼ pound mushrooms, sliced
6 green onions, 4 made into brushes
2 to 3 tablespoons soy sauce

1 tablespoon sherry (optional)
1 teaspoon sesame oil
Salt
Freshly ground black pepper
8 to 12 Chinese pancakes or flour tortillas, warmed
¼ to ⅓ cup hoisin sauce or Dijon mustard
2 cucumbers, peeled and cut into finger lengths

Place a large frying pan or wok over high heat. Add 2 tablespoons of the oil, the garlic, and the ginger. In a few seconds add the pork, and stir-fry until lightly browned. Add the carrot, cabbage, and mushrooms and toss briefly. Slice 2 of the green onions, including the tops, and add to the pan; toss a few minutes more. Add the soy sauce, sherry, and sesame oil and mix well. Taste for seasoning and add salt and pepper to taste. Take an onion brush and brush the warmed pancakes with hoisin sauce. Add 3 tablespoons of the meat/vegetable filling and 1 piece of cucumber. Wrap up like a burrito. Serve immediately.

To heat the pancakes, five minutes before serving, place them in a heatproof dish in a steamer or on a rack in the wok. Cover and steam until heated through. The pork is also good just by itself, with no wrapper, but of course will serve fewer people.

Pasta

Pasta Dough

MAKES $^3/_4$ POUND, SERVING 4 TO 6

I roll my pasta in a small hand machine because extruded pasta from electric machines has a doughy texture.

1 cup bread flour
1 extra large egg
1 tablespoon olive oil

1 teaspoon salt
1 to 3 tablespoons water

Mix together the flour, egg, olive oil, and salt until you have a loose dough, adding water as necessary to keep the dough smooth, moist, and pliable, but not sticky. Knead by hand on a floured board or place the ingredients in a food processor and process. The total kneading time will be a little more than 1 minute in the processor; 5 to 10 minutes by hand. Place the dough in a plastic bag and let it rest at room temperature for 30 minutes.

Feed the dough through a hand pasta machine at the widest opening. Repeat, reducing the width each time, stretching the dough until it is ⅛ inch thick, or as thick as you want it. The dough may be cut by hand for specific sizes or by using the linguine or fettuccine cutter of a hand machine. To prevent sticking, let the cut strips dry on a rack or a floured surface for up to 30 minutes before cooking. The cut pasta may also be placed in a plastic bag and refrigerated up to 2 days or frozen to be cooked later. If frozen, place directly into a pot of boiling water and cook 3 to 5 minutes.

To cook, drop the fresh pasta into a large pot of rapidly boiling water for a very brief time, 2 to 3 minutes if very thin. The thinner and fresher the pasta, the shorter the cooking time. Dried pasta can take up to 10 minutes in boiling water. Taste to test doneness. When cooked it will be slightly resistant to the bite. Drain and serve with any of your favorite pasta sauces.

Dudley's Lasagna

SERVES 4 TO 6

When my friend Dudley, a new bachelor at forty-five, started entertaining, this tomatoey, garlicky, cheesey, herby, traditional lasagna is the recipe he used for his first small dinner party. He was very proud, and why not? It made a very good supper with salad and French bread. And, oh yes—brownies or ice cream with fresh-cut strawberries and seasonal fruit. I have made this lasagna using half ground beef and half ground turkey with delicious results.

1 (6-ounce) package lasagna or ½ pound Pasta Dough (page 53)
2 pounds lean ground beef
1 onion, chopped
4 garlic cloves, chopped
1½ tablespoons dried or fresh thyme
2 tablespoons dried or fresh oregano
1½ teaspoons dried fennel seed
1 teaspoon dried red pepper flakes
1 teaspoon salt
Lots of freshly ground black pepper
3 to 4 cups spaghetti or Marinara Sauce (page 38) or 2 (15½-ounce) jars spaghetti sauce
1½ cups ricotta cheese or cream-style cottage cheese
1 to 2 (6-ounce) packages sliced Mozzarella cheese
¼ to ½ cup imported Parmesan cheese

Preheat oven to 375 degrees. Cook pasta in a large quantity of boiling salted water for 9 or 10 minutes. Drain. In a skillet, brown the ground beef; and add the onion and garlic to any remaining fat. Cook until soft. If there is excess fat, pour off the fat. Add the thyme, oregano, fennel seeds, pepper flakes, salt, pepper, and spaghetti sauce. In a greased 12- × 8- × 1½-inch baking dish, make layers in this order: pasta, spaghetti sauce, ricotta, Mozzarella. Repeat. Bake for 20 minutes. Sprinkle with the Parmesan. Return to oven for 10 minutes.

The lasagna freezes well.

Other Choices

Eggplant "Lasagna"

SERVES 4 TO 6

These layers of eggplant and zucchini, filled with gooey cheese and tomatoes and the kiss of herbs, do not miss meat. Serve as a side dish as well. It goes to covered dish suppers too. I frequently make a double batch and freeze half. Note that there are no noodles.

4 to 6 tablespoons olive oil
2 heaping teaspoons finely
    chopped fresh oregano
1 heaping teaspoon finely
    chopped fresh basil
Salt
Freshly ground black pepper
1 (12-ounce) eggplant, sliced
    ½ inch thick
1 (8-ounce) zucchini, sliced ½
    inch thick

8 ounces sliced Mozzarella
    cheese
1 cup ricotta cheese, drained
2 cups homemade spaghetti
    sauce or 2 (8-ounce) jars
2 tablespoons fennel seed,
    crushed
1 cup freshly grated imported
    Parmesan cheese

Combine the oil with the oregano, basil, salt, and pepper. Brush it onto both sides of the eggplant and zucchini. Lay the eggplant and zucchini in single layers on separate baking sheets. Broil 2 inches from the heat for 4 or 5 minutes, or until cooked. Turn, brush the other side with the herbed oil, and broil until done. Remove.

Preheat oven to 350 degrees. Layer half the eggplant slices in a wide, shallow 2- or 3-quart baking dish. Top with half the zucchini, then layer in half of the Mozzarella, ricotta, spaghetti sauce, fennel seed, and Parmesan. Repeat the layers with the remaining ingredients. Cover and bake 20 to 25 minutes, or until hot and bubbly.

May be made ahead several days. The "lasagna" freezes well.

Pasta or Rice with Pesto

SERVES 4

Pesto, the Italian sauce with the taste of basil, garlic, and Parmesan, has won a permanent place in America's heart. Use in starters, entrées, or side dishes.

1 pound pasta or rice, cooked according to package directions	⅓ to ½ cup Pesto Sauce (recipe follows)

In a large serving bowl, toss together the hot pasta or rice and the pesto sauce. Serve at once.

Pesto Sauce

MAKES 1 1/2 CUPS

Pesto is the answer of an era to an on-hand sauce suitable for any-thing. Try it with pasta, shrimp, clams, oysters, chicken, pork ten-derloin . . . then keep going inventing more uses. I make a large batch several times a year but always at summer's end to have it on hand throughout the winter. This mixture refrigerates well for several days and also freezes.

2 tablespoons chopped fresh
    basil leaves
3 tablespoons chopped fresh
    oregano (optional)
2 tablespoons chopped fresh
    parsley (optional)
3 tablespoons olive oil
3 tablespoons pine nuts
    (optional)

3 to 5 garlic cloves, crushed
1 cup freshly grated imported
    Parmesan cheese
3 tablespoons butter, at room
    temperature
Salt

Blend the herbs, olive oil, nuts, garlic, Parmesan, and butter together in a blender or food processor, or pound in a mortar until nearly a paste. Before spooning the pesto over cooked pasta, thin the sauce by adding 1 tablespoon of the hot water in which the pasta has been boiled.

To Freeze Pesto

- **Place pesto in freezer bag or freezer container, or freeze table-spoon measurements of it on a baking sheet. When frozen, pop into freezer bag as individual servings. Use to zip up stock, soups, sauces, or thawed, with butter, as a spread.**

Simply

Smart

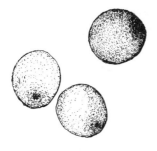

"Simply Smart" is a collection of recipes that can be used for either an upscale everyday family meal or for inviting the boss. Some of the meals are more expensive than those in Everyday Fare, but the main difference is one of style. These are great, somewhat tony, ideas for cozy dinners that invite conversation.

It is my philosophy that we should eat well at home. The recipes in this chapter are a little more intricate than those in the last.

I'm often asked about how to entertain—as if it is separate from daily life. So perhaps I need to say that there is an enormous difference between entertaining and "having company." Entertaining is for when everything is perfect because you need to impress. Having company is for expression of the joy and pleasure of company.

Perfect for home dining or casual entertaining, these recipes still also call for easily obtained ingredients. These are interesting, different, simple but elegant, recipes to wow your guests without going to lots of trouble.

Appetizers and Soups

Camembert Surprise

Nestled inside a lovely pecan coating studded with black olives and
pretzels is a Camembert cheese. I learned this recipe many years ago
at the London Cordon Bleu and still love using it.

1 (8-ounce) ripe Camembert
⅓ cup butter, softened
3 tablespoons white wine or
    lemon juice

¼ cup dry white bread crumbs
Salt
Freshly ground black pepper
½ cup chopped pecans, toasted

Garnish
Black olive halves
Small pretzels
Toast points

Line a quiche pan with a circle of wax paper. Remove the rind of
the Camembert. Beat the butter and Camembert in a food processor

or by hand until soft. Work in the wine and bread crumbs, a little at a time, and season with salt and pepper. Spoon into the prepared pan. Cover with plastic wrap and chill until firm. Use a knife to loosen the edges. Turn the mold out onto the ground pecans. Coat the mold all over, pressing the nuts in with a knife. Mark the top into wedges with the back of the knife and decorate with the black olive halves. Garnish the sides with the pretzels. Serve with the toast points.

Hot Cheese Croquettes

MAKES 50

Use natural cheeses for these delicious, spicy finger foods or the balls will flatten out. Good for a large party or as a snack.

½ pound Cheddar cheese, grated
½ pound Swiss cheese, grated
3 tablespoons flour
¼ teaspoon cayenne pepper
1½ teaspoons salt
4 egg whites, stiffly beaten
2 cups dry bread crumbs
Vegetable oil

Fold together the Cheddar, Swiss cheese, flour, cayenne, salt, and stiffly beaten egg whites. Roll into balls about the size of small nuts. Roll in the bread crumbs. Chill, covered, or freeze. When ready to cook, in a skillet heat the oil to 375 degrees. Add the thawed cheese balls and fry, turning them, until brown on all sides.

The croquettes freeze in an airtight container. Defrost thoroughly before deep frying.

Warm Pasta Salad with Feta and Spinach

SERVES 6

George Heery, who is the godfather of my goddaughter, sent me this recipe, which is one of his favorite things to cook after a hard day at the office. Fast, easy, pretty, with a bit of verve—what more do you need for a quick appetizer or supper on its own?

George uses pancetta—a salted but not smoked bacon—in place of the bacon. If you can find it, you'll love it!

2 heaping tablespoons finely chopped fresh basil, rosemary, parsley, or oregano
Freshly ground black pepper
1½ cups feta cheese (preferably sheep, but goat is okay)
½ cup extra virgin olive oil
1 (16-ounce) box of fusilli (corkscrew-shaped pasta) or other pasta
6 to 8 slices bacon, fried and crumbled, drippings reserved
4 cups (1 pound) loose, fresh, clean, picked-over uncooked spinach leaves, cut into ½-inch slices

1 cup diced fresh tomatoes
2 to 3 garlic cloves, finely chopped
2 tablespoons capers
1 roasted red pepper, peeled, seeded, and cut into ¼-inch strips (page 99)
Salt
¼ cup red wine vinegar
1 cup freshly grated imported Parmesan cheese

Sprinkle the basil, rosemary, parsley, or oregano and pepper over the feta, then drizzle 1 tablespoon of the olive oil over that mixture.

Meanwhile cook the fusilli in a large pot of boiling salted water 8 or 9 minutes, until al dente. Drain.

Place the crumbled bacon, spinach, tomatoes, garlic, capers, and red pepper in a large serving bowl. Put the hot pasta on top and toss until the spinach wilts. Top with the herbed feta and some of the reserved bacon drippings to taste. Season with salt and pepper. Add the remaining olive oil and the vinegar. Toss and sprinkle with the Parmesan. Serve warm.

Black Bean Pâté

MAKES 3 TO 4 CUPS

Even your meat-eating friends will be surprised at how much they love this delicious pâté. The chicken broth adds a lot of flavor. If you use canned beans, drain and purée them before adding the remaining ingredients.

1 pound dried black beans or
  2 (15-ounce) cans
6 to 8 cups chicken broth or
  stock, fresh or canned
  (optional)
6 to 8 garlic cloves, chopped

4 to 6 tablespoons grated fresh
  ginger
1 lemon, juiced
Salt
Freshly ground black pepper

Garnish
Chopped greens of green onions
  or chives, or chopped fresh
  cilantro

Crackers (optional)
Lettuce (optional)

If using dried beans, soak the beans overnight in water to cover. Or place the beans in water to cover, bring to the boil, boil 1 minute, and let rest 1 hour. Drain. Place the beans in a heavy pan with the chicken broth and add water, if necessary, to cover. Simmer until soft, 1½ to 2 hours. (Or use canned beans.) Remove 1½ cups of the beans and purée them. In a bowl, combine the beans, drained, and the purée and add the garlic and ginger to taste. Mix in the lemon juice, salt, and pepper. Garnish with the chopped onion greens, chives, or cilantro. Serve with the crackers as an appetizer or on the lettuce as a starter.

Italian Loaf

MAKES 24 1/2-INCH SLICES

Meat and spaghetti sauce fill this dough, making it a particularly pretty, interesting bread—good for a main course with soup, salad, and dessert, with picnic fare, or cut up into small servings as an appetizer.

The Dough
1½ to 3 cups bread flour
1 package active dry yeast
1½ teaspoons sugar
1 teaspoon salt

¾ cup water, heated to 125 degrees
1 egg
5 tablespoons olive oil

The Filling
3 tablespoons oil
1 large onion, chopped
3 garlic cloves, chopped
1 pound ground beef
1 cup homemade spaghetti sauce, Marinara Sauce (page 38), or 1 (8-ounce) jar spaghetti sauce
⅓ cup chopped dried tomatoes
1 heaping teaspoon finely chopped fresh oregano
1 heaping teaspoon finely chopped fresh basil

1 heaping teaspoon finely chopped fresh rosemary
Salt
Freshly ground black pepper
6 ounces ricotta cheese, drained
1 egg
2 heaping tablespoons finely chopped fresh parsley
½ cup freshly grated imported Parmesan cheese

Glaze
1 egg, beaten, mixed with 1 tablespoon water

Make the dough: In a food processor or mixing bowl, combine 1½ cups of the bread flour, the yeast, sugar, and salt. Add the water, egg, and olive oil to the yeast mixture. Process or knead in enough additional flour, in ½-cup increments, to make a soft dough. Knead until elastic and smooth as a baby's bottom, 1 minute in a food processor; 10 minutes in a mixer or by hand. Place in a greased plastic bag or turn in a greased bowl, cover with plastic wrap, and let rest 15 minutes or, if you have time, let it double.

Meanwhile, make the filling: In a large skillet, heat the oil. Add the onion, garlic, and ground beef, and brown. Drain. Add the spaghetti sauce and reduce until thick, almost to a paste. Add the dried tomatoes, oregano, basil, rosemary, and salt and pepper to taste.

On a lightly floured board, roll the dough to a 11- × 15-inch rectangle. Place on a greased baking sheet. Spread the filling lengthwise down the center third of the dough. Combine the ricotta, egg, and parsley. Spoon on top of the meat filling. Top with the Parmesan.

Preheat oven to 375 degrees. To enclose the filling and form a loaf, starting at the corners, cut the dough on opposite diagonals into 1-inch strips down the length of each side. Fold up the uncut ends and then crisscross the strips, bringing one strip over the filling, then a strip from the other side, until the length of the filling is covered with overlapping strips. Let the loaf double, uncovered, in a warm place for 30 minutes.

Brush the glaze on the loaf. Bake until done, about 25 minutes. Remove from the pan and cool on a wire rack placed over a pan to catch the drippings. Slice. Will keep several days covered in the refrigerator. Serve warm or at room temperature sliced into ½-inch pieces.

Red Bell Pepper Dip

MAKES 3 TO 4 CUPS

This is a pretty, colorful dip (or spread) with a rich full flavor from the peppers, baked garlic, and fresh herbs.

2 whole heads garlic
4 red bell peppers, roasted (page 99) peeled, seeded, and chopped
1 pound Yogurt Cheese (page 11), Montrachet cheese (without the ash), or other mild, soft goat cheese
5 tablespoons olive oil, plus oil for drizzling

½ cup finely chopped fresh basil
1 heaping tablespoon finely chopped fresh thyme
2 heaping tablespoons finely chopped fresh rosemary
¼ teaspoon cayenne pepper
Salt
Freshly ground black pepper

Preheat oven to 400 degrees.

Peel off the papery layer around the garlic heads, place the heads on an oiled baking sheet, and drizzle them with oil. Bake for 1 to 1½ hours. To cook in a microwave, drizzle the peeled garlic heads with oil and cook 1 to 1½ minutes on full power. Or, cook in a pan of boiling water for ½ to ¾ hour, until soft. Press or pop the garlic out of the individual cloves.

Place the red peppers, roasted garlic, and cheese in a blender or food processor. Purée until smooth. Add the oil, basil, thyme, rosemary, cayenne, and salt and pepper to taste. Cover and chill. Serve with crackers or raw vegetables.

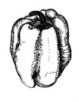

Miniature Bread Thimbles

MAKES 25 TO 30

In this case, smaller is better. These bread thimbles are ideal for fillings, such as Smoked Salmon Dip or Red Bell Pepper Dip. Sometimes I add crushed garlic or herbs to the oil. If a smaller loaf is used, you may only get one thimble per slice. Use leftovers to make bread crumbs.

12 slices very thin white bread (approximately 3¾- × 4¼-inch), crusts removed

3 to 4 tablespoons olive oil or vegetable oil

Preheat oven to 425 degrees

Roll out each slice of bread ⅛ inch thick. Cut into 2- to 2½-inch circles. Press into miniature muffin tins with 1¾- × 1¼-inch depressions. Press any torn spots together with your fingers. Trim off excess. Brush the bread with the oil. Bake 10 minutes, or until brown and crisp. Let the tins cool on a rack for 10 minutes, remove the thimbles from the tins, and cool the thimbles on the rack.

The cases freeze in a hard airtight container for up to 3 months. Crisp them before using in a low oven.

Mussels Julia

SERVES 2 AS A MAIN COURSE OR
4 TO 6 AS AN APPETIZER

Mussels are a special treat—extraordinarily easy to cook, once cleaned, and boldly beautiful in their glistening black shells. I love sipping sauce from their little boats.

This non-garlic recipe was developed by Julia Martin, who adores mussels but is allergic to the garlic usually used in mussel recipes.

To Clean Mussels

- **Mussels can vary considerably in saltiness and grittiness, depending on their source. Some grocery stores clean their mussels before selling them; others sell them as muddy as you can imagine. To clean, place the mussels in a pan or sink with lukewarm water. Using a stiff brush, scrub each shell. If you are serving them in the shell, you may need to scrape the barnacles off them with a knife. With your hands, pull off the beard, if there is one. (The beard is aptly named. If you don't see anything that looks like a beard, there isn't one!) Scoop the cleaned mussels out of the sink, being careful not to tip the mussels out, thereby pouring the gritty water back over them. Do not store mussels in tap water. They will stay alive a week or so if wrapped in wet newspaper and refrigerated, although the longer you keep them the more the flesh will shrink (as they will have nothing to eat).**

2 tablespoons extra virgin
    olive oil
½ medium onion, chopped
¼ cup Dijon mustard
1⅓ cups white wine or non-
    alcoholic wine

½ teaspoon salt
2 pounds mussels, cleaned
2 tablespoons finely chopped
    fresh parsley

Heat the olive oil in a large pot. Add the onion and cook until transparent. Stir in the mustard. Add the wine and salt and bring to the boil over high heat. Add the mussels and parsley, cover, reduce heat to medium, and steam until mussels open, about 6 minutes. Lift mussels out with a slotted spoon. Tip pot and ladle out sauce, leaving any grit from the mussels in the bottom. Serve with crusty bread.

Au Shucks Oysters

SERVES 6 TO 8

This is a winner either as a cold starter or as a cocktail hors d'oeuvre. You may substitute 1½ cups *Pico de Gallo* (page 83) for the marinade. To serve hot, marinate the oysters raw, then run them under the broiler. Serve with crackers or lavash.

2 pints shucked oysters and
    their liquor

Marinade

½ cup fresh lemon juice
¼ cup salad oil or olive oil
5 garlic cloves, chopped
Salt
Freshly ground black pepper

¼ cup finely chopped fresh
    thyme (optional)
¼ cup finely chopped fresh
    parsley
1 head leaf lettuce (optional)

Place the oysters and their liquor in a heavy saucepan. Bring to the boil, reduce heat, and simmer a few minutes, until their edges just begin to curl. Drain and place in a bowl.

To make the marinade, combine the lemon juice and oil. Add the garlic, salt, pepper, and herbs. Pour marinade over the oysters. Cover bowl with plastic wrap and marinate overnight in refrigerator or up to 2 days. Drain if necessary. Arrange in a serving bowl lined with lettuce (for a large party), or on lettuce-lined salad plates (for a starter).

Anytime/Anywhere Shrimp

SERVES 6 TO 8

This dish is popular because it's tangy and has personality. I learned how portable it is when my student Ann Kay brought it to a stand-up party for my cooking class. It also works wonderfully well for a sitdown meal. Serve with sliced black bread or French bread.

¾ cup olive oil
2 or 3 garlic cloves, chopped
2 medium onions, chopped
2 pounds shrimp, peeled
6 scallions or green onions,
    including green part,
    chopped

½ cup red wine vinegar
1 teaspoon dry mustard
¼ teaspoon cayenne pepper
Salt
Freshly ground black pepper

Heat ¼ cup of the olive oil in a heavy skillet. Add the garlic and onions and cook until soft and translucent. Turn up the heat. Add the shrimp and sauté 3 to 5 minutes, until they turn pink. (Do in 2 batches if necessary.) Cool.

Make the marinade with the remaining ½ cup oil, scallions, vinegar, mustard, cayenne, salt, and pepper. Add the shrimp mixture and toss thoroughly. Chill from 6 to 24 hours, stirring occasionally. Serve very cold.

Tarragon Shrimp on Zucchini Rounds

SERVES 4 TO 6 AS A STARTER

One time I had this all ready to serve for dinner at home, and we decided to go to a ballgame instead. I wrapped it in a towel and off we went with our covered dish supper!

1½ pounds zucchini, sliced into
  ¼-inch-thick rounds
¼ cup olive oil
¼ cup butter
4 green onions, chopped
1 shallot, chopped
½ cup sliced almonds
1 cup heavy cream
¼ cup dry sherry (optional)

1 to 2 teaspoons chopped fresh
  tarragon
1 pound large shrimp, cooked
  and peeled
Salt
Freshly ground black pepper
½ cup freshly grated imported
  Parmesan cheese

Preheat the broiler. Place the zucchini rounds on an oiled baking sheet. Brush with some of the oil and broil until soft, about 3 minutes.

Melt the butter in a frying pan, add the green onions and shallot, and cook until soft. Add the almonds and cook, stirring, until lightly browned. Add the cream, bring to the boil, and boil until reduced by half. Add the sherry, tarragon, shrimp, salt, and pepper. Toss to coat.

Preheat oven to 375 degrees.

Arrange the zucchini rounds in the bottom of a greased 1½-quart casserole. Top with the shrimp mixture and dust with the Parmesan. Bake 10 to 15 minutes, until just heated through.

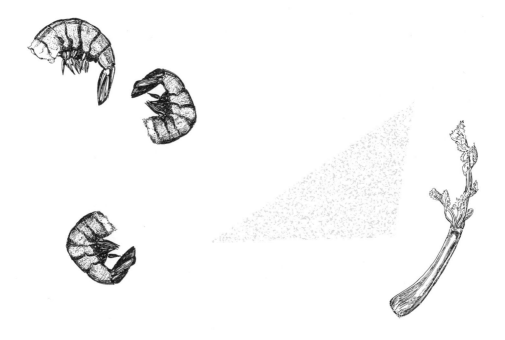

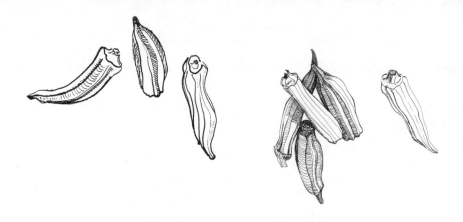

Crab Meat Quesadillas

MAKES 48 WEDGES

Make these full-flavored *quesadillas* as hot as you want with the optional jalapeño peppers. Serve them in wedges as cocktail party appetizers, a starter for a dinner party, or Sunday night supper for the family with a bowl of soup and a salad. They are very popular with all ages from teenagers to the golfing set!

1 cup fresh crab meat
½ cup sour cream
1 teaspoon lemon juice
3 green onions, chopped
¼ cup green chilies
1 heaping tablespoon finely
    chopped fresh cilantro
1 teaspoon chili powder
¼ teaspoon red pepper

1 to 2 fresh jalapeño peppers,
    chopped (optional)
12 tortillas
1 egg white
1 tablespoon vegetable oil
1 cup grated Cheddar cheese
1 cup grated Monterey Jack
    cheese

In a bowl, combine the crab meat, sour cream, lemon juice, green onions, green chilies, cilantro, chili powder, red pepper, and optional jalapeño peppers. Place 2 tablespoons of the mixture on a tortilla, spreading to ¾ inch of the edge. Top with a tablespoon each of Cheddar and Monterey Jack. Brush the rim of the tortilla with egg white. Place a second tortilla on top and press the edges to seal. Repeat with the remaining tortillas. Heat vegetable oil in a large frying pan. Brown the tortillas on both sides, about 1 minute per side. Remove from the pan and let cool. Cut each *quesadilla* into 8 wedges.

Parmesan Chicken Wings

SERVES 4 AS A MAIN COURSE;
8 APPETIZERS OR SNACKS

Tasty, crunchy, and meant for satisfying nibbling cravings, these wings are very popular as pick-up food for a party or for watching television. If dried oregano or marjoram is all that's available, I find that chopping it along with the parsley gives it a fresher taste and renders it acceptable much of the time. I hardly ever use dried parsley, as fresh is so easy to find in grocery stores all over the United States.

1 cup freshly grated imported
    Parmesan cheese
1 heaping tablespoon finely
    chopped fresh parsley
1 tablespoon fresh or dried
    chopped oregano or
    marjoram

1 teaspoon salt
½ teaspoon freshly ground
    black pepper
2 pounds chicken wings, cut up
½ cup butter, melted

Preheat oven to 375 degrees.

Mix the cheese, parsley, oregano, salt, and pepper together and place on a dry tray or baking sheet. Dip each piece of chicken into the butter, then roll in the cheese mixture, coating well. Place on a greased baking sheet. Bake for 45 minutes, turning when brown.

The wings freeze well. Thaw in the refrigerator, and heat in a 375-degree oven.

Tenderloin of Pork with Southwestern Apple Chutney

SERVES 4 TO 6 AS A MAIN COURSE;
10 TO 15 SLICES FOR A PARTY

Pork lovers will like this lean recipe. The chutney sauce is an unusual twist and should be made ahead.

2 tablespoons butter
2 tablespoons oil
2 (½-pound each) tenderloins
    of pork

3 cups Southwestern Apple
    Chutney (recipe follows)

Preheat oven to 400 degrees.

Heat the butter and oil in a roasting pan on top of the stove until sizzling. Add the tenderloins and brown all over. Place in the oven and roast 20 to 30 minutes, or until a thermometer registers 140 degrees for rare, 160 degrees for well done. Let the meat rest 10 minutes, then cut into 1-inch cubes. When ready to serve, stir the cubed meat into 3 cups apple chutney. Serve at room temperature. The chutney may be made months ahead. The roast may be made 2 days in advance and refrigerated.

The roast freezes, well wrapped. Defrost thoroughly, then cut into cubes.

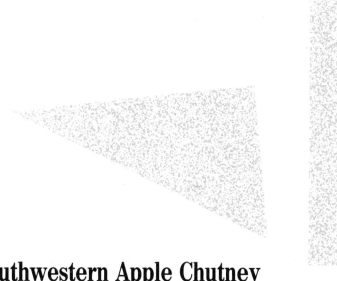

Southwestern Apple Chutney

MAKES 4 PINTS

2 quarts peeled coarsely
   chopped tart apples
2 medium-to-large red bell
   peppers, cored and seeded
2 onions, chopped
2 garlic cloves, chopped
1 pound seedless raisins
2 cups dark brown sugar
2 cups apple cider vinegar

1 tablespoon ground ginger
1 tablespoon cinnamon
1 tablespoon ground cumin
   seed
2 teaspoons dry mustard
2 teaspoons salt
¼ to ½ teaspoon crushed dried
   hot red chili peppers

Place the apples, bell peppers, onions, garlic, raisins, sugar, vinegar, ginger, cinnamon, cumin, mustard, salt, and red chili peppers in a large stainless steel pot or kettle. Cover and bring to the boil over high heat. Uncover, reduce heat, and cook, stirring occasionally, 1 to 1½ hours, until thick. May be used right away, or be frozen. Let cool completely before freezing.

If you'd like to can it, wash and sterilize 4 (1-pint) jars and their closures. Place the jars on a baking sheet in a 250 degree oven until needed. Ladle the boiling hot chutney into the jars, filling them to within ⅛ inch of the tops. Wipe the rims and seal. When cool, check to see if sealed properly. Label. Store in a cool, dark, dry place. If possible, let stand 1 month before serving.

Take-Along Onion Tart

SERVES 10 TO 12 AS A FIRST COURSE

Onions enhance the rich custard and incredibly light, flaky crust of this tart. Cut into small pieces and serve as an appetizer or as a first course. It is also wonderful to take on a picnic or tailgating.

1 recipe Sour Cream Flaky
    Pastry, chilled (recipe
    follows)
3 or 4 tablespoons butter
4 onions, sliced
1½ tablespoons flour
3 eggs
1½ cups heavy cream

Salt
Freshly ground black pepper
½ cup freshly grated imported
    Parmesan cheese
2 heaping tablespoons finely
    chopped fresh thyme
    (optional)
Cayenne pepper

Garnish
Fresh sprigs of thyme (optional)

Turn the pastry out onto a lightly floured surface or wax paper. Roll into a circle slightly larger than a 12-inch metal pie pan with removable bottom. Carefully fit the pastry into the pan and trim the edge. Chill ½ hour.

Preheat oven to 400 degrees. Fit crumpled wax paper or aluminum foil into chilled pastry shell, and fill it with raw rice or beans as weights. Bake for 20 minutes. Remove the pie pan from the oven, and remove the paper and rice or beans. Reduce the heat to 375 degrees.

Heat the butter in a large skillet until sizzling. Add the onions, lower the heat, and cook until soft. Sprinkle the flour over the onions, and cook, stirring, 1 to 2 minutes. Spread the onions in the prebaked pie shell.

In a bowl, beat together the eggs, cream, salt and pepper, Parmesan, optional chopped thyme, and cayenne. Pour custard mixture over the onions. Bake 30 to 40 minutes, until the custard is set in the center. Cool tart slightly on a rack, then unmold it by pushing up the removable bottom. If desired, lay the sprigs of thyme on top. Serve warm or chilled.

Sour Cream Flaky Pastry

MAKES ONE 10- OR 12-INCH TART

This is an exciting recipe to tackle once you feel secure with pastry making. Take a day when you are relaxed and have a few hours. Keep your kitchen cool. The pastry is flaky, tender, and will melt in your mouth. It rises similar to puff pastry.

1½ cups flour
¾ teaspoon salt
Pinch sugar
6 tablespoons unsalted butter,
    cut up and chilled

2 tablespoons shortening, cut up
    and chilled
2 tablespoons sour cream
2 to 4 tablespoons cold water

Sift the flour, salt, and sugar together in a large bowl or pulse to aerate in a food processor. Cut in the butter and shortening until the mixture resembles peas. Mix the sour cream with 2 tablespoons of the cold water, and add to the flour mixture to form a dough. Add more water if necessary. Form the dough into a round disk, wrap it, and chill it for 1 hour before rolling it out.

Place the dough between 2 pieces of wax paper, and roll it into a 6- × 15-inch rectangle. Fold in thirds like a business letter, starting with the bottom third. Turn the pastry so the folded side is on the left. Repeat the rolling and folding a second time. Wrap and chill for 30 minutes.

Flour 2 pieces of wax paper or a pastry cloth and use a floured or stockinged rolling pin to roll out the pastry. Place the dough in the center of the floured surface. Starting in the center of the dough, roll to, but not over, the top edge of the dough. Go back to the center, and roll down to, but not over, the bottom edge. Pick up the dough and turn it a quarter circle. This will prevent it from sticking and will help shape it evenly. Repeat the rolling and the quarter turns until you have a round ⅛ inch thick and 1½ inches larger than your pan. Fold the round into quarters.

Place the dough in a pie pan and unfold. Press well into the bottom and sides of the pan, being careful not to stretch the dough. Trim the dough 1 inch larger than the pie pan, and fold the over-hanging pastry under itself. To decorate, press the tines of a fork around the edge. To make a fluted pattern, use your thumbs to pinch the dough all around the edge so that the dough stands up. Place in the freezer or refrigerator for 30 minutes before baking.

To prebake the shell: Preheat oven to 425 degrees.

Prick the dough all over with a fork. Cover it with crumpled wax paper, then fill the paper with rice or beans to weight the bottom and sides. Bake 10 to 12 minutes. Remove the paper and rice. Fill the shell with the desired filling, and bake according to the filling di-rections. If the filling does not need cooking, finish baking the un-filled crust until done, about 20 minutes total.

Cliff's Crab Soup

SERVES 8

When I introduced Cliff Graubart to Cynthia Stevens and they mar-ried, I knew I would be dealing with Cliff's cholesterol fears. As a consequence, many of the soups I make are low in cholesterol. This fattening recipe actually came from him, however. If you are con-cerned about fat, too, this recipe is still very tasty made with a butter substitute, whole milk, and the cooked crab meat substitute made from Alaskan whitefish. If using canned chicken broth, use the lower in salt variety and omit the salt below entirely.

12 ounces cooked fresh, frozen, or canned crab meat

8 ounces mushrooms, stemmed and cut into strips

5 tablespoons butter, divided

3 tablespoons flour

3 cups chicken broth or stock, fresh or canned

1½ cups heavy cream

¾ cup freshly grated imported Parmesan cheese

¼ cup dry sherry (optional)

Salt

Freshly ground black pepper

½ heaping teaspoon finely chopped fresh parsley (optional)

Pick over crab meat for any bits of shell. Sauté the mushrooms in 2 tablespoons of the butter. Set aside. Melt the remaining 3 tablespoons of butter in a heavy saucepan and blend in the flour, making a *roux*. While stirring constantly, add the chicken broth and the cream. Bring this mixture just to the boil as it begins to thicken. Add the crab meat and the mushrooms. Let the soup heat thoroughly, then add the grated Parmesan and the sherry. Season to taste with salt and pepper. To serve, sprinkle parsley over each serving. If making ahead, lay a piece of plastic wrap directly on the surface of the soup to prevent it from forming a skin. May be made ahead a day and reheated gently.

Florida Gazpacho

SERVES 10 TO 12

When I was a restaurant chef in Majorca, I had an abundance of lush fresh red tomatoes. The gardener placed the extra ones on a long string rope, which he hung in a cool hallway near the kitchen. (This is similar to the way Southerners keep Vidalia onions.) Now, I fight for every good tomato I get!

Since there are only a few months a year when good tomatoes are available, I often compromise and use canned plum tomatoes, or I purchase some peeled and seeded prepacked fresh ones from the farmers' market. I call this recipe Florida gazpacho because that way anything goes, and I can use limes, which I never saw in Spain!

(continued)

2 onions, cut up
4 garlic cloves
1 red or green bell pepper,
    cored, seeded, and chopped
2 medium cucumbers, peeled
½ cup red wine vinegar
¼ to ½ cup fresh lime juice
½ cup bread crumbs

1½ pounds very ripe tomatoes,
    peeled, seeded, and chopped
    or 1 (1-pound) can Italian
    plum tomatoes, chopped
3 quarts tomato juice, fresh or
    canned
Salt
Freshly ground black pepper

Garnishes

1 onion, chopped
1 red or green bell pepper,
    cored, seeded, and chopped
1 cup bread cubes, fried in 3
    tablespoons olive oil

½ unpeeled cucumber, chopped
1 cup sour cream or plain
    yogurt

Purée the onions, garlic, bell pepper, and cucumbers in a blender or food processor. Add the vinegar, ¼ cup of the lime juice, and the bread crumbs, and process. Add the chopped tomatoes and tomato juice and process. Season to taste with salt and pepper and the remaining lime juice if desired. Serve hot or chilled, with the garnishes in separate bowls to be added at serving time.

Without the garnishes added, this will last, covered, in the refrigerator a week or so.

Southwestern Peanut Soup with *Pico de Gallo*

SERVES 6 AS A FIRST COURSE

With the *pico de gallo*, this is a particularly jazzy peanut soup and a filling first course.

2 tablespoons butter
1 medium onion, chopped
2 tablespoons flour
4 cups chicken broth or stock,
    fresh or canned

¾ cup creamy peanut butter
½ cup heavy whipping cream
Salt
Freshly ground black pepper

Pico de Gallo

½ ripe tomato, peeled, seeded,
    and finely chopped
¼ medium red onion, chopped
½ green onion or scallion,
    including green part,
    chopped
1¼ tablespoons vegetable oil

1 fresh hot green chili, seeded
    and finely chopped
½ tablespoon chopped fresh
    cilantro
1 tablespoon tomato juice
Salt
Freshly ground black pepper

Garnish
Chopped toasted peanuts

Melt the butter in a heavy large saucepan, add the onion, and cook until soft, about 10 minutes. Stir in the flour and cook, stirring, until lightly browned. Add the broth, stirring; and bring to the boil over high heat. Whisk in the peanut butter. Reduce heat, cover, and simmer, stirring often, for 20 minutes. Add the cream, heat gently, and season with salt and pepper to taste. The soup may be made ahead 2 days and kept covered and chilled.

Make the *pico de gallo*. Mix the tomato, red and green onions, oil, chili, and cilantro in a large bowl. Add the tomato juice and salt and pepper as needed. Cover and refrigerate. The sauce will keep up to 5 days.

Serve the soup hot, at room temperature, or chilled. Garnish with peanuts and pass the sauce separately.

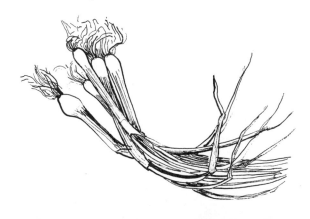

Pistou Soup

MAKES 3½ QUARTS, SERVING
8 TO 10 AS A STARTER

When my foster daughter Audrey was married in a small town of Provence, France, we took the train from Paris to Avignon, then had an hour's drive, arriving in Roussillon hot and tired. Audrey's soon-to-be mother-in-law, Jozette Thiault, had this ready for us for supper. The soup hit the spot perfectly, and I always think of that meal when I serve it.

This dish is good either as a starter or as a main course soup—in cool weather or hot. Traditionally, in France, it is made of various vegetables and vermicelli, with a binding agent of egg, oil, pounded garlic and herbs, and thick tomato purée. I've omitted the egg and simplified it some overall. The soup freezes wonderfully without the cheese. Leftovers freeze well for a casual get-together but do not serve them for important occasions.

1 cup chopped onion
White part of 1 leek or scallion, sliced
2 tablespoons butter
1 cup green beans, cut into 2-inch pieces
1 cup shelled butter beans or small lima beans
1 cup peeled potatoes, cut into 2-inch pieces
1½ cups chopped, peeled tomatoes or 1 cup canned tomatoes, broken up
8 cups chicken broth or stock, fresh or canned
½ cup vermicelli, spaghetti, or small pasta, broken into 1-inch pieces
Salt
Freshly ground black pepper
2 tablespoons tomato purée or paste
¼ cup olive oil or vegetable oil
2 garlic cloves, very finely chopped
2 heaping tablespoons finely chopped fresh basil
2 heaping teaspoons finely chopped fresh thyme or ½ teaspoon dried thyme
1 cup freshly grated imported Parmesan cheese

In a large pot, cook the onion and the leek in the butter until soft. Add the green beans, butter beans, potatoes, tomatoes and their juice, and the broth. Cover and bring to the boiling point over high heat. Reduce the heat and cook for 30 minutes, or until the vegetables are soft. Add the pasta after 15 minutes. Season with salt and pepper.

Place the tomato purée or paste in a bowl. With a fork or whisk, beat in the oil, drop by drop, as in making mayonnaise. Add the garlic, basil, and thyme. Stir into the soup. May be made several days in advance. To serve, sprinkle with the Parmesan.

The soup freezes in an airtight container. Defrost, heat, then add the cheese.

From the Sea

Grilled Orange-Basil Tuna Steak

SERVES 4

Every time I serve this to someone new I am reminded of how many people have never eaten tuna steak. Tuna is as close to red meat in flavor and texture as you can get in fish. Chances are if you didn't know you were eating fish you wouldn't—couldn't—guess, particularly if the tuna has been marinated. Substitute amberjack or swordfish steaks or fillets if tuna is not available.

4 (½-pound each) tuna steaks,
   1½ inch thick, or fillets
1 orange, juiced
1 lemon, juiced

½ cup oil
6 heaping tablespoons finely
   chopped fresh basil

Put tuna steaks in a plastic bag or in a deep plate. Combine the orange juice, lemon juice, oil, and basil. Pour over the fish, and let marinate, covered, 30 minutes to overnight.

   Oil the grill or broiler and preheat it. Shake off the marinade, reserving it, and grill or broil the fish 5 to 7 minutes per side, or a total of 10 minutes per inch of thickness. Meanwhile, bring reserved marinade to the boil, and reduce it slightly. To serve, pour the hot marinade over the fish.

Baked Oysters Casino

SERVES 2 OR 3 AS A MAIN COURSE;
4 TO 6 AS AN APPETIZER

Although oysters are very pretty baked and served in their oval shells, it's a nuisance to scrub the shells. I recommend coquille dishes as a substitute. Containers of fresh shucked oysters, far superior to canned oysters, are now readily available in grocery stores. Sealed carefully, the oysters will last in the refrigerator varying times, according to the date on the container. Frequently they may be frozen in the packages as well.

1 pint oysters, fresh or frozen, well drained
4 slices bacon, cut into ¼-inch strips
6 tablespoons chopped onion
3 tablespoons chopped green bell pepper

3 tablespoons chopped celery
1 to 2 teaspoons lemon juice
½ teaspoon salt
½ teaspoon Worcestershire sauce
Freshly ground black pepper
2 drops hot pepper sauce

Preheat oven to 350 degrees.

Place the oysters in individual coquille dishes or in a well oiled baking dish large enough to hold the oysters in one layer. Fry the bacon until crisp, remove from pan, and crumble, leaving the fat in the pan. Add to the pan the onion, green pepper, and celery. Cook until the vegetables are nearly tender. Add 1 teaspoon of the lemon juice, the salt, Worcestershire, pepper, and hot pepper sauce and mix well. Taste for seasoning and add more lemon juice, salt, and pepper if needed. Spread the mixture over the oysters, and top with the crumbled bacon. Bake for 8 to 10 minutes, or until oysters are done and the edges curl. Serve hot.

Shrimp Scampi

SERVES 2 AS A STARTER

For a main course, serve this garlic-coated shrimp with rice and pour the pan juices over each serving.

To Freeze Shrimp
- **To freeze freshly caught shrimp, dehead the shrimp and place them, unpeeled, in a freezer container or an empty clean milk carton. Pour water over the shrimp to cover and freeze immediately. Defrost in the container. You can also freeze seafood in milk. Crab meat is especially wonderful frozen that way.**

½ pound medium shrimp, in the shells
¼ cup butter
¼ cup olive oil
2 garlic cloves, crushed with salt

2 tablespoons chopped fresh parsley
Pinch cayenne pepper
1 lemon, juiced

Peel the shrimp, leaving on the tails. Heat the butter, oil, and garlic in a broiler-proof pan. Stir in the parsley, cayenne, and lemon juice. Add the shrimp, tossing to coat. Place under the broiler 6 inches from the heat, and broil until done, about 5 minutes. Check halfway through the cooking time and turn as necessary. Serve with crusty bread for dipping in the sauce.

Barbara Morgan's Cold Curried Shrimp

SERVES 2 AS A STARTER

Barbara Morgan, press secretary for Georgia's Governor Joe Frank Harris, uses this recipe as a cold starter, as it is easily made ahead. If you are going to take it on a picnic or constant refrigeration is not possible, storebought mayonnaise is preferred, as it has a preservative effect on the salad. For serving this straight from the refrigerator, you may prefer the flavor of homemade mayonnaise.

3 tablespoons butter
1 Granny Smith or Golden
   Delicious apple, chopped
1 small onion, chopped
1 garlic clove, chopped
2 tablespoons flour
1 cup stewed tomatoes
2 teaspoons curry powder
Salt
Freshly ground black pepper

2 cups mayonnaise (recipe
   follows)
1 tablespoon lemon juice
1 to 1½ pounds shrimp, cooked
   and peeled
5 leaves lettuce (optional)
2 cucumbers, thinly sliced
¼ cup slivered almonds, toasted
1 green onion, green part only,
   chopped

Melt the butter in a skillet. Add the apple, onion, and garlic and sauté until the onion is golden. Stir in the flour. Add the stewed tomatoes, curry powder, salt, and pepper. Bring to the boil. Remove the sauce from the heat, let cool slightly, and stir in the mayonnaise, lemon juice, and shrimp. Chill. The sauce may be made 1 to 2 days ahead and kept refrigerated, covered. When ready to serve, place the shrimp on the lettuce leaves if desired and serve surrounded by the sliced cucumbers and topped with the almonds and green onion.

Mayonnaise

MAKES 3 CUPS

Salmonella can be a problem with uncooked eggs, particularly for the aged and very young. So use your best judgment when making homemade mayonnaise.

3 egg yolks or 1 whole egg and 1 yolk
Salt
Freshly ground white pepper

3 tablespoons lemon juice
1½ cups vegetable oil or olive oil
Boiling water (optional)

In a small bowl, blender, or food processor, beat the egg yolks with a pinch of salt, pepper, and 1 tablespoon of the lemon juice until thick. Gradually whisk or beat in the oil, drop by drop at first, until the mixture thickens. Continue whisking, adding the oil in a slow, thin stream until the mayonnaise is thick. Season with the remaining 2 tablespoons lemon juice, salt and pepper to taste. Thin with water if too thick.

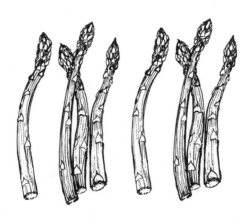

Grilled or Oven-Steamed Hard-Shell Clams

SERVES 4 AS A STARTER

Scrub the clams under cold running water. If necessary, then soak them in cold tap water for 30 minutes maximum to remove remaining sand. Do not leave the clams any longer as they will die in the fresh water.

Cleaned mussels (see page 70) may also be prepared this way but shorten the cooking time to 10 to 15 minutes, until the shells open. It's by far the most flavorful method of cooking them, as all the juices are captured. Serve with a crusty bread or rolls.

2 to 4 pounds cleaned littleneck
    or cherrystone clams or 3
    pounds cleaned butter clams
4 garlic cloves, chopped
2 onions, chopped
½ cup lemon juice or dry
    white wine

4 tablespoons chopped fresh
    parsley
4 tablespoons chopped fresh
    basil

Heat a grill or preheat oven to 450 degrees. Cut 8 pieces of heavy-duty wide aluminum foil into 18-inch squares.

Divide the cleaned clams among the foil squares. Sprinkle with the garlic, onion, lemon juice, parsley, and basil. Fold the foil loosely over the clams to allow them to open, then fold the edges together to seal the 8 packets. Place in the refrigerator. May be made to this point several hours ahead.

When ready to cook, place the clam packets on the hot grill or on the middle rack of the oven and cook until the clams open, 15 to 30 minutes, depending on whether they are coming from the refrigerator. (Littlenecks cook faster than cherrystones.) Check by opening a package. Turn out into a large bowl or individual bowl to eat.

Sautéed Soft-Shell Crabs

SERVES 2

Several times in their lives crabs shed their shells. For this brief period, the whole crab is edible. We did a television segment showing the process—the crabs backing out of their shells. It was fascinating seeing the empty shell next to the crab, for all the world looking like two identical crabs.

Usually soft-shell crabs are sold ready to cook. If not done already, cut off the eyes, remove the "dead-men" (the spongy gray gills), the sand sac, and the lower mouth of the crab. Crabs vary in size according to their age, from "small" to "large" to "jumbo." Three large or two jumbos make a good dinner portion. Fresh soft-shell crabs are superior to frozen. These crisp soft-shell crabs are served glistening with butter and sprinkled with nuts. They are great for the last minute.

1 to 2 tablespoons oil
¼ to ½ cup butter
4 to 6 soft-shell crabs, cleaned
    and dried

2 to 3 tablespoons slivered
    almonds

Heat the oil and 3 tablespoons of the butter in a heavy skillet until hot and sizzling. Add the crabs and sauté a few minutes on each side. Remove to a warm serving plate. Meanwhile, brown the almonds in 1 to 2 tablespoons of the remaining butter. Pour over the crabs and serve at once.

Spicy Shrimp and Cucumbers

SERVES 2 TO 4 AS A STARTER

This beautiful shrimp coated with spicy peanut butter sauce, accompanied by cool cucumbers, then topped with green onions is delicious. Nearly a salad, the textures and flavors are varied and exciting.

The entire dish can be made several hours or up to a day in advance; although the sauce does become a little watery, it still tastes good! I prefer getting everything ready a day ahead, storing the components in separate plastic bags or containers in the refrigerator, then combining them several hours in advance.

Spicy Peanut Butter Sauce

4 tablespoons peanut butter
½ cup soy sauce
1½ tablespoons rice or white wine vinegar
¼ to ⅓ cup sugar
1 to 2 teaspoons hot sauce

2 (quarter-size) slices ginger, chopped
1 to 1½ tablespoons ground Szechwan peppers
3 garlic cloves, chopped

1 long or 2 small cucumbers, thinly sliced
Salt
1 pound shrimp, cooked and peeled

6 to 8 green onions or scallions, thinly sliced

To make the sauce, blend together the peanut butter, soy sauce, vinegar, sugar, hot sauce, ginger, peppers, and garlic cloves.

Sprinkle the cucumbers with salt, and let stand in a colander 15 to 30 minutes to remove the bitter juices and soften. Rinse and drain. Dry with paper towels. Put the cucumber slices on the outside rim of a platter on the diagonal. Place the shrimp in the center, pour the sauce over, and sprinkle with the green onions.

Steamed Soft-Shell Clams

SERVES 4

Treat yourself to a bucket of these tiny jewels of the sea that are steamed in broth, then served with melted butter. The brittle shells never completely close as the necks stick out. There are many kinds of steamer or soft-shell clams, which are also called softs and gapers.

2 garlic cloves, finely chopped
1 onion, finely chopped
1 cup lemon juice or dry white wine
4 pounds soft-shell clams, cleaned
3 tablespoons chopped fresh parsley

1 tablespoon chopped fresh thyme or ½ tablespoon dried thyme
Freshly ground black pepper
1 cup butter, melted

Place the garlic, onion, and lemon juice in a large non-iron skillet. Bring to the boil over high heat, cover, reduce heat, and simmer 3 to 5 minutes. Add the clams, arrange in one even layer, cover, and bring back to the boil. Reduce the heat, and simmer until the shells open wide, about 3 to 5 minutes. Use a slotted spoon to remove the clams. Strain the broth through a very fine strainer into a bowl. Add the parsley, thyme, and pepper. Serve the broth and butter in separate bowls. Remove the clams from the shells, dip them in the broth, then in the melted butter. Put the empty shells in a separate bowl.

Uncle Ben's Grilled Stuffed Trout

SERVES 4

Fresh sea trout and rainbow trout are quite different, but both are delicious. This recipe was given to me by my producer, Cynthia Stevens, just as this book was going to the publisher. The recipe belonged to her uncle who died this past summer.

1 (4- to 5-pound) fresh sea trout, with head on, or 4 small trout (⅔ to ¾ pound each)
½ heaping teaspoon finely chopped fresh dill
Salt
Freshly ground black pepper
2 tablespoons bacon fat or drippings

1 medium onion, chopped
½ cup chopped celery
1 cup sliced fresh mushrooms
1 cup crumbled cornbread
1 (4½-ounce) can ripe olives, chopped
½ cup sour cream
¼ cup butter, melted
8 thin slices lemon

Preheat the grill.

Wash and drain the fish. Sprinkle the outside and inside of the trout with the dill, salt, and pepper. In a medium skillet, heat the bacon fat, add the onion, celery, and mushrooms, and sauté until soft. Add the cornbread, olives, sour cream, and melted butter. If necessary moisten with water slightly to make the stuffing hold together. Stuff the cavity of the fish with the mixture and close securely. Arrange 4 lemon slices on each side of fish. Place trout in oiled fish basket. Place basket on grill and cook until done, 10 minutes per inch of thickness, including stuffing, or about 15 minutes per side. Or place the fish in 2 greased rectangular baking pans, garnish the fish with the lemons, and bake at 400 degrees for 10 minutes per inch of thickness, including stuffing, about 15 to 20 minutes.

Poultry and Meats

Lemon and Garlic Broiled or Grilled Chicken Breasts

This is a simple, quick dish that received extraordinary acclaim from my students for its ease of preparation. It is really good served with baked garlic and baked onions (recipes follow).

4 chicken breasts, on the bone
Salt
Freshly ground black pepper
2 tablespoons olive oil or
    vegetable oil

2 lemons, juiced
4 large garlic cloves, chopped
1 heaping tablespoon finely
    chopped fresh rosemary

Place the chicken breasts, skin side up, in a dish or plastic bag. Season with salt and pepper. Mix together the oil, lemon juice, garlic, and rosemary. Pour the juice mixture over the chicken, and cover or seal bag. Marinate, refrigerated, as long as possible, up to 2 days. When ready to serve, place the chicken, skin side turned to the heat, under the broiler or on a preheated grill 6 inches from the heat, and cook 15 minutes. Turn; and continue to cook until done, about 15 minutes. The juices should run clear when chicken is pierced with a fork. May be made ahead and reheated, but is best hot off the grill.

Chicken Breasts with Mustard Sauce

SERVES 4

I bone and skin chicken breasts in batches, then wrap each individually, and store in the freezer. The breasts defrost quickly and are wonderful for fast, tasty "emergency" meals like this one. For the family I do the low-cal version; for other occasions, I've been known to add the cream!

1 (8-ounce) jar Dijon mustard
1 slice ginger (quarter size),
    chopped
3 tablespoons dry white wine
3 heaping tablespoons finely
    chopped fresh chives or
    green part of green onions
    or scallions

1 garlic clove, chopped
6 chicken breasts, boned,
    skinned, and flattened with
    a mallet
¼ to ⅓ cup heavy whipping
    cream (optional)

Garnish
1 tablespoon mustard seed
    (optional)

In a pan, heat the mustard with the ginger, white wine, 1 tablespoon of the chives, and the garlic. Preheat a grill. Add the chicken breasts, and grill 2 minutes on each side; or place in a hot non-stick skillet and brown, turn, and brown the other side. Remove from the heat. Reheat the sauce, adding the cream if desired. Serve the sauce separately or pour over the chicken. Garnish with the optional mustard seeds and the remaining chives.

Chicken Breasts with Apples and Cranberries

SERVES 4

This very unusual dish is a hit with my students. It speaks of fall dinners with good friends. The ginger adds a sort of "sweet" hotness that makes an interesting contrast to the tart cranberries. And it freezes. You'll love it. Incidentally, when cranberries are in season, buy extra bags of them and pop them, as is, into the freezer until needed.

1 cup flour
1 teaspoon cayenne pepper
½ teaspoon cinnamon
Salt
Freshly ground black pepper
3 Granny Smith apples, peeled, cored, and cut into small wedges
1 lemon, juiced
2 garlic cloves, chopped
1 tablespoon chopped ginger
2 tablespoons butter
1 small onion, chopped
4 boneless chicken breasts with skin

2 to 3 tablespoons olive oil
½ cup apple cider
¼ cup apple cider vinegar
1 cup chicken broth or stock, fresh or canned
1 heaping tablespoon finely chopped fresh rosemary
1 heaping tablespoon finely chopped fresh thyme
1 cup sour cream
½ cup whole berry cranberry sauce

Garnishes
Fresh thyme leaves
½ cup chopped cranberries (optional)

Combine the flour, cayenne, cinnamon, salt, and pepper. Set aside. Toss the apple wedges with the lemon juice, garlic, and ginger. Heat the butter in a large skillet. Add the apple mixture and cook over low heat for 6 to 8 minutes, until tender. Remove the apple mixture from the pan. Turn up the heat. Add the onion, and cook over medium heat until soft. The recipe may be made ahead to this point, 2 to 3 days, if desired.

Meanwhile, dredge the chicken in the flour mixture. Heat the olive oil in another skillet. Add the chicken, and cook until golden brown on one side; turn and brown the second side. Cook through, about 15 to 20 minutes. Remove the chicken from the skillet and keep it warm. Add to the skillet the apple cider, vinegar, chicken stock, rosemary, and thyme. Bring to the boil, and reduce liquid by half. Add the sour cream and cranberry sauce. Simmer 1 to 2 minutes. Add the apple mixture to the skillet and reheat until heated through. Adjust seasonings.

Meanwhile, arrange the chicken on a heated platter, pour the hot apple-sour cream mixture over it. Garnish with the fresh thyme and cranberries and serve immediately. May be made ahead and reheated in a 325-degree oven.

Chicken Breasts with Eggplants and Roasted Red Pepper Sauce

SERVES 4

This is a great last-minute lunch or dinner if you keep roasted and peeled peppers on hand. I can't always find the tiny eggplants but I love them when I do! Serve these breasts with plain or herbed rice. For a decadent meal, cut one or two potatoes into wedges, and brown them in olive oil. Finish off in the oven until crisp, then add rosemary and garlic.

To Roast Peppers
- **To roast peppers, place the peppers on the grill or under the broiler, turning them, until charred all over, nearly black. Re-**

move and place in a plastic bag to steam off skin. When cool enough to handle, remove charred skin and seed them.

2 small Italian or Chinese eggplants
2 to 4 tablespoons olive oil
4 chicken breasts, boned and skinned
1 onion, sliced
1 garlic clove, chopped
2 red bell peppers, roasted and peeled (see above)

¼ cup sherry vinegar or red wine vinegar (can be Balsamic)
1 to 2 heaping tablespoons finely chopped fresh herbs, such as thyme or parsley (optional)

Preheat the grill or broiler.

Halve the eggplant, score in 2 or 3 places, and brush with some of the oil. Place on the grill, cut side toward the heat. Turn after 5 minutes. Cook until almost soft. Add the chicken breasts and cook 3 minutes on each side, until done. Remove to a plate.

Heat the remaining oil in a large frying pan until singing. Add the onion and garlic, and cook until soft. Purée the peppers and vinegar in a food processor or blender until smooth. Add the purée, eggplants, and chicken to the frying pan, and heat together, about 5 minutes. Place the chicken mixture on a platter surrounded by the eggplants and sauce. Sprinkle with the herbs if desired.

Chicken Salad with Grapes

SERVES 4 TO 6

In the early 1970s when I had a restaurant in Social Circle, I quickly whipped up a salad for a last-minute guest and her friends. Martha Summerour always remembered that lunch and asked for the recipe. This is as close as I can get. I think it is good enough for her to remember for another twenty years! Perfect for a hot summer ladies' lunch or Sunday night supper.

1 whole chicken, cooked,
    skinned, boned, and meat
    shredded
4 tablespoons orange juice
1 cup Mayonnaise (page 90)
½ cup heavy cream, whipped

1½ cups halved seedless grapes
¼ cup sugar
Salt
Freshly ground black pepper
¼ head Boston or Bibb lettuce
    (optional)

Garnish
1 to 2 tablespoons julienned
    strips, no white attached,
    orange peel

In a bowl, combine the chicken, orange juice, mayonnaise, whipped cream, and grapes. Season to taste with sugar, salt, and pepper. Chill, covered. Arrange on lettuce leaves if desired or on salad plates. Top with the slivered orange peel.

Baked or Grilled Onions

SERVES 6

Baked or grilled onions are a comfort food to me. I eat them when I crave a lot of flavor as well as when I'm sad. To get them cooked faster, quarter them.

6 medium onions, peeled
6 tablespoons butter or oil

Salt
Freshly ground black pepper

Preheat oven to 400 degrees.

Halve the onions and arrange in a greased baking dish or on a greased grill rack, dot with the butter, and cook until tinged with black and brown, nearly charred, for 45 minutes to 1 hour and 15 minutes, brushing with more butter or oil as necessary to keep moist. Season with salt and pepper. Serve hot or chilled.

Whole Baked Garlic

SERVES 4

Whole garlic, cooked in its peel, has a full, nutty flavor quite different from raw garlic, chopped or crushed.

4 whole heads garlic   Salt
3 tablespoons olive oil or butter   Freshly ground black pepper

Preheat oven to 350 degrees.

Remove the thin papery outer skin that covers each whole head of garlic. (Either peel it off starting from the root or take a knife and cut around the covering midway up the head, then peel off the outer skin.) Place the heads in a small baking dish. Drizzle a little oil or butter over them and sprinkle on salt and pepper. Bake 1 to 2 hours, depending on size, until tender. Serve one head per person.

To cook in a microwave, drizzle the peeled garlic heads with oil and cook 1 to 1½ minutes at full power.

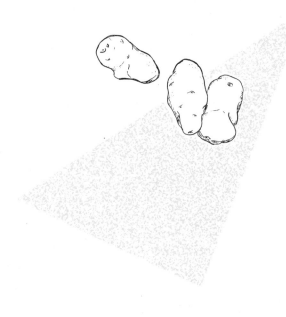

Chicken with Oriental Sauce

SERVES 4

My buddy John Markham served this incredibly tasty chicken full of Oriental verve as a main course with Oriental (Szechwan) noodles at an informal dinner party. If using wings, they may also be cut into joints to serve as an hors d'oeuvre. Have on hand plenty of napkins or even finger bowls.

⅓ cup olive oil
1 (3-pound) chicken, jointed, or
    4 pounds chicken wings

Oriental sauce

5 tablespoons tomato sauce
3 tablespoons dry sherry or
    lemon juice
3 tablespoons dark brown sugar
3 tablespoons flour

3 tablespoons dark soy sauce
1 tablespoon red wine vinegar
1 teaspoon hot sauce
1½ tablespoons chopped ginger
2 garlic cloves, chopped

Garnish
⅓ cup sliced green onions

Heat the oil in a frying pan. Add the chicken, skin side down, without overloading the pan. Brown, turn, and brown the other side. Reduce heat to medium, cover, and cook until done, about 20 minutes. May be done ahead.

To make the Oriental sauce, mix together in a bowl the tomato sauce, sherry or lemon juice, sugar, flour, soy sauce, vinegar, hot sauce, ginger, and garlic. Stir until well combined. Place in a pan, and bring to the boil, stirring, until the sauce has thickened. When ready to serve, combine the chicken and the sauce and heat through, making sure all the chicken is coated. Garnish with the green onions. May be made ahead 1 day, but best served immediately.

Cindy's Turkey Stuffed Under the Skin

SERVES 8 TO 10

This beautiful dish combines the traditional flavors of Thanksgiving with an unusual and elegant presentation. As a result of placing the stuffing under the skin, the turkey is extremely moist. Although you may think that the process of putting the stuffing under the skin is a time-consuming one, it is not. It only takes about ten minutes longer than stuffing the turkey cavity and the extra effort is worth it for something that tastes this great. Return the turkey to the kitchen for carving; it's infinitely easier that way. I learned this from Cindy Morgan, who worked for me in the early sixties in my restaurant.

1 (12- to 14-pound) turkey,
    thawed

The Stuffing

1 onion, chopped

3 garlic cloves, chopped

3 cups unsweetened cornbread crumbs, flavored or plain (page 361, omitting the red peppers)

¾ cup ricotta cheese

1 cup chicken broth or stock, fresh or canned

½ cup butter, melted

¾ cup chopped pecans

1 heaping tablespoon finely chopped fresh sage

1 heaping tablespoon finely chopped fresh thyme

2 (10-ounce) packages frozen spinach, defrosted and chopped

Salt

Freshly ground black pepper

¼ cup butter, softened

2 to 4 cups chicken stock or broth

The Gravy

3 tablespoons butter (optional)

3 tablespoons flour

1 cup heavy cream

Preheat oven to 325 degrees.

    Remove the neck and giblets from the turkey cavity. Set aside.

Gently loosen the skin from the turkey flesh, including the skin around the legs and thighs. Be careful not to tear the skin.

Prepare the stuffing by combining in a large bowl the onion, garlic, crumbs, cheese, broth, butter, pecans, sage, and thyme. Mix well. Gently add the chopped spinach and salt and pepper to taste. Press the mixture under the skin of the bird, distributing it evenly. If you see flesh under the skin, then the stuffing needs to be evened out. When completely stuffed (do not place stuffing in the main cavity), massage the surface of the skin to insure uniform distribution of stuffing underneath. Don't stuff too fully around the opening as this may make it difficult to truss. Truss the skin to enclose the stuffing, using kite string or non-waxed dental floss. Remove pop-up thermometer and truss the opening. Place turkey in a large roasting pan. Brush with the butter and season with salt and pepper. Pour enough stock around the bird to come up 1 inch around the sides. Bake 3 to 4 hours, basting as needed, or until a meat thermometer inserted in the thigh registers 170 degrees. Check after 1½ hours and cover very loosely with foil if brown. Test. Uncover if not completely brown. Turkey should register 170 degrees on a meat thermometer. If not done in 3 hours, increase oven temperature to 350 degrees and roast 30 to 60 minutes more. Remove the turkey to a platter and allow to rest 20 minutes before carving or remove from pan and refrigerate, covered, up to 2 days. To reheat, place in a 325-degree oven and cook about 1 hour from refrigerator temperature.

Remove the fat from the stock in the pan. Add any remaining stock and bringing to the boil, reduce it by half. Serve with the turkey.

If you like gravy, in a saucepan melt the butter, add the flour, and cook several minutes until pale brown. Add the hot stock, whisking briefly. Bring to the boil and boil briefly. Add the cream if desired, bring back to the boil, and boil until it reaches the desired consistency. Season with salt and pepper. Cover with plastic wrap until needed. The gravy may be made up to 2 days ahead.

Beef Braised with Mahogany Onions

SERVES 4 TO 6

This is what I cook when I'm home working on the computer and want an occasional excuse to get up, to turn the meat! The house smells wonderful all day long.

The beef is very tender braised in its own juices and smothered with onions and garlic. It's also good cold and in sandwiches. And the recipe multiplies up very well for a crowd. To serve 20 to 25 people, increase the ingredients to 1 (10-pound) sirloin tip, ½ pound bacon, 10 garlic cloves, and 10 onions. Proceed as below, but cook 5 to 6 hours.

2 pounds boneless chuck or
  round roast
¼ pound bacon, cut into slivers
4 medium onions, very thinly
  sliced

5 garlic cloves, chopped
Freshly ground black pepper
Salt

Preheat oven to 325 degrees.

Choose a heavy casserole large enough to accommodate the meat snugly. Put the bacon, sliced onions, and the garlic on the bottom of the pot. Top with the meat, and season with pepper. Cover tightly, and cook for 2½ to 3 hours, turning the meat after the first hour and every half hour after that, until the meat is very tender and brown, and the onions are a lovely mahogany. Season with salt and more pepper if necessary. Slice the meat very thin, pour the juices and onion mixture over it, and serve hot. May be made several days ahead and reheated.

Rosemary Rubbed Beef

SERVES 4 TO 6

Family and friends will enjoy this very flavorful, pretty braised beef—nearly a pot roast—but one full of excitement.

2 tablespoons chopped fresh
    rosemary
4 garlic cloves, chopped
6 black olives, pitted and
    chopped
2 plum tomatoes, seeded and
    chopped

1 teaspoon prepared
    horseradish
¼ cup olive oil
Salt
Freshly ground black pepper
1 (3-pound) beef round tip roast

Combine the rosemary, garlic, olives, tomatoes, horseradish, olive oil, salt, and pepper. Rub over the roast and marinate, covered, for 24 hours in the refrigerator.

Preheat oven to 325 degrees. Place roast in a shallow baking pan, and top it with the marinade. Cover. Bake 2 to 2½ hours. Remove, let cool 10 minutes, and slice. Serve sauce on top. May be made several days in advance and reheated.

The beef freezes well.

Breaded Veal Scallopine

SERVES 4

For a crisp crust on the outside and soft tender meat on the inside, be sure the butter and oil are "singing hot," and that you use a heavy large skillet or frying pan for this recipe. Add butter and oil in batches, as needed, so the meat doesn't swim in fat.

2 eggs
2 tablespoons water
¼ cup flour
Salt
Freshly ground black pepper

2 pounds veal or turkey
   scallopine, cut ¼ inch thick
1 cup fine bread crumbs
¼ cup butter
4 tablespoons oil

Garnish
3 lemons, cut into wedges

Beat the eggs lightly with the water. Season the flour with salt and pepper. Dip the scallopine into the flour, shake off the excess, then dip them into the beaten eggs. Finally dredge the veal in the bread crumbs. Gently shake any excess crumbs. Refrigerate, covered, for ½ hour to 6 hours.

   Heat enough butter and oil to coat the bottom of a heavy 12-inch skillet until sizzling. Add enough scallopine to fill the pan without their touching. Brown, then turn, and brown the second side. This should take only a few minutes per side. Remove from pan to a warm plate. Repeat with more butter, oil, and scallopine. To serve, squeeze a little lemon juice over the veal and garnish with the lemon wedges.

Saltimbocca alla Romana

SERVES 4

Saltimbocca means "jump in the mouth." Rome, Italy, claims the recipe, but others say it originated in Brescia. The preparation is amazingly easy and quick, allowing just enough time to cook rice and a vegetable, as well as toss a salad. It's a great last-minute dish.

8 slices veal scallopine or turkey cutlets
8 slices Parma ham (or prosciutto)
8 fresh sage leaves
1 tablespoon butter
¼ cup olive oil
Salt
Freshly ground black pepper
1 cup dry white wine or ¾ cup chicken broth or stock and ¼ cup lemon juice

Pound veal or turkey slices thin. Put a slice of ham and a sage leaf on each slice. Lace in place with a toothpick. Heat the butter and oil until hot and singing in a large skillet. Add the veal and brown on one side. Turn and brown other side. Season to taste with salt and pepper. Add the wine or chicken broth and lemon juice and bring to the boil over high heat. Reduce heat, and simmer 10 minutes. Remove the meat to a plate and keep warm. Remove the toothpicks. Bring pan juices to the boil, boil until reduced by half. Pour over the meat, and serve hot.

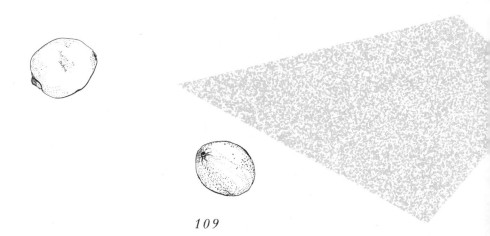

Lamb Chops with Mustard Mint Sauce

SERVES 2 OR 3

It's becoming quite usual to accompany a hot dish with a cold or room temperature sauce. This one may be made several days ahead if desired, and it is also good with grilled tuna steaks.

6 (1- to 1½-inch-thick) lamb chops
3 garlic cloves, chopped
4 heaping tablespoons finely chopped fresh mint
1 cup olive oil or vegetable oil, divided
3 tablespoons lemon juice
2 tablespoons Dijon mustard
2 tablespoons heavy cream, sour cream, or drained plain low-fat yogurt
Salt
Freshly ground black pepper
Sugar

Rub the chops with 2 teaspoons of the garlic and 2 tablespoons of the mint. Mix ¼ cup of the oil with 2 tablespoons of the lemon juice. Drizzle on the chops. Cover and marinate up to 2 hours at room temperature or longer in the refrigerator. Place the chops on a pre-heated hot grill and grill 5 to 6 minutes on each side, or until desired doneness.

Meanwhile, make the cold sauce. Place the mustard in a blender or food processor with the remaining 1 tablespoon lemon juice and 1 teaspoon garlic. Slowly add the remaining ¾ cup oil as you would to make mayonnaise and blend until emulsified and thick. Add the remaining 2 tablespoons mint. Quickly blend in the cream or yogurt. Taste, season with salt and pepper, and add sugar as necessary. Pour some sauce over the meat and pass the rest separately.

Country Ham

SERVES 16

When country hams or Smithfield hams have been cured they are very salty. It is terribly important, therefore, to scrub them well, then soak them several days, changing the water regularly to remove the excess salt. Don't worry about mold. It scrubs off and doesn't mean the meat is bad. If you don't have a galvanized tub for soaking, use a large cooler—it's the perfect size. Or if you are fortunate enough to have a pan large enough, you may simmer with enough liquid to cover to an internal temperature of 180 degrees.

1 (12- to 15-pound) country
   ham, scrubbed, soaked 1 to
   2 days, changing water after
   first 4 hours, then daily
10 (quarter-size) slices ginger
1 teaspoon peppercorns
½ gallon apple cider

1 gallon water
1 cup chunky applesauce
3 tablespoons Dijon mustard
1 tablespoon prepared
   horseradish
1 cup dark brown sugar
1 cup bread crumbs

Preheat oven to 350 degrees.

Place ham in a large pan, fat side up. Add sliced ginger and peppercorns. Then add enough cider and water to come 2 to 3 inches up the side of the ham. (Reserve remaining cider/water to add to pan as liquid evaporates.) Cover and place in oven. Cook about 20 minutes per pound, or until internal temperature on a meat thermometer registers 160 degrees. Remove from oven halfway through cooking and turn ham over. Replace in oven and continue cooking. When done, remove ham to broiler rack and let rest 10 minutes. Remove skin and fat. Taste at this point. If ham is still terribly salty, it may safely be immersed in more apple cider and water to draw out more of the salt. Let sit a couple of hours. Taste again and proceed. Drain. You may refrigerate until ready to glaze.

Increase oven temperature to 400 degrees. Combine the applesauce, mustard, horseradish, and ½ cup of the brown sugar. Spread over the ham. Bake 20 minutes, or until ham is heated through and sauce is bubbly. Remove from oven and turn on broiler. Mix together remaining ½ cup brown sugar and bread crumbs and spread on ham. Broil 5 minutes, or until crisp.

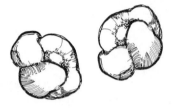

Grilled Ham with Asian Barbecue Sauce

SERVES 6

When precooked ham is on sale, I have the butcher cut steaks for me. It's a fast supper and good for company. This sauce has Asian ingredients and keeps well in the refrigerator. Hoisin sauce is a sweet Chinese combination made from soybeans. Hoisin as well as dark Oriental sesame oil are available in the gourmet or Oriental sections of most grocery stores. Use for grilled ham, in marinades, and sauces.

1 (7½-ounce) bottle hoisin sauce
¼ cup soy sauce
¼ cup packed brown sugar
2 tablespoons dark Oriental sesame oil
3 tablespoons apple cider vinegar
⅓ cup freshly squeezed orange juice
1 teaspoon ground ginger
2 teaspoons dry mustard
2 green onions, white part only, chopped
1 (3-pound) precooked ham steak, 1½ to 2 inches thick

Combine the hoisin sauce, soy sauce, brown sugar, sesame oil, vinegar, orange juice, ginger, mustard, and green onions. Marinate the ham in the sauce several hours at room temperature or overnight, if possible, in an airtight container in the refrigerator. (I like a plastic bag.)

Preheat the grill or broiler. Drain the steak, saving the marinade, and grill or broil, 2 to 3 inches from the heat, 5 to 8 minutes on each side, or until heated through and lightly scored with brown from the grill. Meanwhile, heat the marinade until boiling. Serve over the ham.

Spicy Pork Tenderloin with Marinara Sauce

SERVES 4 TO 6

I keep long-cooking sauces like marinara sauce in the freezer, then I can pull it out for an occasion and dress it up a bit. This sauce may also be served with pasta and is particularly lovely on green fettuccine.

2 tablespoons olive oil
2 (1-pound each) pork
    tenderloins, trimmed
2 cups Marinara Sauce (page
    38)
1 teaspoon chopped fresh thyme
½ teaspoon cinnamon
½ to 1 teaspoon cayenne pepper
Freshly grated nutmeg

1 bay leaf, crumbled
1 lemon, juiced
½ cup red wine vinegar
Salt
Freshly ground black pepper
Sugar
5 cups cooked white rice, still
    warm (page 262)

Preheat oven to 300 degrees.

Heat the oil in a large pan with a lid. Add the pork and brown on all sides. Add the marinara sauce, thyme, cinnamon, half of the cayenne, the nutmeg, bay leaf, half of the lemon juice, and half of the red wine vinegar. Cover tightly, and bake 35 minutes. Remove the meat and carve. Taste the sauce and add lemon juice and vinegar as needed. Bring the sauce to the boil, scraping the sides and bottom of the pan to get all the goodness. Taste again, and add salt and pepper, the remaining cayenne, and sugar as needed. Serve over the rice.

Ray's Cassoulet

When my nearly daughters Audrey and Gail moved in with me, they were teenagers. They were totally unfamiliar with the foods I was teaching and brought home from the cooking school, so I didn't bore them with the fancy names. They just reheated them casually, usually in the microwave, as they were hungry and wanted to eat. Years later, after Audrey had lived in France, she came home and said, "One day I was eating cassoulet in a marvelous restaurant. Everyone was praising it. All of a sudden I realized the dish we called 'stuffing' was really cassoulet. No wonder we loved it!"

This recipe is easy when taken step by step, and may be done in stages over several days. It freezes well. I usually choose a long rainy day when I have ironing to do. I turn on the opera, and alternate ironing and cooking, smelling, and listening as I cook.

This famous French country "casserole" of beans has many variations. I like the combination of meats here, but some people use chicken only—others *kielbasa* sausage rather than Italian. Now I see it in Southwestern restaurants, using cumin and coriander as seasonings.

The cassoulet may be put in the oven frozen but needs to be watched carefully. Be sure to place it on a baking sheet to catch the drippings.

2 pounds dry white beans

1 pound fat and lean salt pork, streak-o-lean, or 2 ham hocks

1 tablespoon olive oil

2 large onions, sliced

6 large garlic cloves, chopped

8 cups chicken broth or stock or water

1 to 2 tablespoons salt

Freshly ground black pepper

15 parsley stalks

2 to 3 stalks fresh thyme

3 bay leaves, crumbled

The Duck

1 (4- to 5-pound) duck

2 to 3 tablespoons kosher salt

1 teaspoon freshly ground black pepper

1 to 2 teaspoons ground allspice

1 teaspoon chopped fresh thyme

Duck fat, melted to render (page 171)

The Lamb/Pork Mixture

2 pounds lamb shoulder with bones

2 pounds pork shoulder (Boston butt) with bones

3 large onions, sliced

5 large garlic cloves, chopped

1 (28-ounce) can plum tomatoes, coarsely chopped, with juice

3 cups dry white wine

2 cups beef stock or broth

Salt

Freshly ground black pepper

2 bay leaves, crumbled

1 teaspoon chopped fresh thyme

2 to 3 cups duck or chicken stock

2 pounds Italian sweet sausage, cut into ½-inch chunks and browned

5 cups fresh bread crumbs, finely sieved

1 cup packed chopped fresh parsley

¼ cup chopped fresh thyme

Pick over the beans. Rinse them, changing the water several times. Place the beans in a large pot with enough water to cover. Cover and bring to the boil and boil 5 minutes. Remove from the heat and set aside 1 hour. Drain the beans, and return them to the pot.

Meanwhile, place the salt pork in boiling water and cook 15 minutes to remove excess salt. Cut into ½-inch cubes, including one rind, if desired. Heat a large skillet. Add the olive oil and the salt pork, and cook 10 to 15 minutes. Remove the salt pork with a slotted spoon and drain. Add the onions and garlic to the skillet and cook until soft and translucent, 6 to 8 minutes. Add the salt pork, onion, and garlic mixture to the beans. Add enough broth or water to cover. Add the salt, pepper, parsley, thyme, and bay leaves. Bring to the boil over high heat, reduce the heat, and simmer slowly, partially covered, until the beans are tender, 1½ to 2 hours, adding more broth or water as needed. May be done in advance and refrigerated until needed.

To prepare the duck: Cut the duck into 8 pieces, separating it at all the joints. Set the backbone, gizzard, and heart aside. Rub the other pieces with the salt, pepper, allspice, and thyme and place in a plastic bag. Seal. Refrigerate for 4 to 6 hours or up to 2 days. Preheat the oven to 400 degrees. Remove the duck from the bag, and pat dry. Place in the hot oven in a roasting pan and roast for 1 hour. Set aside to cool, reserving all the fat. When cool enough to handle, take the meat off the bones and set the meat aside. May be done in advance and refrigerated until needed.

Heat enough of the duck fat to cover the bottom of a large pot. Brown the backbone, gizzard, and heart of the duck. Remove, leaving the fat in the pot. Chop the bones, gizzard, and heart into 1-inch pieces, place in a stock pot and cover with 2 to 3 cups of water to make stock. Bring to the boil over high heat. Reduce heat, partially cover, and cook 1 to 2 hours. Strain. Reserve the duck stock until needed.

To prepare the lamb/pork mixture: Brown the lamb pieces in the duck fat. Remove. Add more fat if needed and brown the pork pieces on all sides. Remove. Add the onions and garlic and cook until golden brown, about 15 to 20 minutes. Add the tomatoes, wine, and beef stock to the pot. Add the salt, pepper, bay leaves, and thyme, lamb, and pork. Bring to the boil over high heat, then reduce to a simmer. Cook, covered, adding beef stock as needed, 2 hours, or until the meat is tender and falls off the bones. When done set solids aside. Boil the liquid to reduce by half, about 30 minutes. Take the meat off the bones, and return it to the pan.

Add the duck meat and the sausage to the lamb/pork mixture. May be done ahead and refrigerated until needed.

Preheat oven to 400 degrees. Combine the bread crumbs, parsley, and thyme. Layer about ⅓ of the bean mixture, saving the liquid, into the bottom of a 6- to 8-quart flameproof casserole. Add ½ of the meat mixture, saving the liquid, on top of the beans. Continue layering, beginning and ending with beans. Pour in enough bean liquid and duck stock to barely cover the beans. Put 2 cups of bread crumb mixture on top of the beans, pressing down slightly. Drizzle with rendered fat. May be done ahead to this point and refrigerated until needed.

Bake, uncovered, 20 to 30 minutes. Then reduce the heat to 300 degrees. Press the crumbs into the mixture, coat with more crumbs, drizzle on more rendered fat, and continue to cook for 1½ hours. Remove from the oven and push the crust back into the cassoulet. Add stock and liquid as needed to keep moist. Top with 1 more cup of bread crumbs. Drizzle the top with fat from the duck. Bake 2 more hours.

The cassoulet may be served now or frozen. If you have more time, remove, break the crumbs into the mixture, add more stock if needed, and top with more bread crumbs. Bake 2 more hours. Repeat the topping, adding stock as needed, finish with 1 cup of bread crumbs, and return to the oven for 1 hour more. Remove.

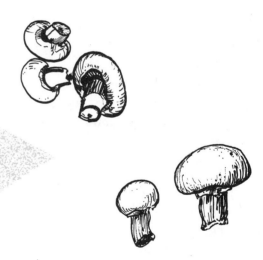

Sweet Italian Sausage and Chicken Stew

SERVES 6

This earthy, yummy stew is just right for casual entertaining around the fireplace in fall or winter or on a cool spring evening. Over the years fennel has become one of my favorite vegetables. Unfortunately, it is sometimes hard to find so when I can't I just omit it.

2 tablespoons peanut, canola, or olive oil
1 pound sweet Italian sausage, cut into 1-inch pieces
1 (3-pound) chicken, cut into 8 pieces
1 onion, chopped
2 garlic cloves, chopped
3 teaspoons chili powder
1 (28-ounce) can crushed tomatoes with purée or chopped tomatoes and 2 teaspoons purée
2 teaspoons ground cumin seed

2 heaping tablespoons finely chopped fresh fennel or California anise bulb (optional)
½ to 1 tablespoon fennel seed
1 heaping teaspoon finely chopped fresh marjoram
1 heaping tablespoon finely chopped fresh rosemary
1 teaspoon red wine vinegar
Salt
Freshly ground black pepper
Sugar
10 ounces dried rotini, cooked

Place the oil in a large heavy skillet with a lid. Add the sausage and brown. Remove and drain the sausage. Add the chicken, skin side down, to the hot fat and brown. Turn and brown on the second side. Remove from the skillet. Add the onion, garlic, and chili powder and cook 2 minutes. Stir in the tomatoes, cumin, fennel, fennel seed, marjoram, rosemary, and vinegar. Return the sausage and chicken to the skillet. Cover. Bring to the boil, reduce heat, and cook 30 to 45 minutes, until the chicken is done. Remove the chicken, boil down the sauce briefly, and return the chicken to the skillet. Season with salt, pepper, and sugar. Serve over the rotini.

May be made ahead several days.

The stew freezes in an airtight container.

Pasta and Pizza

Sausage and Cheese Calzone with Tomato Sauce

MAKES 4 CALZONE

This pizza dough, filled with sausage and cheese, folded, then surrounded with a tomato sauce, may be served hot or cold, which makes it great for a picnic as well as a casual supper. I prefer fresh herbs, but if you need to, use dried—just use dried sage in place of the fresh basil. And if you have a baking stone, by all means use it in place of the skillets, following the manufacturer's directions. It will give a great crust, but must be preheated about 20 minutes.

(continued)

The Dough

1 package active dry yeast
2 teaspoons sugar
1 cup warm water (105 to 115 degrees), divided
3 tablespoons milk
2 tablespoons olive oil
2 heaping tablespoons finely chopped fresh basil or dried chopped sage

2 tablespoons finely chopped fresh or dried oregano
2 teaspoons salt
2 to 3 cups bread flour

The Filling

1 pound sweet or hot Italian sausage links
8 ounces grated Mozzarella cheese
1 cup freshly grated imported Parmesan cheese
¾ cup ricotta cheese
3 ounces goat cheese (Montrachet or feta) or Monterey Jack cheese, cut into pieces

Cornmeal
1 egg beaten with 1 tablespoon water
Olive oil
Uncooked Fresh Tomato Sauce (page 148) or Marinara Sauce (page 38)

To make the dough, dissolve the yeast and sugar in ¼ cup of the warm water. Place the remaining water, milk, olive oil, herbs, and salt with the yeast mixture in a mixer or food processor. Mix in enough of the flour to make a soft dough. Process, adding more flour if necessary, until the dough is elastic and smooth as a baby's bottom, about 1 minute in a food processor; about 10 minutes by hand or in a mixer. Place the dough in a greased bowl and cover it with plastic wrap, or place in a plastic bag. Let dough rise in a warm place until doubled in volume. Punch the dough down. Return it to the oiled bowl or bag and let it double again, about 1½ hours.

To make the filling, cut the sausage into ¼-inch slices and fry over medium heat until browned. Mix the Mozzarella, Parmesan, ricotta, and goat cheese in a bowl and set aside.

Preheat oven to 475 degrees. Sprinkle 2 (10-inch) cast-iron skillets or baking pans with sides with the cornmeal. Divide the dough into 4 equal pieces. Roll out each piece into a circle about 7 inches in diameter and ¼ inch thick. Place some of the cheese and sausage on one half of each dough circle, leaving a ½-inch border along the round edge. Brush the egg wash around the entire circumference, and fold the dough over to form a semi-circle. Crimp the edges of the calzones by pressing them with the tines of a fork. Brush the top lightly with olive oil. Place 2 calzones back to back in each of the 2 skillets. Bake on the bottom rack of the oven until golden brown, about 12 minutes. The recipe may be doubled. Serve with fresh tomato sauce or marinara sauce, heated.

The dish freezes well.

Fancy Pizza with Dried Tomatoes and Pesto

SERVES 2 OR 3

It certainly is fun to see all the ways pizza is being served these days. Although I love a traditional pizza, I also enjoy the dried tomatoes here, which add a strong tomato dimension, and the basil of the pesto sauce.

1½ packages active dry yeast
1 teaspoon sugar
1 cup warm water (105 to 115 degrees)

2 tablespoons olive oil
1 teaspoon salt
3 cups bread flour
1 tablespoon cornmeal

The Topping
¾ cup tomato sauce
½ cup Mozzarella cheese
1 medium onion, sliced
3 dried tomatoes, chopped with 2 tablespoons oil (optional)
2 tablespoons Pesto Sauce (page 58)

1 cup freshly grated imported Parmesan cheese
Salt
Freshly ground black pepper

Dissolve the yeast and sugar in the warm water. Place in a mixer bowl or food processor. Add the olive oil, salt, and enough of the flour, ½ cup at a time, to make a soft dough. Process 1 minute in food processor or 10 minutes by hand, until dough is elastic and smooth as a baby's bottom. Shape into a ball. Place in a greased bag, turn to coat, and let rise until double in volume, about 1 hour. Refrigerate or use right away.

Preheat oven to 450 degrees. Roll dough into a 14-inch round on a floured surface and place on a greased pizza pan that has been sprinkled with the cornmeal. Top with the tomato sauce, Mozzarella, onion slices, optional dried tomatoes, pesto sauce, and Parmesan. Bake 15 to 20 minutes or until edges are browned and cheese is bubbly. Add salt and pepper to taste. Serve immediately.

And for Brunch

Creamed Chipped Beef

SERVES 4

When Richard Lands returned to the United States after finishing La Varenne, he helped with my television series. One day the crew got a craving for something familiar and homey, so while we were taping he whipped up this chipped beef. It's a wonderful Sunday night supper. There are many varieties of chipped or dried beef on the market, both in jars and frozen. If the meat is very salty, rinse it in hot water, then drain it well.

5 ounces chipped beef
3 tablespoons butter
3 tablespoons flour
2 cups milk

Tabasco sauce
Freshly ground black pepper
4 pieces toast or 4 baked
    potatoes (optional)

Coarsely chop the beef. Melt the butter in a heavy saucepan. Stir in the flour and cook briefly, without browning. Stir in the milk and bring it to the boil, stirring constantly. Cook until thickened. Season with a few drops of Tabasco and some pepper. Stir in the chipped beef and heat thoroughly. Serve over the toast or potatoes if desired.

Early Bird Buttermilk Pancakes

MAKES 15 (4-INCH), 25 (3-INCH),
OR 36 DOLLAR PANCAKES

Julius Walker is a good friend as well as husband to my friend Savannah and father to LuLen, Stuart, and Savannah Waring Walker. Julius gets up early on Saturday when the family is asleep and starts breakfast. By the time the juice is squeezed and the coffee ready, he's got a good start on a stack of pancakes.

A non-stick pan reduces the amount of oil needed. To make a substitute for buttermilk, combine 1 tablespoon lemon juice or vinegar and enough whole milk to make 1 cup. Let stand 5 minutes before using. The pancake batter will separate when made ahead. Whisk lightly to bring back. However, it does last several days in the refrigerator.

1½ cups flour	1 egg, beaten
1 tablespoon sugar	2 tablespoons cooking oil
½ teaspoon salt	Oil for pan
2¼ teaspoons baking powder	½ cup milk for thinning batter
½ cup buttermilk	as needed
⅔ cup milk	

Sift together the flour, sugar, salt, and baking powder. Beat together the buttermilk, milk, egg, and oil. Pour the liquid ingredients into the dry ingredients and stir until well mixed. (A few small lumps in the batter will cook out.) The first pancake is a test pancake. The batter should be thin, so dilute it, if necessary, with milk (not buttermilk). The pan should be lightly oiled and hot enough to make a sprinkling of water dance, not just sit and sizzle. Ladle about ⅛ cup of the batter into the hot pan. When the top of the pancake is full of bubbles and the bottom is golden, turn the pancake. Cook on second side until done. Continue to make pancakes in the same manner.

Orange-Flavored French Toast

SERVES 4

If my feet were put to the fire, I would admit I prefer French toast to pancakes. I think it is due to the buttery, brown, eggy outside. And in this recipe I love the hint of sweetness and spice. Using the right bread is important. The wrong one will fall apart. Bob Coram served this one Sunday with his own adaptations from a recipe he got from the newspaper.

2 eggs
1 cup freshly squeezed orange
    juice
¼ cup heavy cream
¼ teaspoon ground ginger
¼ to ½ cup butter, preferably
    unsalted

6 to 8 slices Italian or French
    bread, thickly sliced,
    preferably a bit stale
1 orange, sliced, and the slices
    halved
Confectioners' or brown sugar
Freshly grated nutmeg

Beat the eggs into the orange juice, then add the cream and ginger, and combine completely. Melt the butter in a large heavy frying pan until bubbling. Soak the bread slices thoroughly in the egg mixture. Slide each slice carefully into the bubbling butter. Fry one side until golden brown. Turn and cook other side until golden. Serve topped with the orange slices and sprinkled with the sugar and nutmeg.

French Toast

SERVES 2

One of my favorite memories when I was young was of my mother making French toast on Saturday morning. We had a large floor-model radio, and my sister and I would curl up in front of it, listening to our favorite programs, eating our special breakfast.

Bread and eggs are staples in any cupboard. Sugar and jam make this egg-coated bread a true sweet treat. You might want to use eggnog in place of the milk. It's very festive for Christmas breakfast, especially with rum flavoring in it.

2 eggs
½ cup milk, light cream, or
    heavy cream
½ teaspoon vanilla
Salt (optional)
2 to 3 tablespoons butter

4 slices bread, preferably a
    dense, homemade type
Confectioners' sugar
Butter
Jam

To make the batter, beat together the eggs, milk, vanilla, and salt. Melt 1 to 2 tablespoons of the butter in a large skillet. Dip each slice of bread into the batter, turn to soak, and let soak 10 to 15 minutes. Fry the bread in the skillet over medium heat until very lightly browned. Turn once. Keep the cooked slices warm in a 250 degree oven while frying the remaining slices. Serve warm, sprinkled with the Confectioners' sugar and topped with plenty of butter and good jam.

Hocus-Pocus Oven-Baked Pancake

MAKES 8 WEDGES

Here is a puffy pancake that hollows out to hold fruit and cream. It's easy to do on the spur of the moment and nice, too, as a dessert for a simple Sunday night supper. A bit of sugar in the pancake and waffle batter makes the crust brown quickly and evenly.

½ cup flour
Pinch salt
1 teaspoon sugar
Pinch freshly grated nutmeg
2 eggs, lightly beaten

½ cup milk
1 teaspoon vanilla
2 tablespoons butter
¼ cup Confectioners' sugar
½ lemon, juiced

Garnish
4 cups sliced strawberries and
    bananas
1 cup heavy cream, whipped

Preheat oven to 425 degrees.

Sift the flour with the salt, sugar, and nutmeg. Combine the eggs, milk, and vanilla and pour into the flour mixture. Stir until batter is just blended. Melt the butter in a 9-inch non-stick skillet or a 9-inch round cake pan, coating bottom and sides. Pour the batter into the hot pan and bake for 15 to 20 minutes, or until golden brown. The pancake puffs and rises on the outside edges, but collapses when removed from the oven. Fold edges over in a scalloped fashion. Dust with the sugar, then sprinkle with the lemon juice. Fill or garnish with fresh fruit and whipped cream. Cut into wedges and serve immediately.

Piperade

SERVES 6 TO 8

This colorful Basque dish—softly scrambled eggs cooked with garlic, tomatoes, onions, and peppers— is one of my favorite Sunday night suppers or Saturday lunches. I always serve it with hot buttered garlic toast and frequently with prosciutto or Jambon de Bayonne. To spice the dish up, add 2 small hot green chilies, chopped, when cooking the onions and garlic.

The Sauce

3 tablespoons olive oil, butter, or drippings

2 onions, chopped

4 garlic cloves, chopped

3 large red bell peppers, cored, seeded, and sliced into ¼- × 3-inch strips

1 green bell pepper, cored, seeded, and sliced into ¼- × 3-inch strips

1 pound tomatoes, seeded and chopped

2 tablespoons chopped fresh basil or thyme

16 eggs, beaten lightly

Salt

Freshly ground black pepper

4 slices bread, toasted and brushed with butter or oil and garlic

Heat the oil in a heavy frying pan. Add the onions and garlic, and cook over medium heat until soft and golden. Add the bell peppers and cook 15 minutes. Add the tomatoes and the basil. Cover and cook until very soft. Remove the cover and add the eggs. Stir gently, until lightly cooked and scrambled, but not hard. Season to taste with salt and pepper. Serve with the toast.

Teacher's Omelet

Anne Willan, owner of La Varenne Cooking School, has largely been responsible for the melting pot cooking of today in the United States. La Varenne's students are now America's editors, chefs, caterers, and writers. This recipe was adapted from a lovely little book of hers, *Classic French Cooking*. An untraditional omelet, it is sprinkled with cream and cheese and broiled until golden. Use a pan that can be placed under the broiler.

4 or 5 eggs	3 tablespoons heavy cream
Salt	¾ cup grated Gruyère or Swiss
Freshly ground black pepper	cheese
1 tablespoon butter	

Preheat the broiler.

Whisk the eggs lightly with salt and pepper. Heat the butter in a 9-inch omelet or non-stick pan over high heat until it stops foaming and begins to brown. Add the eggs immediately. Stir briskly for 8 to 10 seconds, until the eggs start to thicken. Then quickly pull the egg at the sides of the pan to the center, rolling and tipping the pan to pour uncooked egg to the sides. When half the eggs are set, take the pan from the heat.

Spoon the cream over the eggs and sprinkle them with the cheese. Broil until golden. Cut the omelet in half, slide onto plates, and serve at once with hot buttered toast.

Putting on
the Ritz

Here are recipes for those really special occasions, when you don't mind spending a little extra time and effort. They're festive, elegant, unusual, and definitely impressive. And they're all within reach—ingredients are available at almost any market, and the cost never becomes astronomical. So for that extra-special celebration—birthday, anniversary, good friends, loving family, put your best foot forward and enjoy the compliments!

Appetizers and Soups

Pretty Fancy Baked Brie

MAKES 1 ROUND

Brie wrapped in puff pastry with a surprise center is a luscious taste sensation. Use a sweet preserve for a brunch or dessert party, and the chutney or pepper jelly for a cocktail party. You can make your own puff pastry (see page 320) or buy the frozen sheets (see page 135). Freezing the Brie and pastry before baking helps.

Nora Crawley has been one of my loyal students for many years. She brought this wonderful dish to the class party.

1 round Brie (any size) cheese, cut horizontally into 2 rounds

2 sheets puff pastry

½ cup black raspberry preserves with Chambord, apple chutney, red pepper spread, or hot pepper jelly

1 egg, beaten

Cut 2 circles of pastry about 1½ inches larger than the Brie. Place the bottom round of Brie on 1 circle and spread preserves on the cut side. Top with the other Brie half. Lightly brush the bottom pastry circle with water. Place the second pastry circle on top and press the two circles together. Wrap the entire round in plastic wrap and store in the freezer up to 2 months.

When ready to use, preheat oven to 425 degrees. Unwrap the Brie, and brush with the beaten egg. Place the Brie on a baking sheet and bake until light brown, about 15 minutes. Cool on wire rack.

Dried Tomato Palmiers

MAKES 40 PALMIERS

Palmiers are sweet or savory pastries that puff into the shape of palm leaves. This recipe looks difficult, but isn't once the rapid or puff pastry is made. And there is commercially made puff pastry; it comes in a 1-pound 1¼-ounce package of 2 sheets. If frozen, defrost before rolling out. If using homemade puff pastry, roll out a 10- × 12-inch sheet ⅛ inch thick.

Dried tomatoes are one of the most flavorful items to have on hand in the kitchen. Store in a tightly closed container, and they freeze indefinitely.

½ cup Pesto Sauce (page 58) or the storebought variety
4 tablespoons dried tomatoes, chopped
1 large garlic clove, chopped
½ cup freshly grated imported Parmesan cheese

2 heaping tablespoons finely chopped fresh herbs, such as basil or thyme
1 teaspoon lemon juice
1 sheet puff pastry (see above) or Rapid Puff Pastry (page 320)

Preheat oven to 350 degrees.

In a bowl, combine well the pesto, tomatoes, garlic, Parmesan, herbs, and lemon juice. Roll the pastry into a 10- × 12-inch rectangle. Spread the filling to ¼ inch of the sides of the puff pastry. Fold in each long side to the center, then fold again toward the center to finish with a 10- × 2½-inch piece. Chill, wrapped in plastic wrap. Slice ¼ inch thick to make 40 pieces. Place each palmier, cut side up, on greased baking sheet, leaving space in between, or on parchment paper on a baking sheet and chill for 30 minutes. Bake until golden brown, a total of 10 to 12 minutes, turning once. Reduce heat if necessary. If they get too brown, the cheese will taste scorched. Cool on a rack for 5 minutes. Serve at room temperature.

The palmiers keep in an airtight container for a few days in the refrigerator, or for up to 3 months in the freezer. Reheat in a 300-degree oven for 10 minutes.

To make 80 bite-sized pieces, cut the sheet of pastry in half to make two 10- × 6-inch rectangles.

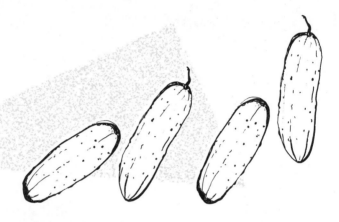

Pesto Palmiers

MAKES 40 PALMIERS

The French named this pastry after the palm leaf, which it resembles. Serve these along with Dried Tomato Palmiers for an interesting red and green contrast.

1 sheet puff pastry or Rapid
    Puff Pastry (page 320)
¼ cup Pesto Sauce (page 58) or
    the storebought variety

½ cup freshly grated imported
    Parmesan cheese

Preheat oven to 375 degrees.

Roll pastry into a 10- × 12-inch rectangle. Spread the pesto to ¼ inch of the sides of the puff pastry. Sprinkle heavily with the Parmesan. Fold in each long side to the center, then fold each long side again toward the center to finish with a 10- × 2½-inch piece. Chill, wrapped in plastic wrap. Slice ¼ inch thick to make 40 pieces. Place the palmiers on greased baking sheet or on parchment paper on a baking sheet. Chill for 30 minutes. Bake until golden brown. Turn. Bake other side. Reduce heat if necessary. If they get too brown, the cheese will taste scorched. Cool on a rack.

To make 80 bite-sized pieces, cut the sheet of pastry in half to make two 10- × 6-inch rectangles.

The palmiers keep in an airtight container for a few days in the refrigerator, up to 3 months in the freezer. Reheat for 10 minutes in a 300-degree oven.

Smoked Salmon Dip

MAKES 1 CUP

This dip may also be used as a filling for little tea sandwiches. And it is particularly pretty garnished with tiny sprigs of parsley or dill or a sprinkling of capers.

8 ounces smoked salmon, trout, or bluefish

½ cup cream cheese, softened

3 tablespoons finely chopped green onion

¼ teaspoon Worcestershire sauce

2 teaspoons lemon juice

Water wafers, thin melba toast, or cucumber rounds

Blend 7 ounces of the salmon, the cream cheese, 2 tablespoons of the onion, the Worcestershire sauce, and lemon juice in a food processor or blender until thick and smooth. Store in a covered container in the refrigerator for up to 3 days or freeze. To serve, garnish with the remaining salmon by rolling it into a tiny cylinder, then opening it out as the petal on a flower. Sprinkle with the remaining green onion. Serve with the crackers, melba toast, or cucumber.

Pine Mountain Cheese Loaf

MAKES ENOUGH SPREAD FOR
20 SMALL APPETIZERS

Soft cheese is layered with pesto in this particularly pretty recipe.

Pine Mountain is a low Georgia mountain, where my student Annie Audsley lives. She brought this dish to a party I had for the students, and there were many raves. We made a book of the students' recipes—they were all so good—and I've cooked most of them. With this, I substitute yogurt when I'm thinking slim, and when I can't find cheesecloth, I use Handi Wipes. You can also make the loaf in 1 or 2 smaller dishes. Freeze what you don't need for a later treat.

8 ounces cream cheese or
    Yogurt Cheese (page 11),
    softened
1 cup unsalted butter, softened
1¼ cups lightly packed finely
    chopped fresh basil
2 to 3 garlic cloves, chopped

½ cup freshly grated imported
    Parmesan cheese
3 tablespoons olive oil
Salt
Freshly ground black pepper
1 French baguette, thinly sliced

Garnish
Sprigs of basil

Beat the cream cheese and the butter until smooth. Set aside. Make the pesto by blending the basil leaves, garlic, Parmesan, and olive oil to a paste in a food processor. Season to taste with salt and pepper.

Moisten two 12-inch squares of cheesecloth with water and wring dry. Lay the squares out flat, one on top of the other, and use them to smoothly line a 2½-cup plain mold or plastic container with straight sides. Spread ⅙ of the cheese mixture in the prepared mold. Cover with ⅕ of the pesto filling, extending it evenly to the sides. Repeat layering until the mold is filled, finishing with the cheese mixture. Fold the end of the cloth over the top of the cheese-pesto loaf and press down lightly to compact it. Chill the loaf until it is firm, 1 to

1½ hours. Invert it onto a serving dish and gently pull off the cloth. If the loaf is allowed to stand any longer, the cloth will dry out and will cause the green of the filling to bleed into the cheese. May be made up to 5 days ahead if unmolded, covered with plastic wrap, and kept refrigerated. Garnish with additional sprigs of basil. Serve on French baguette slices.

The loaf freezes well wrapped in plastic wrap.

Randy Harris's Shrimp Cocktail

MAKES 10 TO 12 SERVINGS

Simple and delicious! This is a variation of a shrimp cocktail my student, Randy Harris, made on one he tasted in Tijuana, Mexico. Spicy but not hot, it's like a basic piece of wearing apparel. It can be dressed up or down and is suitable for a large party or smaller gathering. If you wish it hotter, leave the seeds in the peppers and add Tabasco.

3 pounds cooked medium
   shrimp, peeled
6 Key limes, juiced (about
   ½ cup)
2 to 3 jalapeño peppers, seeded

2 medium onions, diced
1½ cups cocktail sauce
½ cup white wine vinegar
3 tomatoes, peeled, seeded, and
   diced

Garnish
Sprigs of parsley or cilantro

For a large gathering, combine the shrimp, lime juice, peppers, onion, cocktail sauce, vinegar, and tomatoes in a serving dish and mix thoroughly. Chill, covered, 1 hour. Garnish and serve.

For a more intimate gathering, arrange a layer of shrimp in the bottom of a stemmed glass. Top with a layer of peppers and onions, then tomatoes, then cocktail sauce. When layered to within an inch of the top of the glass, add lime juice and vinegar to taste. Chill 1 hour, or up to 2 days, garnish, and serve.

All Gone Snails and Butter

SERVES 4

Once the snails are gone, there is nothing better than dipping into the flavorful butter in the snail pan. In fact, many people like the garlicy melted butter best, tipping the shell into their mouths to get the very last drop. Vary the shellfish, by substituting clams, mussels, shrimp, or oysters and change the cooking time to coordinate with the selection. The butter may be made in advance, may even be frozen, making this a ridiculously easy dish to serve for something considered so glamorous. Serve with crusty French bread.

Snail butter
3 shallots, chopped
2 garlic cloves, chopped
½ cup butter, at room
   temperature
2 heaping tablespoons finely
   chopped fresh parsley

Salt
Freshly ground black pepper
Lemon juice (optional)

24 snail shells
24 snails, canned
1 loaf French bread

Preheat oven to 400 degrees.

To make the butter, place the shallots, garlic, butter, and parsley in a food processor or mixer bowl and cream until combined. Stir in salt, pepper, and lemon juice to taste. May be made ahead several days or be frozen, wrapped in plastic wrap.

Put a little of this butter into each snail shell. Slip the snail into the shell. Put more of the butter on top and put the shell into a snail pan or baking dish. (If you don't have the special snail pans, use crumpled foil or rock salt to keep the round shells from overturning.) When ready to serve, heat thoroughly, about 6 minutes. Serve with the French bread. Freeze excess butter for another occasion.

Ballottine

MAKES 20 SLICES AS AN APPETIZER

Ballottine is now a catch-all term for a boned fowl or fish. In this case, a beautiful stuffed and rolled chicken, which when sliced is a mosaic of ham and nuts sprinkled with herbs. The word probably derived from the French term "bundle," but I hardly think "chicken bundle" would whet your appetite! It is, however, very impressive to serve. (Fry any leftover stuffing as a sausage treat for yourself!)

How to Bone a Whole Chicken

- Usually the butcher will bone a chicken for you, but you can do it yourself. Boning a whole chicken is understandably terrifying the first time. After you've boned two, you will wonder why you were afraid. After boning seven, it will take you only 5 minutes. Cut off the wings at their joints and reserve for another use. Lay the chicken on its breast and cut down the flesh over the backbone, to the bone. Peel back the flesh, leaving the flesh attached to the skin. Keep your knife to the bone, going from backbone to breast on either side. Run your knife down the keel bone. Bone the legs by cutting around each at the ankle with the knife. A good twist should pull out the leg bone. Cut down the thigh and scrape off the bone. Don't worry if it looks messy or tears. With tears, sew them up with a trussing needle and thread. I prefer kite string, but unwaxed dental floss works fine.

(*continued*)

1 (3½-pound) chicken
Salt
Freshly ground black pepper
½ pound lean pork, ground
½ pound lean turkey breast or
    veal, chopped
¼ to ½ pound salt pork, cubed
1 egg
5 shallots or 1 small onion,
    chopped
5 garlic cloves, chopped
2 tablespoons ground fennel
    seed
2 heaping tablespoons finely
    chopped fresh parsley

2 heaping tablespoons finely
    chopped fresh thyme
2 heaping tablespoons finely
    chopped fresh marjoram or
    oregano
¼ cup shelled blanched
    pistachio nuts
⅛ to ¼ pound sliced boiled
    ham, cut into ¼-inch strips
3 to 4 cups chicken broth or
    stock, fresh or canned
3 fennel fronds (optional)
1 recipe Uncooked Fresh
    Tomato Sauce (page 148) or
    Mustard and Cream Sauce

Mustard and Cream Sauce
¼ cup Dijon mustard
¾ cup sour cream

Bone the chicken. Place it, skin side down, on a plastic or non-wooden board and sprinkle with salt and pepper. Mix the pork, turkey or veal, salt pork, egg, shallots, garlic, fennel seed, parsley, thyme, and marjoram. Fry a tablespoon of the mixture to taste for seasoning and season heavily with salt and freshly ground pepper. Spread the mixture all over the inside of the chicken, leaving about 1 inch for the rest of the stuffing. Press the pistachios into the stuffing so that they are distributed in an interesting pattern. Press the ham strips lengthwise into the stuffing. Do not let the ham slices butt up against each other as they will cause the chicken to break unevenly when sliced. Fold the sides of the chicken together and sew up the overlapping edges including the neck and tail flaps with white kitchen thread or unwaxed dental floss. (This is probably self-evident, but do not use plastic string or waxed floss, which will melt.) Place the chicken in a large saucepan with the chicken broth. Cover and bring to the boil. Reduce the heat and cook slowly 1½ hours, or 25 minutes per pound, or about 6 hours in a crock pot on low, until the chicken registers 170 degrees. Drain, and put into a loaf pan. Cover with plastic wrap. Put a brick weight on top. Refrigerate overnight.

Next day remove the weight, wipe the chicken free of fat, remove the string, and slice ¼ inch thick. Serve cold. Garnish with fresh fennel, if desired.

To make the mustard sauce, mix the mustard with the sour cream. Serve as is or heat slightly.

Smoked Tea Duck

SERVES 4 AS AN APPETIZER

This steamed then smoked duck is marvelous. I sliver the meat and use it at ladies' lunches as well as cocktail buffets. The recipe looks like a lot of work, but it isn't; it just takes planning ahead to have time for the marinade, and then being home while the duck cooks. Consider adding to the salad stir-fried red peppers and snow peas or cooked asparagus.

1 (4- to 5-pound) duck or
  2 wild ducks

Dry Marinade I

1 tablespoon ground ginger	½ teaspoon freshly ground
4 teaspoons ground star anise	black pepper
2 tablespoons soy sauce	
1 tablespoon oil	6 slices fresh ginger, julienned
1 teaspoon salt	6 scallions, julienned

Dry Marinade II

3 tablespoons kosher salt	2 teaspoons five-spice powder
1 tablespoon whole Szechwan peppercorns, roasted and crushed	

Smoking Mix

1 cup raw long-grain white rice	½ cup light brown sugar
1 cup dark Chinese tea leaves	

(continued)

Dressing

¼ cup sherry vinegar

1½ teaspoons ground cumin
   seed

¼ teaspoon five-spice powder

½ teaspoon red pepper flakes

1 large garlic clove, chopped

⅛ teaspoon ground ginger

¼ cup peanut oil

¼ cup Oriental sesame oil

½ head radicchio lettuce, torn
1 head Bibb lettuce, torn

Trim the duck. Press down hard on the duck breastbone to crack it. Combine the ingredients for Dry Marinade I and rub the marinade over the duck and inside the cavity. Stuff the cavity with the ginger and scallions. Let stand 2 hours. Combine the ingredients for Dry Marinade II and rub over duck. Place the duck on a baking sheet and cover with another baking sheet. Weight the top baking sheet to flatten the duck and to release its moisture. Marinate in the refrigerator up to 2 days.

Place the duck in a steamer. If not available, improvise your own. In a large Dutch oven, invert a small soufflé dish or other small heatproof dish that can support a larger baking dish with the duck on it. Pour water around the small dish and place the larger baking dish on top. Put the duck on the dish and cover. Steam over medium heat 1 to 1½ hours, adding additional water to steamer as needed. Cool the duck slightly and pat dry.

Prepare a wok (or stove-top smoker) for smoking: Line with heavy duty aluminum foil. Place the ingredients for the smoking mix in the bottom of wok. Place duck on a rack in the wok. Cover and wrap foil around the top of the wok so as not to allow any smoke to escape. Heat until mix smokes, then smoke 10 minutes on medium-high heat. Reduce to medium heat and smoke 15 minutes longer. Cool duck. Remove meat from bones, and shred. The meat may be frozen at this point. Mix together the dressing ingredients with a whisk. Pour over the duck meat.

When ready to serve, arrange the duck salad over the lettuce.

Red Bell Pepper Mousse

SERVES 8 AS FIRST COURSE

This is a dazzling first course, beguilingly pink with a soft texture and a subtle, delicious red bell pepper flavor, all encased in sparkling aspic. It requires some organization, but can be made over a period of several days. It will keep one or two days in the refrigerator, covered. Once the aspic is made, it is a snap!

I learned a variation on this recipe at the Paris Ritz Cooking School, the Ecole de Gastronomie Française Ritz-Escoffier. There they use small metal rings with taut plastic wrap stretched across as the bases, which makes unmolding much easier than with ramekins.

1½ pints Aspic, still liquid (recipe follows)
8 large black olives
1 pound 5 ounces red bell peppers, scraped of all white, trimmed, halved, cored, and seeded, trimmings reserved
1⅓ cups chicken broth or stock, fresh or canned
Bouquet garni of 1 bay leaf, 2 stalks parsley, 2 tablespoons thyme, and sprigs of leek, both white and green parts

Salt
Freshly ground black pepper
1 envelope powdered gelatin, soaked in ¼ cup water
½ cup heavy cream, whipped to a mousse-like consistency
Sugar (optional)
1 recipe Uncooked Fresh Tomato Sauce (page 148)

Chill eight 2-inch round ramekins. Slowly pour a little of the liquid aspic into each. Turn the ramekins slowly to coat the sides with a layer about ⅛ inch thick. Check to be sure there are no air bubbles. If there are, pierce with a needle. Chill the ramekins in the refrigerator or over ice and salted water to set, about 10 minutes. Make tiny cutouts of the olives and pepper trimmings, scraping thinner if necessary, and place each in a bowl with 1½ tablespoons of the remaining liquid aspic. Remove the ramekins from the refrigerator, decorate each one with some of the olive and pepper cutouts in gelatin. Pour another layer of aspic over the cutouts, and chill again for a few minutes.

Meanwhile, place the trimmed bell peppers in a saucepan with the chicken stock, bouquet garni, salt and pepper; cover and simmer for 15 to 20 minutes. Drain the peppers, purée finely in a food processor, and strain through a sieve to remove the skins.

Melt the gelatin over low heat or in the microwave and stir the gelatin into the purée. Set aside. Add 3 tablespoons of the unset liquid aspic to the red pepper mousse, and stir over crushed ice until nearly set, the consistency of the cream. Stir a portion of the mousse into the cream, then fold the cream mixture into the mousse. Taste for seasoning. Add salt, pepper, and sugar if desired. Spoon over the set aspic in each ramekin, smooth the surface, and chill for 1 hour to 2 days. Invert onto an oiled plate and surround with Uncooked Fresh Tomato Sauce.

Aspic

MAKES 1¹/₂ PINTS

Making aspic always looks and sounds daunting, but it is really easy and a lot of fun. It gives me immense satisfaction to see the diamond-like sparkle of the finished jelly. Good stock, whether meat, chicken, or fish, is essential for aspic and must be well flavored and seasoned before clarifying. If enough salt and pepper are not added before, you cannot add them later, because they will cloud the aspic. If the stock is very greasy, additional egg whites will be needed.

1 quart cold stock (meat, chicken, or fish), well skimmed and free of grease	Salt
	Freshly ground black pepper
	3 egg whites or more
2 packages powdered gelatin	2 egg shells or more

Choose a pan big enough so that the stock fills it by no more than a third. Scald the pan, 2 dish towels, and 2 large bowls with boiling water to remove any residual detergent or grease. Wring the towels damp carefully. Do not let them get greasy from your hands. Double them, and spread each one over one of the bowls. Set aside ¼ cup of the cold stock in a small pan with the gelatin.

Turn the remaining cold stock into the scalded pan. Taste for seasoning and add salt and pepper if necessary. In a bowl whisk the whites to a light froth and add them and the egg shells to the large pan of stock. Set it over gentle heat and whisk the whites into the liquid. Turn up the heat. When just hot, but not boiling, add the unmelted, spongy gelatin mixture and continue to whisk until the liquid reaches the boiling point. Take out the whisk and allow the contents of the pan to boil up through the egg whites to the top of the pan. Take the pan off the heat, without disturbing it, and let settle for 4 or 5 minutes. Repeat this process again, bringing the liquid rapidly to the boil without whisking. Check to see if liquid is clear by ladling out a small amount into a small glass. Repeat the process 2 or 3 times if necessary. When clear, pour the clarifying ingredients onto the cloth all at once. Lift up the cloth carefully and set over the other clean bowl; pour the liquid that has come through the cloth into the first bowl over the "filter" of egg whites on the cloth. This clarifying process may be repeated once more, into the other bowl at which time the aspic should be crystal clear. If it is not, then the stock was too cloudy to begin with or the whisking was not adequate. At this point, line the molds or chill the aspic until set, either in the refrigerator or by stirring in a pan set over ice.

Aspic will keep in the refrigerator for several days. Once set, run a little cold water over the top to prevent drying and losing flavor. Cover with plastic wrap. Carefully pour off the water before use. Make cutouts or remelt and reset if using for a mold.

Uncooked Fresh Tomato Sauce

MAKES 2 CUPS

Sometimes called a *coulis*, this very thin uncooked sauce is more like juice, a perfect foil for Red Bell Pepper Mousse (page 145). The garlic is deliberately very subtle. Boost it up, if you like.

1¾ pounds vine-ripened
    tomatoes
Salt
Freshly ground black pepper

Lemon juice
3 garlic cloves
1 tablespoon tomato paste
    (optional)

Cut off the ends of the tomatoes, core them, then chop the tomatoes. Crush them in a bowl, season with salt, pepper, lemon juice, and garlic. If the tomatoes are not perfectly ripe, the tomato paste can be added to the pulp when it is left to marinate. Marinate, covered, for several hours. Remove the garlic and push the tomatoes through a fine sieve, pressing hard on the pulp to extract the maximum amount of juice. Taste for seasoning and chill.

Happy Host Tenderloin of Beef with Fennel

MAKES 60 TO 75 HORS D'OEUVRES;
OR SERVES 10 TO 12 AS A MAIN COURSE

This is a beautiful, exciting fall and winter buffet dish. The tender, juicy red beef is surrounded with a salad of fennel and arugula and topped with Parmesan shavings—all my favorite Italian foods. Use Parmigiano Reggiano, which is expensive but worth it. Serve with sliced bread if you want the option of sandwiches.

    The time I most enjoyed serving this was when PBS chefs Martin Yan and Jeff Smith came to Atlanta to do autographings and demonstrations at Rich's Department Store. Each had crowds lined up to see him so their arrival for dinner was uncertain. With a dish like this, it doesn't matter. A happy host—everything was done early in the morning—I could wait, relaxed, until they were able to arrive.

1 (3-pound after trimming) beef tenderloin
1 cup olive oil
½ cup lemon juice
1 tablespoon Dijon mustard
1½ cups finely chopped fresh parsley
⅓ cup finely chopped fresh basil
3 to 4 tablespoons grated or chopped, no white attached, lemon peel
2 red onions (1 pound total), chopped

4 garlic cloves, chopped
4 to 5 bulbs (2 pounds total) fennel, cut into thin wedges, fronds reserved, or California anise
Salt
Freshly ground black pepper
5 (4-ounce) bunches watercress or arugula, washed and dried thoroughly
¾ pound imported Parmesan cheese, cut into long shavings with a wide cheese slicer or vegetable peeler

Preheat oven to 400 degrees.

Place the tenderloin in a mixture of ¼ cup of the olive oil and ¼ cup of the lemon juice. Marinate, covered, ½ hour or overnight in the refrigerator.

When ready to cook, flip about 2 inches of the tail under, and tie up the tenderloin with string, making it all nearly the same diameter as the center portion. Place the beef and its marinade in a baking dish. Roast until a meat thermometer registers 125 degrees for rare, approximately ½ hour. Let rest for 20 minutes. Slice into 12 to 15 slices. For an hors d'oeuvre, quarter every slice. Bring the pan juices to a quick boil and pour over the beef.

Mix together the remaining ¾ cup olive oil, the remaining ¼ cup lemon juice, mustard, parsley, basil, lemon peel, onions, and garlic. Add the fennel. Season with salt and pepper. May be made and refrigerated up to 1 day.

To serve, arrange the tenderloin on a large platter. Spoon the marinade over it. Surround with the watercress or arugula. Top the greens with the fennel and onion mixture and the Parmesan shavings. Garnish with the reserved fennel fronds.

Serve at room temperature.

Ginger and Curry Beef

MAKES 2½ TO 2¾ CUPS BEEF FILLING;
ENOUGH FOR EIGHTY 1½-INCH PHYLLO TRIANGLES

I wrap this beef curry in phyllo triangles for cocktail parties, ladies lunches, or even as a Sunday night supper, varying the triangle sizes according to the occasion. I usually keep some triangles in the freezer, ready to pop out for drop-ins. The beef can also serve as a main course with rice or pasta and a vegetable.

¼ cup butter
1 large onion, finely chopped
3 garlic cloves, chopped
2 to 4 tablespoons curry powder, preferably Madras
2 to 3 teaspoons fresh ginger, peeled and grated or chopped

Salt
½ to ¾ teaspoon cayenne pepper
1 pound ground beef
½ cup cooked and chopped fresh or frozen spinach, thawed, and squeezed dry
Freshly ground black pepper

Garnish
Green onions, sliced on the diagonal (optional)

Heat the butter in a large skillet until singing. Add the onion and garlic and cook until soft. Add the curry powder, ginger, salt, and cayenne. Add the ground beef, stirring, and cook until brown. Taste for seasoning and add salt, the spinach, and pepper. May be made ahead. Serve as a main course, garnished with the green onions, or wrap in phyllo (directions follow).

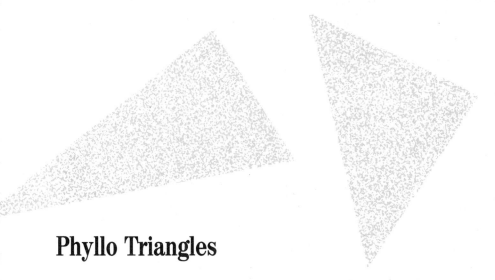

Phyllo Triangles

Stuffed phyllo triangles are easy to make once you get the hang of it. And larger ones can serve as a main course.

To Clarify Butter
- **Cut the butter into pieces. In a saucepan melt over low heat. Skim the froth off the top. Carefully pour off the clear clarified butter, leaving the milk solids, the sediment, behind. You can also melt the butter in the microwave on high for 30 seconds. Be careful not to burn the sediment. Clarified butter will keep, covered, in the refrigerator indefinitely.**

1 package (1 pound) phyllo
    dough
1 cup butter, clarified

Preheat oven to 375 degrees.

Defrost dough if frozen and unroll it, 1 sheet at a time. (Keep the remaining phyllo covered with a slightly damp, light-weight dish towel). Place the first sheet of phyllo on a work surface or baking sheet. Brush with butter. Place a second sheet of phyllo on top of the first and brush it with butter. Cut the 10-inch side of the sheets into 6 strips. Put 1 teaspoon of filling at the top of each strip. Fold each dough strip down like a flag, making triangles. Brush again with butter. Transfer to baking sheet. Bake 20 minutes.

The triangles freeze, well wrapped in aluminum foil. Reheat them directly from the freezer at 350 degrees for 5 minutes.

Asparagus Crab Soup

SERVES 8

This pretty, quick, and easy soup is very flavorful and fresh-tasting. Good as a starter or as a main course with a hot bread and a salad.

1 teaspoon butter or vegetable oil
1 garlic clove, finely chopped
2 shallots, finely chopped
6 cups chicken broth or stock, fresh or canned, boiling

1 pound small green asparagus, cut into 1-inch pieces
½ pound flaked crab meat
Salt
Freshly ground black pepper

Garnish
¼ cup chopped green onion greens

¼ cup chopped fresh cilantro (optional)

Heat the butter in a pan, add the garlic and shallots, and cook until soft. To the boiling stock, add the asparagus and cooked garlic and shallots. Boil 2 or 3 minutes and remove from the heat. When ready to serve, bring the soup back to the boil, add the crab meat, reduce heat, and simmer briefly to heat through. Season to taste with salt and pepper. Garnish with the green onions and cilantro.

Basil and Shrimp Won Ton Soup

SERVES 8 TO 10

This soup looks exciting on the table. Clear broth with nearly bursting white won tons, green basil and snow peas, and pink shrimp.

I frequently double the won ton filling to use all of the one-pound package of wrappers (60 in all) found most often in the stores. Sometimes I fry the extras in 360 degree fat and serve them as appetizers or freeze them for another time. You may want to use a reduced-salt canned broth for this recipe. In the winter, I like adding the soy sauce as it imparts a hearty flavor. But in the summer I don't.

The Filling

¼ pound cooked shrimp, peeled and deveined

2 green onions or scallions, white and green parts, separated

3 tablespoons chopped fresh ginger, divided

2 ounces canned water chestnuts

1 tablespoon Pesto Sauce (page 58)

¼ cup freshly grated imported Parmesan cheese

Salt

Dash Tabasco sauce

Freshly ground black pepper

The Soup

½ pound (30) won ton wrappers

1 heaping tablespoon chopped fresh basil

10 ounces snow peas, strings, tips, and tails removed

1 pound raw shrimp, peeled and deveined

10 cups chicken broth or stock, fresh or canned, boiling

Soy sauce (optional)

To make the filling, mince the cooked shrimp, the white part of the green onions, 2 tablespoons of the ginger, and the water chestnuts. Combine with the pesto, Parmesan, salt, Tabasco, and pepper in a food processor or by hand to make a paste.

Place 2 teaspoons of the filling in the center of each won ton wrapper. Use your finger or a brush to dampen the outer rim of the wrapper with water. Fold the won ton into a triangle. Seal. Twist the won tons to look like a nun's cap. Press the ends together. Set aside until needed. You can then place the won tons in a plastic bag and refrigerate them 1 or 2 days, or freeze them.

Slice the remaining green onions. Add them with the won tons, the basil, the remaining 1 tablespoon ginger, the snow peas, and the raw shrimp to the boiling broth. Reduce heat, and simmer 2 or 3 minutes, until the shrimp turn pink. Season with the optional soy sauce just before serving.

Cold Borscht

SERVES 8 TO 10

This is a stunningly beautiful crimson soup, which may be served hot or cold. Many years ago my favorite former husband, David, and I went to Africa on a Russian cruise ship. The food was dreadful, except for the cold borscht, which was terrific! I loaned the maître d' a cookbook I had with me. In those days, Russians had no access to English cookbooks. At the end of the trip, he was reluctant to part with it, so in exchange he sent a bottle of champagne to the table and I pried this recipe out of him. To cook beets, preheat the oven to 400 degrees. Cut off the greens, leaving a inch or so on top to prevent bleeding. Bake the unpeeled whole beets for 30 to 45 minutes, until tender. Let cool and peel. Beet juice stains, so use rubber gloves and a non-wooden board to peel and chop them.

2 to 3 quarts chicken broth
    or stock, fresh or canned
6 beets (2 pounds) fresh cooked
    beets, or canned beets
2 red onions, chopped
1 red cabbage, grated or sliced
    thinly
½ cup lemon juice
Salt
Freshly ground black pepper

1 teaspoon sugar
1½ pounds (2 medium)
    cucumbers, peeled and
    sliced
½ cup sour cream
2 green onions or scallion
    greens, chopped
3 heaping tablespoons finely
    chopped fresh dill

Bring the chicken broth to the boil and add the cooked beets, red onions, and cabbage and cook until soft, about 1 hour. Purée the solids in a blender or food processor, then add the broth and lemon juice. Taste for seasoning and add salt, pepper, and sugar. Chill, covered, if serving cold. May be refrigerated up to 3 days. Reheat thoroughly if serving hot. To serve, ladle into individual bowls and top with the sliced cucumbers, then garnish them with the sour cream, green onions, and dill.

The soup freezes covered in an airtight container.

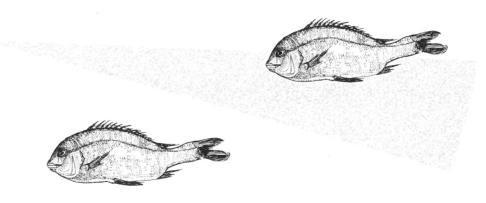

Georgia Bouillabaisse

SERVES 6 TO 8

Bouillabaisse is Southern France's kettle of fish, a peasant soup served with a peppery, garlicky sauce and croutons. For Georgia bouillabaisse nearly anything goes! Figure 3 to 4 pounds of total fish or shellfish for 3 quarts total broth. You may use all fish, or as I've indicated part fish, mussels, shrimp, and/or lobster. Everything can and should be prepared in advance. Then all that is left to do is add the fish to the broth and cook it quickly. This is actually a very simple dish to prepare. Don't let the steps intimidate you. The stock freezes well and can be reheated; the fresh fish you have selected the day of your party. Although I have a friend who serves this in a copper chafing dish in the living room, I love having my guests crowd into the kitchen to watch the final additions! Be sure to serve lots of napkins!

I usually get my fish man to steam the lobsters for me, then I crack the tail and remove the meat. I leave the claws whole, but cracked, to add to the bouillabaisse at the last minute.

To clean mussels, see page 70 for instructions.

3 quarts Enhanced Fish Broth Base (recipe follows)
½ pound each of 3 different kinds of firm, white fish such as halibut, grouper, red snapper, bass, haddock, rock cod, orange roughy, or scallops, cut into 2-inch pieces, or 3 pounds whole fish (see note on Enhanced Fish Broth Base), skinned, boned, and cut into 2-inch pieces

1 pound mussels in the shells (optional)
1 pound shrimp, peeled
2 (1-pound) cooked lobsters, cracked, tail and claws separated (optional)
Rouille (page 158)
Garlic Croûtes (page 158)

Bring the fish broth base to the boil in a large stockpot, then add the fish and the mussels. If the shrimp are large, add now. Add smaller shrimp in 1 minute. Reduce heat, if necessary, to a simmer and simmer for 2 to 5 minutes, until the mussels open and the shrimp are cooked. Do not stir as the fish will break up. Add the cooked lobsters and remove from the heat. Taste for seasoning. Ladle the soup into a large tureen.

Thin the Rouille with 2 or 3 tablespoons of the soup base and pour into a sauceboat. Place a garlic crust in each soup bowl, add a dollop of Rouille, and ladle the soup with much fish over it. Pass more Rouille and Croûtes separately.

Enhanced Fish Broth Base

MAKES 3 QUARTS

This broth is what gives Georgia bouillabaisse its full flavor. It's very important to have it fabulous tasting. Unfortunately, sometimes no fish bones are to be found. Once we could find only fillets for sale in Atlanta—no bones! Desperate, but aware of the financial invest-ment we already had in the kettle of fish, we bought two pounds of the cheapest fish we could find. It had been frozen but tasted and smelled fine. We cooked it as we would have the bones. The broth was as flavorful as one made with bones, but not quite as replete in texture, as the gelatin in the bones provides fullness.

Some people use a mixture of clam juice and water as the base and that is fine, too. The fish we used was too overcooked for me to enjoy, but the cat loved it, and it was only slightly more expensive than clam juice and *much* more tasty! On a whole fish the bones and flesh on the fish are of equal weight. Not only is this economical, but you will have a wonderful broth from the bones, which add body, and the fish.

¾ cup olive oil
2 cups sliced onions
2 large carrots coarsely chopped
1 cup sliced leeks
½ cup finely chopped fresh
    fennel (optional) or
    ½ teaspoon fennel seed
3 pounds canned Italian plum
    tomatoes, or very fresh
    tomatoes, coarsely chopped
4 garlic cloves, chopped
3 pounds cleaned bones, heads,
    and trimmings of the fish
    you are using in the
    bouillabaisse, well washed

6 sprigs parsley
1 teaspoon fennel seed
2 bay leaves
½ teaspoon dried tarragon
½ teaspoon dried thyme
12 black peppercorns
Peel, no white attached, of
    1 small orange
Pinch saffron threads
Pinch cayenne pepper

Heat the olive oil in a heavy 12-quart stockpot. Add the onions, carrots, leeks, fennel, tomatoes, garlic, and the fish bones and cook over medium heat for 10 minutes. Add the parsley, fennel seeds, bay leaves, tarragon, thyme, peppercorns, orange peel, saffron threads, and cayenne to the pot with cold water to cover. Bring to the boil, reduce the heat to a simmer, and cook for 30 minutes, uncovered. Let the broth base settle off the heat for 15 minutes, then strain it through a large fine sieve into a soup pot or kettle, pressing hard on the solids to extract all the juices.

The broth freezes in a freezer container.

Rouille (Garlic Red Pepper Sauce)

MAKES 1½ CUPS

This garlicky, near mayonnaise is marvelous as a dip or sauce for fish, chicken, and potatoes, as well as grilled foods. It has a special relationship to bouillabaisse, to which it is traditionally added at the end. Jarred red peppers or pimientos may be substituted for the fresh roasted.

1 thin slice French bread, crust removed, torn apart
¼ cup strained fish broth
Pinch saffron
¼ teaspoon cayenne pepper
3 egg yolks
6 to 8 garlic cloves, crushed to a paste

1 cup olive oil
2 medium sweet red bell peppers, roasted, peeled, and seeds removed (page 99)
Salt
Freshly ground black pepper
Tabasco sauce

Soak the bread in the fish broth with the pinch of saffron and half the cayenne until soft. In the food processor with the metal blade or in a mixer, beat the 3 egg yolks with the bread mixture and garlic. Slowly pour in the olive oil in a thin steady stream until a mayonnaise consistency forms. When thick, add the red peppers. Purée. Season well with salt, pepper, the remaining cayenne, and Tabasco.

Garlic Croûtes

MAKES 24 PIECES

These homemade toasts, much like thick melba toasts, are a wonderful snack as well as a good accompaniment to soup. They keep very well in a sealed container for weeks, and they can be frozen.

2 or 3 garlic cloves, put through a garlic press

¼ to ½ cup olive oil

24 slices French bread, each about ½ inch thick

Preheat oven to 400 degrees.

Mix the garlic with the oil and let stand 30 minutes. Lightly brush the slices with the flavored oil and bake for 15 to 20 minutes, turning as necessary until golden brown.

The croûtes freeze in an airtight container. Crisp in the oven before serving.

Ginger Vichyssoise

SERVES 4

Vichyssoise, the famed cold soup, is a wonderful summer starter. The addition here of yogurt and ginger adds snap. Like any vichyssoise, be sure to taste for seasoning carefully. I devised this soup for Cliff Graubert who worries about his cholesterol. Hence, the absence of milk or cream.

¾ pound potatoes, peeled and sliced

2 leeks, with some green, chopped

4 to 6 garlic cloves, chopped

2 onions, chopped

2 teaspoons chopped fresh jalapeño pepper (optional)

4 green onions or scallions, sliced, greens reserved for garnish

½ to 1 tablespoon chopped fresh ginger

5 cups chicken broth or stock, fresh or canned, skimmed of fat

1 cup plain yogurt

2 cucumbers, seeded and finely diced

Salt

Freshly ground black pepper

Put the potatoes, leeks, garlic, onions, optional jalapeño pepper, green onions, ginger, and the chicken broth in a large saucepan. Bring to the boil, reduce heat, and cook, covered, until the potatoes, garlic, and onion are very soft, about 25 minutes. Skim off any scum. Remove the solids with a slotted spoon and purée in a food processor or blender with a little of the liquid until very smooth. Return the purée to the liquid, whisking vigorously until the mixture is cool. Whisk in the yogurt until well incorporated. Chill. Add the cucumbers. Season to taste with salt and pepper, adding more ginger if necessary. Garnish with the sliced green onions. Serve very cold.

From the Sea

Baked Fish with Moroccan Spices and Spinach

SERVES 8 TO 10

This spectacularly pretty dish, with its incredible perfume of spices, is easily prepared and is great party fare. Greens and reds predominate, and the whole fish is breathtaking and delicious.

I developed this recipe when I returned from Seattle with a lovely three-pound salmon. I cast around for a recipe, and I took some ideas from *A Taste of Morocco* by Robert Carrier, to come up with this Moroccan-Georgian invention. Serve the fish directly from the baking dish. Leave the skin on as the dry marinade is delicious! If you have a fish larger than three pounds, increase the marinade and spinach mixture by at least half again. A five-pound fish will need six packages of spinach and will easily serve fifteen. The herbs are in two different places in the ingredients list, so when shopping be sure to get them all; it's frustrating to run short! Be sure to help your guests serve themselves as they may be intimidated until they get the hang of it.

(continued)

Moroccan Fish Dry Marinade

1 large onion, finely chopped
4 garlic cloves, finely chopped
½ teaspoon turmeric
1 teaspoon ground cumin seed
2 tablespoons finely chopped
   red bell pepper
½ teaspoon finely chopped hot
   red pepper (fresh or dried)
½ teaspoon ground saffron

6 heaping tablespoons finely
   chopped fresh cilantro
6 heaping tablespoons finely
   chopped fresh parsley
6 tablespoons olive oil
3 tablespoons lemon juice
Salt
Freshly ground black pepper

The Fish

1 whole sea bass, sea trout, or
   small salmon (3 to 5
   pounds), cleaned, scaled,
   with head on
3 to 5 tablespoons olive oil
3 medium onions, chopped
3 garlic cloves, chopped
4 (10-ounce) packages spinach,
   defrosted, or 2 pounds
   blanched spinach, squeezed
   lightly (page 219)
3 tomatoes, peeled and cut into
   ½-inch cubes

4 heaping tablespoons finely
   chopped fresh cilantro
2 heaping tablespoons finely
   chopped fresh thyme
4 heaping tablespoons finely
   chopped fresh parsley
Grated peel, no white attached,
   and juice of 1 lemon
1 teaspoon salt
1 teaspoon freshly ground black
   pepper

To make the dry marinade, mix the onion, garlic, turmeric, cumin, bell pepper, hot red pepper, saffron, cilantro, parsley, olive oil, lemon juice, salt, and pepper.

Rub the fish with the marinade and leave 2 hours or more, covered, in refrigerator.

Preheat oven to 400 degrees.

Oil a large baking and serving pan. Heat 3 tablespoons of the oil in a large frying pan. Add the onions and garlic and sauté until soft, about 5 minutes, adding oil if needed. Place the spinach in a layer on the bottom of the baking pan, then add a layer of the onion and garlic mixture, then top with tomato. Sprinkle with the cilantro, thyme, parsley, lemon peel and lemon juice, salt, and pepper. This may be done several hours in advance to this point, depending on the quality of the tomatoes.

Measure the thickness of the fish, reserving the marinade. Place on top of the layered vegetables. Cover the body of the fish with the reserved marinade. Cover with aluminum foil. Bake for 12 minutes per inch of thickness, plus 5 minutes more, approximately ½ hour in all. This recipe takes longer to cook than most fish dishes because of the layered vegetables. Serve in the baking dish, or transfer as is to a large platter. Cut down to the bone of the fish to serve. Pull up the bone to serve the underside of the fish.

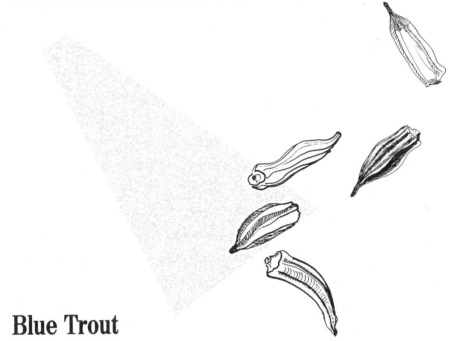

Blue Trout

SERVES 4

There is nothing like the taste of freshly caught fish. If you are careful to leave on the coating, freshwater trout will turn a brilliant blue when dropped in acidulated water. Well worth the care. You may cook any fresh fish in simmering water this same way; it just won't turn blue!

To Clean Trout

- **To clean trout, with one hand hold the live trout securely from the bottom, placing your fingers in the gills without letting the fish rub against anything, including your hands. With your other hand, club the fish. Insert a small knife in the vent and cut from**

the vent to the head. Pull out the gills and innards in one tug. Rinse out gently, without splashing water on the skin. Return the fish to the vat of lake water until ready to cook.

4 freshly caught whole rainbow trout (each 8 to 10 inches long) in a holding vat of lake water	Vinegar or lemon juice 2 lemons, halved and cut decoratively

Bring 1 or 2 pots of water to the boil, being sure the pots are large enough so that the fish will not touch one another as you slide them in. Add 2 tablespoons of vinegar or lemon juice per fish to each pot. Remove the fish from the holding vat. You may choose to also sprinkle the fish with vinegar or lemon juice at this time to ensure that they turn blue. Measure the trout for thickness. Add the fish to the boiling water, belly down. Let the water return to a simmer. It takes about 3 to 5 minutes to cook a 10-inch-long by ½-inch-thick trout. (In brief, cook 10 minutes to each inch of thickness. The eyes bulge when done.) Remove with a slotted spoon or strainer. Drain. Place on plates and serve with the lemon halves. If desired, add a sauce of your choosing—hollandaise, *beurre blanc*, Rouille (page 158), or *Pico de Gallo* (page 83).

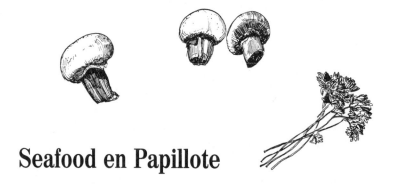

Seafood en Papillote

SERVES 4

The nice thing about dishes cooked in parchment paper is the flurry of excitement they cause at presentation. Sometimes aluminum foil is used as a substitute. It works, but is not as dramatic. Either way, the whole package can be made ahead and refrigerated, ready to pop in the oven. The sauce here is a variation of a *velouté*. If using thick fillets, you may have to add 5 minutes of cooking time. Also, add 5 minutes of cooking time if the package has been prepared in advance and refrigerated. The mushrooms dilute the thick sauce and give a nice crunch!

4 medium (about ¼-inch-thick) flounder fillets, or other flat fillets such as lemon sole
½ pound shrimp, shelled and deveined
½ pound sea scallops
2 tablespoons butter
4 tablespoons flour
2 cups fish stock, clam juice, or chicken broth or stock, fresh or canned
¼ cup dry white wine

Salt
Freshly ground black pepper
2 egg yolks, lightly beaten
Parchment paper
Vegetable oil
¼ pound mushrooms, rinsed and sliced
2 green onions, sliced on diagonal, with green part saved
2 tablespoons finely chopped fresh parsley

Preheat oven to 400 degrees.

Rinse the flounder, shrimp, and scallops and set aside on a paper towel. Melt the butter in a skillet, stir in the flour, and cook until tan. Stirring constantly, gradually add the fish stock. Bring to the boil, reduce to a simmer, and cook until reduced by half, stirring as needed. Add the wine and season to taste with salt and pepper. Add a little of the hot sauce to the egg yolks and then stir the yolks back into the sauce. Stir for a moment over low heat without overcooking the yolks. Strain if necessary.

You can make 4 individual packages or 1 large one. Cut 8 small or 2 large sheets of parchment paper or aluminum foil. Brush half with the oil. Place the fillets side by side in the middle of the large sheet, or 1 fillet on each small sheet. Place ¼ of the shrimp, scallops, mushrooms, green onions, and parsley on top of each fillet. Spoon the sauce liberally over the seafood and top with the green onion. Top with a similar sheet of parchment paper, securing tightly, so that no juice can escape. Make packages with the remaining ingredients in the same manner. May be made ahead to this point and refrigerated. Place the packages on an oiled baking sheet and bake until the paper browns, about 10 minutes. Serve in the package slitting it at the table, or open the package and turn onto a plate or the serving platter just before serving.

Seafood Stew

SERVES 6 TO 8

It's too bad there are so many ingredients in this recipe, since, like Georgia Bouillabaisse, this brings the scent and charm of the sea to your home, with very little effort. Once the base is ready and the fish cut, there is really not much to the final cooking and serving, which is done in less than 10 minutes. The sauce, however, can and should be made at the convenience of the cook. Serve with angel hair pasta, a nice salad, and homemade bread.

5 tablespoons olive oil
2 large onions, chopped into
   ½-inch pieces
4 garlic cloves, chopped
2 (1-pound 12-ounce) cans
   peeled plum tomatoes,
   chopped, including juice
2 bay leaves, crushed
1 teaspoon sugar (optional)
Salt
Freshly ground black pepper
2 heaping tablespoons finely
   chopped fresh basil

2 heaping tablespoons finely
   chopped fresh oregano
1 heaping tablespoon finely
   chopped fresh rosemary or
   cilantro (optional)
1 pound sea bass, grouper,
   salmon, mahi-mahi,
   monkfish, or red snapper,
   cut into 2-inch pieces
1 pound shrimp
1 pound sea scallops
Freshly grated imported
   Parmesan cheese

In a large Dutch oven, heat the oil. Add the onions and garlic and cook until soft. Add the tomatoes and their juice and bay leaves and simmer, uncovered, until thickened, about 1 hour. Taste and add sugar, salt, and pepper as necessary. Add the basil, oregano, and rosemary or cilantro. Continue cooking to blend the flavors, about 10 minutes more. The sauce may be made ahead to this point, and refrigerated or frozen. When ready to serve, bring the sauce to the boil, add the fish, reduce the heat, and simmer 5 minutes. Then add the shrimps and scallops, and cook just until the shrimp are pink and the scallops are opaque, about 2 or 3 minutes. Serve in soup bowls and sprinkle with the Parmesan.

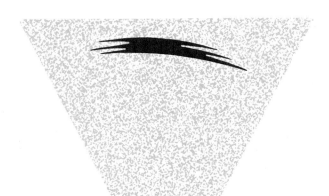

Poultry and Meats

Cornish Hens with Lime Spice Marinade

SERVES 4

These tangy cornish hens are a treat for a special dinner or a picnic. Remove the backbones by cutting down either side of the hens from the neck to the tail. This will enable you to cook the hens evenly and make them easier to serve. For a dinner party you need one per person; for a family with small children or light eaters, sometimes half a hen is sufficient. Serve with Lime-Cilantro Butter (recipe follows).

3 tablespoons lime juice
2 tablespoons olive oil
4 garlic cloves, chopped
2 green onions, finely chopped
Grated peel, no white attached, of 1 lime
1 tablespoon coarsely ground black pepper
1 teaspoon cayenne pepper

1 teaspoon chili powder
1 teaspoon ground cumin seed
1 teaspoon dry mustard
½ teaspoon salt
½ teaspoon ground coriander seed
4 cornish hens, backbones removed and hens flattened

(continued)

Combine the lime juice, olive oil, garlic, green onions, lime peel, black pepper, cayenne, chili powder, cumin, mustard, salt, and coriander. Spread paste evenly over the hens. Cover hens with plastic wrap, then weigh them down. Marinate 24 hours in the refrigerator if possible.

Preheat oven to 400 degrees.

Bake hens, uncovered, for 45 minutes, or until a meat thermometer measures 170 degrees and the juices run clear. May also be cooked on the grill about 20 to 25 minutes per side, turning occasionally to prevent overbrowning. May be made ahead and reheated. Serve hot, with the flavored butter, or cold.

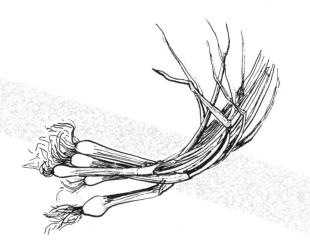

Lime-Cilantro Butter

MAKES 2 CUPS

This is wonderful over cornish hens, grilled fish—particularly salmon—chicken, and even lamb chops.

1 cup butter, softened
½ cup finely chopped fresh
    cilantro

2 tablespoons fresh lime juice
1 teaspoon grated lime peel

Cream the butter with the cilantro, lime juice, and peel. The butter freezes, either in a tub, shaped as a log, or in individual measurements.

Stuffed Cornish Hens with Basil Cream Sauce

SERVES 4 TO 6

This is a dramatic and exciting dish. The hens puff up with a tasty stuffing under the skin, which adds flavor to the flesh as well.

Cornish hens seem to me to be much bigger than they were a few years ago, when one was a perfect serving size for one person. One stuffed hen will serve one and a half to two guests. The stuffing assures everyone half when a hen is split.

½ cup Yogurt Cheese (page 11)
1 (10-ounce) package frozen
   chopped spinach, drained
4 green onions, chopped
½ cup freshly grated imported
   Parmesan cheese
⅓ cup sunflower seeds
3 garlic cloves, chopped
2 heaping teaspoons finely
   chopped fresh thyme
2 heaping tablespoons finely
   chopped fresh basil

½ teaspoon ground coriander
   seed
Salt
Freshly ground black pepper
4 cornish hens
1 cup chicken broth or stock,
   fresh or canned
¾ cup heavy cream
2 teaspoons chopped dried
   tomatoes

Preheat oven to 400 degrees.

Combine the Yogurt Cheese, spinach, green onions, Parmesan, sunflower seeds, garlic, thyme, half the basil, coriander, salt, and pepper. Stuff the mixture under the skin of each hen. Place the hens in a large shallow baking dish. Pour the broth around them and bake, uncovered, for 45 to 50 minutes, or until a meat thermometer registers 170 degrees. Remove the hens from the pan and simmer the juices over high heat until reduced by half. Add the cream, tomatoes, the remaining basil, salt, and pepper and heat until just bubbly around edge of pan. Meanwhile, halve the hens and arrange on a platter. Pass the cream sauce separately.

Roasting Chicken with Garlic

I've always loved the classic recipe for French chicken stuffed with ten garlic cloves, but I've hated peeling the cloves. Now peeled garlic cloves are available in grocery stores and it makes this recipe a snap! If peeled garlic is not available, place the unpeeled cloves in boiling water for 30 minutes. Drain, cool, and pop off the skin. Or cook 1 minute per whole head in the microwave. Cool and peel. When cooked, the garlic loses its strength, becoming soft, with a golden nut-like flavor. This dish is absolutely delicious, so delicious I've upped the garlic. Try to get the large cloves. Don't use elephant garlic as it doesn't soften properly when cooked. The Balsamic vinegar is an "up town" conceit. It is not necessary at all for a great family meal. Homemade stock is preferable as it makes for a thicker richer sauce.

2 tablespoons oil
2 tablespoons butter
50 garlic cloves, peeled
2 onions, peeled and cut into
    quarters
1 (6-pound) roasting chicken
3 tablespoons finely chopped
    fresh rosemary, tarragon, or
    marjoram

2 cups chicken broth or stock,
    preferably homemade
1 cup Balsamic vinegar
    (optional)
Salt
Freshly ground black pepper

Preheat oven to 425 degrees.

Heat the oil and butter in a large frying pan. Add the 50 garlic cloves and the onions and brown slightly for a few minutes. Remove the garlic and onions with a slotted spoon, shaking off excess fat, and stuff them inside the chicken cavity with 2 tablespoons of the herbs. Brush with any remaining oil and butter. Place the chicken in a metal or ovenproof roasting pan. Tie the legs together or truss. Add ½ cup chicken broth. Bake 1 hour. Remove from the oven. Turn. Add 1 more cup of the chicken broth and continue cooking another hour, turning occasionally, until the chicken registers 170 degrees on a meat thermometer. Remove the chicken and set aside. Add to the pan the remaining broth, the remaining herbs, and half the optional vinegar. Remove the garlic mixture from the chicken and add to the pan. Bring to the boil and boil steadily until reduced by half. Taste. Add more vinegar if desired and continue boiling until a thick sauce forms. Skim off the fat. Season with salt and pepper. Serve with the sauce. May be made ahead 1 to 2 days and reheated, but it's best served freshly made.

Duck with Red Wine and Prunes

SERVES 2

In the winter you'll love this hearty company or family dish. Duck has a real affinity for dried fruit. Cutting up the duck prior to browning it also makes serving easier. You need good poultry shears. Also, use a metal spoon to remove the fat, not a plastic spoon or bulb baster, which will melt. Serve with Whole Baked Garlic (page 102) or Baked or Grilled Onions (page 101).

To Prepare the Duck
- **To carve, cut the duck down either side of the backbone; cut off the legs, and bone the breast into 2 portions. Pull off excess fat and remove if desired.**
- **To prepare duck stock, brown the reserved back of the duck, chop up, and add to the pan as the duck browns. It'll add flavor to the mixture.**
- **To render duck fat, remove fat from the duck, cut into pieces, place in a pan with some water, and boil down until water is gone and fat rendered. Use the hard bits of fat like cracklings.**

If you are serving four people, be sure to have a lot of side dishes and vegetables, as one duck really only serves two or three people sufficiently.

(continued)

1½ cups pitted prunes, dried apricots, or cherries

1 cup dry red wine or non-alcoholic wine (Cabernet Sauvignon)

5 tablespoons butter or rendered duck fat

1 onion, sliced

2 garlic cloves, chopped

1 leek, julienned

1 carrot, peeled and julienned or grated

1 (4- to 5-pound) duck, back removed and reserved, quartered

1 bay leaf

½ cup fresh parsley, stems reserved

2 cups chicken broth or stock, fresh or canned

Salt

Freshly ground black pepper

Garnish

¼ cup finely chopped fresh thyme

¼ cup dried fruits such as apricots, prunes, or cherries

Bring the dried fruit and wine to the boil in a small pan, and set aside. Heat 2½ tablespoons of the butter in a large skillet. Add the onion, garlic, leek, and carrot. Cook until the onion is lightly browned. Remove the vegetables, and set aside. Add more fat if necessary to cover the bottom of the pan. Prick the duck skin all over with a fork, but do not pierce the flesh of the breast. Pat dry with paper towels. Add the duck pieces to the hot pan, skin side down. Brown and turn. Reduce heat and cook until the second side is brown, draining fat off as necessary. Remove. Pour excess fat from the pan. Drain the wine from the fruits and add to the pan, reserving the fruits. Deglaze the pan by bringing the wine to the boil and scraping the sides and bottom of pan until all the goodness is incorporated in the sauce.

Place the onion mixture in the bottom of a casserole, and arrange the duck pieces on top. Tie the bay leaf up with the parsley stems for easy removal later. Add them with the reduced wine and the stock. Bring to the boil. Lower heat and simmer, covered, until the duck is tender, 45 minutes to 1 hour, removing fat periodically. Remove the duck and vegetables. Remove the fat, and the bay leaf and parsley stems. Add the fruit. Bring the sauce to the boil and boil until reduced by half. Season with salt and pepper. May be made ahead to this point.

When ready to serve, preheat the broiler. Run the duck pieces and vegetables under the broiler to crisp. To serve, garnish with the parsley and thyme and additional dried fruits. In a saucepan, bring the sauce back to the boil, and serve with the duck.

Duck à l'Orange

SERVES 2; 4 WITH
MULTIPLE ACCOMPANIMENTS

This most famous of duck preparations is a great company dish, sure to dazzle out of proportion to the effort it takes to produce the elegant rich sauce and lustrous brown duck.

One duck will serve four people only if you have a lot of side dishes and vegetables. If you choose to roast it, see the recipe for Honey Vinegar Duck (page 174). Leave duck whole and place orange rind in the cavity; roast as directed. For four to six people, cook two ducks at one time. Use any leftover meat in a wild rice salad.

1 (4- to 5-pound) duck, fat removed and reserved
¼ cup orange-flavored liqueur (optional) or orange juice
4 navel oranges, peel removed, blanched, and chopped; flesh sectioned
3 tablespoons sugar

⅔ cup red wine vinegar
2 tablespoons cornstarch
½ cup Madeira or dry sherry (optional) or ½ cup orange juice
Salt
Freshly ground black pepper

Carve the duck(s) as directed on page 171. Marinate all the parts of the duck but the giblets, neck, and backbone in 3 tablespoons of the orange liqueur and 2 tablespoons of the orange peel.

Meanwhile, make brown stock. In a medium saucepan brown the giblets, chopped (not the liver), neck, and bones. Add water to cover, about 2 cups. Bring to the boil, reduce heat, and simmer, partially covered, 1 to 2 hours. Remove the solids, bring the stock to the boil, and boil to reduce to 2 cups. Skim the fat. This may be done in advance and refrigerated or frozen.

Heat the reserved duck fat in a pan until melted and hot. Add

173

the duck legs, skin side down. Brown and turn. When nearly done, add the breast. Reduce heat and cook 10 to 15 minutes, until duck is done. Drain off fat as necessary. Remove duck.

To make a sweet and sour sauce, boil the sugar and ½ of the red wine vinegar over high heat until the mixture has turned to a rich brown. Immediately remove from the heat and pour into the duck stock. Bring back to the boil, stirring. Mix the cornstarch with 4 tablespoons of the Madeira or orange juice. Add part of the sauce to the cornstarch mixture, then return it to pot, and stir in the remaining orange peel. Simmer for 3 or 4 minutes, or until the sauce is clear and lightly thickened.

Remove as much fat as you can from the duck pan. Add the remaining 4 tablespoons of the wine or orange juice and the remaining vinegar. Boil it down rapidly, stirring to get all the goodness from the meat, until the liquid is reduced to 2 to 3 tablespoons. Strain into the sauce base, and simmer. Add the remaining orange liqueur to taste. Boil 2 minutes to marry the flavors and season to taste with salt and pepper. May be made to this point 1 day ahead. When ready to serve, run the duck under the broiler to crisp. Place some of the orange sections over the duck and pile the rest around it on the serving platter. Spoon a bit of sauce with peel over the duck, and serve with white rice or wild rice.

Honey Vinegar Duck

SERVES 2 OR 3

This crisp roasted duck, its tawny skin sparkling with honey coating, is very tender. The type of wine vinegar and honey will change the sauce. Experiment. It's fun to see the differences. And the long cooking time insures a moist bird.

When I visited my foster daughter and her French husband in Canada, he cooked this for us for dinner, while Audrey fixed a fresh cherry tart. A lovely marriage of people and food.

1 (4- to 5-pound) duck
Salt
Freshly ground black pepper
¼ cup butter
1 large shallot, chopped

3 to 4 tablespoons honey
3 to 4 tablespoons red wine,
    Balsamic, raspberry, or
    sherry vinegar

Preheat oven to 375 degrees.

Rub the duck with salt and pepper. Prick and score the skin at 1-inch intervals. Place the duck on a rack in a pan with 2-inch sides. Roast, uncovered, for 30 minutes per pound until tender.

In a small saucepan melt the butter, add the shallot, and sauté until it turns blond. Add the honey, bring to the boil, and boil for 2 or 3 minutes. Add the vinegar and continue to boil. The sauce is ready when it starts to have a syrupy consistency.

Cut down both sides of the backbone, from neck to tail, dividing the duck in 2 pieces. Pull out the breast and rib bones. When ready to serve, place the halves under the broiler to crisp the skin and warm through. Lightly coat the pieces with the honey sauce. Can be made 1 to 2 days ahead and reheated under the broiler or in a 375-degree oven.

If you prefer to fry the duck, cut it into 6 pieces. Season with salt and pepper. Brown, turn, and continue cooking until done (see Duck with Red Wine and Prunes, page 171).

Roast Goose

SERVES 4

Cooking and serving goose is a treat anytime and should be thought of as a joyous mission! You need a lot of side dishes as there isn't a lot of flesh.

1 (6- to 8-pound) goose
Salt
Freshly ground black pepper

2 apples, quartered
3 onions, quartered

Stock
Neck
Gizzard
Heart
1 onion, sliced
2 (14½-ounce) cans chicken
    broth

2 (14½-ounce) cans water
6 parsley stems
1 bay leaf
2 teaspoons thyme

Sauce
1 cup Cabernet Sauvignon or
    non-alcoholic Cabernet
    Sauvignon

½ cup red currant jelly

Garnish
Red currants or red grapes

Preheat oven to 325 degrees.

Wash and dry the goose, inside and out. Remove excess fat and fry it to extract 2 to 4 tablespoons liquid fat. Sprinkle salt and pepper in the cavity, and place the apples and onions inside. Prick the skin all over with a sharp knife, taking care not to puncture the flesh. Place the goose, breast side up, in a roasting pan, and cook, uncovered, for about 2 hours, or 20 minutes a pound, until dark golden brown and tender and a thermometer registers 175 degrees when placed in the thigh. Drain off the fat from time to time. You may wind up with as much as 6 cups of fat, which may be strained and refrigerated or frozen for another purpose.

While the goose is cooking, make the stock. Heat the 2 to 4 tablespoons rendered goose fat in a saucepan. Chop the neck, gizzard, and heart (not the liver) into 1- to 2-inch chunks. Add to the fat, and brown well. Add the onion and brown. Add the broth, water, parsley stems, bay leaf, and thyme. Cover. Bring to the boil, reduce heat, and simmer 1 to 2 hours, partially covered. Strain the stock.

When the goose is done, remove the goose to a platter. Remove the fat, leaving any juices in the pan. Add the strained stock and the Cabernet Sauvignon to the pan juices and boil until thick and glossy. Add the red currant jelly and whisk or stir until melted. Both goose and sauce may be made ahead 1 to 2 days, refrigerated and reheated. When ready to serve, put the goose on a decorative platter and garnish with the currants or grapes. Serve with the warm sauce.

Marinated Rib Eye

SERVES 4 TO 6

This flavorful, tender, succulent, rare beef kissed with herbs and lemon deserves a special occasion.

1 lemon, sliced thin	Salt
¼ cup olive oil	Freshly ground black pepper
¾ cup lemon juice	2½ pounds rib eye
1 large garlic clove, sliced	
4 tablespoons coarsely chopped	
fresh rosemary	

Combine the sliced lemon, olive oil, lemon juice, garlic, rosemary, salt, and pepper. Pour over meat, cover, and let marinate 4 hours or up to 1 day.

Preheat oven to 400 degrees.

Remove the beef from the marinade and place in roasting pan. If the pan is 1 inch larger around than the roast, add water to cover the bottom of the pan to prevent juices from burning. Place in oven and roast until the beef reaches an internal temperature on a meat thermometer of 125 degrees for rare. Remove from oven and let cool. Serve with the juices poured over it.

Beef Tenderloin with Mock Italian Sauce

SERVES 10 TO 12

Many people ask me how I get my recipes. This one came as a consequence of a class I donated to a local high school auction. Relatives who really didn't want to work too hard cooking bought the class. Ray sat down, made up this simple marinade to replace something complicated, and we all loved it. The combination has real punch—welcome, since tenderloin has so little flavor compared to chuck and round or New York strip. Of course, the tenderloin is the tenderest cut of beef and the easiest to fix.

1 (5-pound) beef tenderloin, after trimming of fat
4 garlic cloves, chopped
⅓ cup tomato juice
3 tablespoons olive oil
½ cup red wine vinegar
2 tablespoons Worcestershire sauce
1 tablespoon packed brown sugar
1½ tablespoons chopped fresh oregano
1½ teaspoons fennel seed, crushed
1 teaspoon crushed red pepper
1 bay leaf, crumbled
Salt
Freshly ground black pepper

Preheat oven to 400 degrees.

Place the tenderloin in a plastic bag or glass bowl. Mix the garlic with the tomato juice, olive oil, red wine vinegar, Worcestershire, brown sugar, oregano, fennel, red pepper, bay leaf, salt and pepper to taste, and and pour over the tenderloin. Seal bag or cover tightly. Refrigerate 2 hours to overnight.

When ready to cook, flip about 2 inches of the tail under, and tie the tenderloin up with string, making it nearly the same thickness as the center portion. Place the beef and the marinade in a baking dish. Roast 25 to 30 minutes until a meat thermometer registers 140 degrees for rare. Remove from the oven and let rest on a platter for 10 minutes. Slice the meat thin and serve with the pan juices.

Grilled Racks or Saddle of Lamb

SERVES 4

Garden herbs, garlic, and shallots imbue this lamb with the hint of spring's promise. This recipe combines grilling with oven cooking, but may be cooked completely in the oven. Be careful of grill flare-ups.

A rack of lamb has seven ribs. Up to two pounds are lost from an untrimmed three and half-pound rack when trimmed. A double rack is sometimes available and makes a stunning presentation, as does a "Guard of Honor," where the bones of the cooked racks cross each other like swords in a military salute. Some like it cooked very rare (I call it "walking") at 125 degrees; 140 to 160 degrees seems in the range most people prefer. You may substitute a five-pound saddle of lamb—the double tenderloin, on the bone from the rump end—cooking it an additional 10 minutes.

2 racks of lamb
5 heaping tablespoons finely
   chopped mixed fresh herbs
   such as thyme, mint, lemon
   balm, or dried or fresh
   rosemary, plus fresh
   rosemary sprigs for garnish
   (optional)

3 large garlic cloves, chopped
3 shallots, chopped
2 tablespoons olive oil
Salt
Freshly ground black pepper
1 cup white wine or white wine
   vinegar, mixed with 3
   tablespoons water

If the racks have not been trimmed, trim off the cap and excess fat, leaving ¼ inch of fat on top. Scrape or "French" the bones clean.

Prepare and heat a grill. Preheat oven to 425 degrees.

Combine the herbs, garlic, shallots, olive oil, salt, and pepper.

(continued)

179

Rub on the lamb. If possible, marinate refrigerated in a plastic bag or covered dish for ½ hour to 2 days.

When ready to cook, wrap the bones on the rack in foil to prevent burning. Brush the grill rack with oil. Place the lamb, fat side down, on the hot grill. Brown and turn. Then place the meat in a small pan with the wine mixture. Place in the oven, and roast 15 to 20 minutes, until pink and medium rare, to an internal temperature on a meat thermometer of 125 degrees for rare, 140 degrees for medium, and 160 degrees for well done. Let the meat rest 10 minutes. Meanwhile, skim excess fat from the pan and boil down juices briefly. Slice the lamb off the rack, and serve with some of the juices on top. Garnish with optional sprig of rosemary.

Variation: Use fennel seed in place of the fresh herbs. Garnish with a fennel frond.

Noisettes of Lamb with Coriander

SERVES 2

Noisette or nut in French, is a boned loin or rib chop cut from a rack of lamb. When I crush coriander seeds for this recipe I think of Australia and my friends the Ledinghams in Mauree, New South Wales. I keep in my mind's eye a beautiful summer day one December when we drove around the farm where they raised lamb as well as fenugeek and coriander. We stood and crushed coriander seeds in our palms, watching the baby lambs running around in the sun.

There are many kinds of lamb with a broad range of sizes of racks available. Allow one to two *noisettes* per person, a total of two to three pounds of meat, trimmed, for four to six people, because so much of the weight is in the bones. If you buy the lamb trimmed, the butcher may have removed the flap of meat that allows you to roll it, enclosing the seasoning. If this happens, just rub the outside of the cylinder of meat firmly with the spices, and cut. If you have a good eye you won't need the string as I do!

Trim only the *excess* fat. Don't take all of it off, because the fat keeps the meat moist while roasting. Besides, many of us consider lamb fat delicious.

2 garlic cloves
Salt
2 tablespoons crushed coriander seed
1 (1½- to 2-pound) rack or loin of lamb, boned and trimmed of skin and excess fat only
1 tablespoon butter
1 tablespoon oil

1 small onion, sliced roughly
1 teaspoon flour
½ cup chicken, beef, or lamb stock, preferably homemade
½ cup dry white wine (optional; replace with additional stock)
Freshly ground black pepper

Garnish
Sprigs fresh coriander

Preheat oven to 400 degrees.

Crush the garlic with salt to a paste and mix with the coriander seeds. Spread the coriander and garlic over the lamb. Roll up the meat, starting at the lean side. Tie at 1- to 1½-inch intervals. Cut between each interval to make a noisette. Heat the butter and oil in a large skillet. Add the lamb. Brown and turn, cooking 5 or 6 minutes on each side, for medium rare. Remove the lamb and set aside.

Tip the corner of the pan and let the fat run out, gently. With the juice that is left, you will have about a tablespoon of fat, about a tablespoon of goodness, and a little sediment. Add the onion, and brown gently to give your sauce flavor and color. Add the flour and brown it, stirring. Add the stock and white wine to the pan. Bring to the boil, stirring, to deglaze the pan. Boil until reduced by half, until thick and glossy. Add salt and pepper to taste. Serve separately, garnishing the meat with the fresh coriander.

Rack of Lamb with Brown Mustard Seeds

SERVES 2

A mustard-seed-and herb-crusted rack of lamb is an easy, romantic dish to make. Because this is a bit skimpy for two, be sure to serve plenty of vegetables and a salad. Racks of lamb vary in size tremendously so adapt the cooking time accordingly, using a meat thermometer to be sure of the doneness.

2 tablespoons brown mustard
    seeds
3 garlic cloves, chopped
1 heaping tablespoon finely
    chopped fresh basil
1 heaping tablespoon finely
    chopped fresh mint

2 teaspoons capers
2 tablespoons olive oil
Salt
Freshly ground black pepper
1 (1½- to 2-pound) rack of
    lamb, trimmed (page 179)

Combine the brown mustard seeds, garlic, basil, mint, capers, olive oil, salt, and pepper. Rub on the lamb, and marinate, covered, 2 days in the refrigerator.

Preheat oven to 375 degrees.

Place the rack of lamb in a shallow baking pan. Bake 25 to 30 minutes for rare, or to an internal temperature on a meat thermometer of 125 degrees; 40 minutes for medium rare, or 140 degrees.

Roasted Leg of Lamb

SERVES 6

Lamb is best cooked rare or medium rare, not well done. One whole leg of spring lamb ideally should be no more than six pounds. Perhaps the best lamb comes from Australia, as it is small in size and sweet. The smaller the lamb, the less dense the meat, and the less time per pound it will take to cook. In comparison, many times half an American leg of lamb weighs over six pounds. Lamb is raised on many of the same farms where rosemary, mint, and coriander grow, so it is usual to see one of them accompanying it as a garnish. The wine or wine vinegar used here in cooking helps keep the house from retaining the strong odor of lamb to which some people object—particularly men who were at sea during World War II and smelled mutton being overcooked.

1 (5- to 6-pound) leg of lamb	Salt
3 to 4 garlic cloves, slivered	Freshly ground black pepper
4 heaping tablespoons finely chopped fresh rosemary, divided	2 tablespoons red currant jelly
	2 heaping tablespoons finely chopped fresh mint or
1 cup dry white wine and ¼ cup water (optional) or ½ cup white wine vinegar and ½ cup water	2 tablespoons crushed coriander seed
	Yogurt-Coriander Sauce (recipe follows) (optional)

Preheat oven to 500 degrees.

Trim off the fell, the lamb's papery skin. Cut small slits in the lamb, and push the garlic and half the rosemary into the slits. Place lamb in a roasting pan and pour in the white wine and water. Place in the oven, reduce temperature to 350 degrees, and roast 10 to 18 minutes per pound for medium rare, or 140 degrees on a meat thermometer. Remove to a platter, and let rest before carving.

Skim the fat from the pan. (To speed removal of fat from pan juices, place in the freezer until the fat congeals.) Taste the pan juices for seasoning, and add salt and pepper. Add the red currant jelly, remaining rosemary, and mint or crushed coriander seed. Bring to the boil, and boil briefly to thicken. Pour over lamb and garnish with sprigs of mint or rosemary. Serve with optional Yogurt-Coriander Sauce.

Yogurt-Coriander Sauce

MAKES 1½ CUPS

This cool yogurt sauce goes well with grilled salmon, chicken, lamb, and grilled vegetables.

1 cup plain yogurt
3 tablespoons sour cream
3 tablespoons freshly squeezed
   lemon juice
3 green onions, white part and
   half the green, chopped
2 garlic cloves, chopped

1½ tablespoons ground
   coriander seed
Pinch sugar
Salt
Freshly ground black pepper
¼ cup chopped fresh cilantro

In a bowl whisk together the yogurt, sour cream, lemon juice, green onions, garlic, and coriander until smooth. Season to taste with the sugar, salt, and pepper. Garnish with the chopped cilantro.

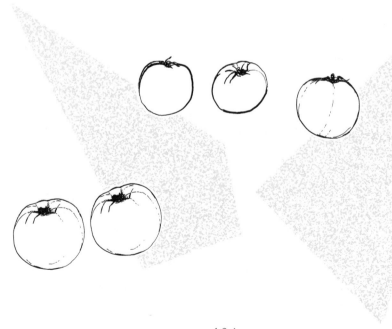

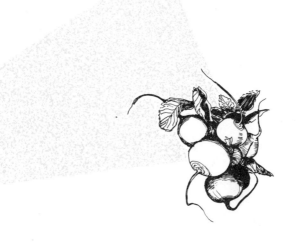

Smoked Saddle of Venison or Lamb

SERVES 8 TO 10

I'm fortunate to receive many gifts of venison, particularly the prime cuts, but farm-raised Texas venison is also available to the consumer. If venison is young and has been properly treated—field-dressed immediately—and kept under refrigeration, it doesn't need marinating, but marinade does add flavor.

Sue Hunter's Marinade

½ cup olive oil
½ cup vinegar
½ cup water

3 tablespoons A-1 Sauce or Worcestershire sauce (optional)

1 saddle of venison or lamb

Combine the olive oil, vinegar, water, and A-1. Marinate the venison or lamb, covered, overnight in the refrigerator.

Preheat a grill.

Place the saddle on the grill over direct heat. Cover the grill. Grill or smoke for 1 hour, or until a meat thermometer registers 125 degrees for rare, 140 degrees for medium, and 160 degrees for well done. Check the temperature every ½ hour. Remove from the heat and let rest 10 minutes. Carve the meat and replace it on the bone for presentation. Serve with cranberry sauce or red currant jelly.

Mustard Pork Tenderloin

SERVES 4 TO 6

Pork tenderloins are one of the easiest meats to prepare. They cook quickly and don't need to be rubbed with any additional fat. They reheat easily. And they are also good cold! What more can I say?

3 garlic cloves, finely chopped
2 tablespoons fennel seed
⅓ cup Dijon mustard
2 (½- to ¾-pound) pork
    tenderloins

Salt
Freshly ground black pepper

Preheat oven to 400 degrees.

Mix together the garlic, fennel seed, and mustard. Spread or rub the mixture over the tenderloins. Place them, side by side, in a greased baking pan and roast 20 to 30 minutes, or until a meat thermometer registers 140 degrees for rare, 160 degrees for well done. Let rest 5 minutes. Season with salt and pepper. Slice the meat on the diagonal. Pour any juices over the meat. May be made 1 or 2 days in advance, covered and refrigerated. Reheat 15 to 20 minutes at 350 degrees until warm.

Pork Tenderloin with Prunes

SERVES 4 TO 6

The presentation of this is particularly pretty: dark prunes contrasting with the pale pink of the pork and the white almonds. Unfortunately there is terrible unwarranted prejudice against anchovies and prunes. But this pork has extraordinary flavor, and once you've tasted it you'll love it. If you do wish to vary the recipe, use dried cherries instead of the prunes. Should you elect not to use wine, soak the prunes in additional stock. I have used anchovy paste instead of anchovy fillets when there were no fillets in the store. Use about ½ teaspoon per prune.

It is easier to slice the pork if it has been made ahead and cooled. Reheat in the sauce or by covering with foil and placing in hot oven for 15 minutes.

2 (preferably 1-pound each) pork tenderloins	3 tablespoons butter
12 anchovy fillets	1 tablespoon flour
12 almonds, blanched	1 cup beef stock or bouillon
18 large dried pitted prunes, soaked in 1 cup Burgundy (optional) or non-alcoholic wine	Salt
	Freshly ground black pepper

Make a slit down the length of each pork tenderloin. Open it out like a butterfly. Wrap an anchovy fillet around each almond. Drain 12 of the prunes and stuff each with an anchovy-wrapped almond. Lay 6 stuffed prunes in a line down the center of each pork tenderloin. Roll and tie or truss each tenderloin firmly up with string. Heat the butter in a large pan. Add the tenderloins, and brown on all sides. Remove to a platter. Stir in the flour. Add the stock, stirring the liquid until smooth. Bring to the boil and boil briefly, stirring. Return the tenderloins to the pan, cover, and simmer gently for about 20 minutes. In a saucepan simmer the remaining 6 prunes in the optional soaking wine until tender and most of the wine has evaporated. (Or add the prunes to the pan with the pork.) Remove the pork from the pan. May be made ahead to this point. Remove the strings and slice thin. Add the prunes and wine reduction to the pork sauce and bring to the boil. Add salt and pepper to taste. Reheat if necessary. Spoon the sauce over the meat. May be cooked ahead 1 to 2 days and reheated covered.

The dish freezes well enough for family leftovers, but not for company.

Ric Lands's Spicy Pork Roast

SERVES 10

I met Ric Lands when he was studying at La Varenne Cooking School in Paris, France. When he returned to Georgia, he started working on my public television show, then driving each Wednesday from Athens, Georgia, to Atlanta to help research this book.

A boned loin is usually in two pieces. For a large roast, tie the pieces together. If you prefer a smaller one, use only one piece, and reduce the roasting time. This nearly "melts," like barbecue. For a different texture, more of a traditional roast, cook at 375 degrees, instead of 250 degrees, to 160 degrees on the thermometer, about 2 hours.

2 cups honey
4 tablespoons Dijon mustard
4 tablespoons prepared
   horseradish
4 tablespoons dried rosemary,
   crushed
10 garlic cloves, crushed

2 teaspoons freshly ground
   black pepper
2 tablespoons chopped fresh
   ginger
1 (4- to 5-pound) boneless pork
   loin roast

Mix together the honey, mustard, horseradish, rosemary, garlic, pepper, and ginger. Pour over the pork roast, cover, and let marinate, refrigerated, 4 to 24 hours.

Preheat oven to 500 degrees.

Remove the pork from its marinade. Shake off excess marinade and reserve. Tie the roast together, if necessary to make 1 piece. Place in a roasting pan and put in the oven. After 15 minutes, reduce the heat to 250 degrees. Roast to an internal temperature on a meat thermometer of 155 degrees, about 5 hours. Turn the roast every hour or so. Remove from the oven and let rest 15 to 30 minutes. Slice.

Meanwhile, bring the marinade to a boil and reduce by about half. Pour the reduced marinade over the meat. Refrigerate until ready to serve. May serve hot, room temperature, or cold.

Pasta

Linguine with Herbed Shrimp

SERVES 2 AS A MAIN COURSE;
4 TO 6 AS A STARTER

This is primarily a pasta dish. If you want an abundance of shrimp, simply double the amount. Serve with a vegetable and salad and you have a great last-minute meal.

½ pound dried linguine or
    spaghetti
3 tablespoons butter
3 tablespoons olive oil
½ pound large shrimp, peeled
    and deveined
1 garlic clove, chopped

⅓ cup freshly grated imported
    Parmesan cheese
¼ cup finely chopped fresh
    oregano, thyme, basil, and/
    or parsley
Salt
Freshly ground black pepper

Boil the pasta in a large pot of salted water for 8 or 9 minutes; drain. In a large skillet, heat the butter and olive oil. Add the shrimp and garlic; cook until shrimp turn opaque or pink. Turn and cook the second side. Combine the hot cooked pasta, shrimp mixture, Parmesan, and herbs. Add salt and pepper to taste. Serve hot. May be made ahead and reheated.

Fix-Ahead Cannelloni Verdi

SERVES 6

This is a very special delicate pasta dish. It can serve as a main course for 6 or a starter for more. Although it looks like a long complicated recipe, it is not, and the result is astonishingly delicious.

A Few Tips About Ingredients
- **Freshly ground nutmeg is far superior to the powdered variety in a jar. Mace is the outer blade of a nutmeg.**
- **Four cups of fresh spinach make 1 cup puréed. To cook, wash thoroughly after stemming. Shake off excess water. Add to a large nonstick frying pan and cook quickly, about 5 to 8 minutes, until soft and wilted and the water has evaporated. Blend or process until puréed. Frozen and defrosted spinach may be used.**
- **Very thin fresh pasta does not always need to be boiled before filling. If you are unsure of your pasta, do a test cannelloni before filling the rest. I find it easiest to cook the pasta in a frying pan with its large surface area. It holds about as much as I can easily handle.**

3½ cups milk
1 onion slice
6 peppercorns
1 bay leaf
1 parsley stalk

1 blade mace
3 tablespoons butter
1½ pounds ground veal or
    turkey

White Sauce

3 tablespoons butter

3 tablespoons flour

2 egg yolks, beaten

Pinch freshly grated nutmeg

Salt

Freshly ground black pepper

2 pounds fresh cannelloni
(24 squares)

Green Sauce

⅓ cup butter

⅓ cup flour

1¼ cups heavy cream

Pinch freshly grated nutmeg

1 (10-ounce) package frozen
chopped spinach, drained
and puréed in a blender or
food processor

Salt

Freshly ground black pepper

1½ cups freshly grated
imported Parmesan cheese

First, infuse the milk by heating it with the onion, peppercorns, bay leaf, parsley stalk, and mace until it bubbles lightly around the sides of the pan. Remove from the heat, cover, and let sit at least ½ hour to absorb the flavors. Strain. Part of the milk will be used in the white sauce; the other part in the green.

Heat the butter in a large frying pan. Add the veal or turkey and cook until light brown. Set aside.

To make the white sauce, melt the butter and add the flour. Cook, stirring constantly, a few minutes over low heat. Stir in 1½ cups of the infused milk and bring it to the boil, stirring. Reduce the heat, and cook the sauce over low heat a few minutes. Add some white sauce to the beaten egg yolks to warm them, then add the egg yolk mixture to the white sauce.

To make the filling, stir in the partially cooked veal or turkey, the nutmeg, salt, and pepper.

Cook the cannelloni in a large frying pan of boiling salted water, adding only 6 to 8 squares at a time so they do not stick together, for 1 to 2 minutes, or until the squares are tender but still firm. Stir them occasionally to prevent them from sticking. Drain the squares and put them in cold water to stop the cooking. Drain again and spread them on a damp cloth to cool. Put about 2 teaspoons of filling on each square of pasta, roll up, and arrange them in a large, shallow, buttered baking dish. Cannelloni can be stacked, if necessary, with green sauce between layers.

To make the green sauce, melt the butter, stir in the flour, and cook briefly over low heat. Add the remaining 2 cups infused milk. Bring to the boil, stirring constantly, then reduce heat and cook over low heat a few minutes. Add the heavy cream, nutmeg, and spinach purée and bring just back to the boil. Season to taste with salt and pepper.

Spoon the green sauce over the cannelloni to coat it. May be made ahead a day or frozen at this point. When ready to use, defrost. Cover the dish with aluminum foil and bake the cannelloni at 350 degrees for 20 to 30 minutes, until heated through. Ten minutes before the end of the cooking time, remove the foil, sprinkle the cannelloni with the Parmesan, and continue baking until the top is lightly browned.

Menus and Other Ideas

Black Bean Pâté
Ric Lands's Spicy Pork Roast
Potatoes Ray
Green Salad
Barbara Robinson's Cheddar Muffins
Orange Caramel Cake or Upside Down Gingerbread

Mussels Julia
Lemon and Garlic Broiled or Grilled Chicken Breasts
Whole Baked Garlic
Baked Onions
Elizabeth Burris's Broccoli Salad
French Bread
Double Chocolate, Chocolate Chip Sandwich Cookies

All Gone Snails and Butter
Quick Chicken Taj Mahal
Boiled Rice
Roberta's Tomatoes and Parsley
or
Will's Three Lettuce Salad
Strawberry Mousse with Crisp Florentine Cookies

Cold Borscht
Seafood en Papillote
Tomato and Fennel Salad
Easy Squash and Corn Pudding
Crisp Dinner Rolls
Strawberry and Orange Dessert

Crudités with Dilly Dip
Honey Vinegar Duck
or
Lemon and Garlic Broiled or Grilled Chicken Breasts
Vicky Mooney's Sautéed Grated Sweet Potatoes
Down East Apple Pie
or
Red-Glazed Poached Pears
Pepper Bread

Randy Harris's Shrimp Cocktail
Chicken Breasts with Mustard Sauce
Green Beans with Tomatoes
or
Spinach with Garlic Pine Nuts
Couscous
French Bread (optional)
Cool Mint-Raspberry Pie
or
Treacle and Blueberry Tart

Broiled Shrimp *p918*
Chicken Breasts with Apples and Cranberries *98*
Butternut Squash and Cheddar Gratin *228*
Curried Wreath Bread *344*
Almond Tart *323*
or
Parisienne Soufflé Omelet

Pine Mountain Cheese Loaf
Roast Goose
or
Honey Vinegar Duck
Wild Rice and Prune Dressing
Orange and Fennel Salad
Free-Form Brown Sugar Apple Tart
or
Pumpkin Cheesecake
Crisp Dinner Rolls

Root Vegetable Soup
Country Ham
Creamed Cabbage
or
Cauliflower Mornay
Garlic Flavored Potato Cake
Banana-Carrot Sheet Cake
Crisp Dinner Rolls

Smoked Salmon Dip with Cucumbers
Grilled Racks or Saddle of Lamb
Speeded-up Oriental Ratatouille
or
Grilled Vegetables
Twice-Baked Potato Casserole with Mushrooms and Cream
Unbelievably Easy, Indestructible Raspberry-Peach Mousse
Basil Crescent Rolls

Babybobs
Grilled Honey-Ginger Fish Steak
Green Beans with Lemon and Onion
Vegetable Couscous Pilaf
Pavlova
Fennel-Raisin Round

Stuffed Artichokes
Sautéed Soft-Shell Crab
Beet Salad Vinaigrette
Charred Green Beans
Free-Form Brown Sugar Apple Tart

Southwestern Peanut Soup with *Pico de Gallo*
or
Country Soup with Potatoes, Green Beans, and Garlic
Roasting Chicken and Garlic
Green Salad with Garlic Cheese Toast
Diet Mashed Potatoes (optional)
Zucchini Strips with Moroccan Spices
Summer Pudding
or
Upside Down Gingerbread

Ginger Vichyssoise
Noisettes of Lamb with Coriander
Grilled Vegetables
or
Spinach with Garlic and Pine Nuts
Quick Yeast Galette
or
Chocolate Marbled Angel Food Cake

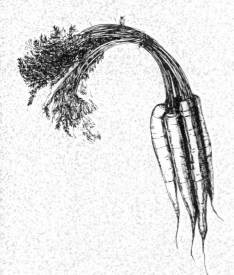

Sassy Crab Spread
or
Crudités with Yogurt Honey Mustard Dip
My Chili
Barbara Robinson's Cheddar Muffins
or
Cornbread with Red Peppers
Will's Three Lettuce Salad
Nearly Brownie Cookies
or
Ginger Ice Cream

Hot Cheese Croquettes
Grilled Ham with Asian Barbeque Sauce
Squash and Zucchini Casserole
Wild Rice, Asparagus, and Pineapple Salad
Fudgy Brownies

Red Bell Pepper Dip
Duck with Red Wine and Prunes
Asparagus Spears with Herbed Lemon Butter
Russ Parsons's Luxurious Diet Mashed Potatoes
Gingered Pumpkin Pie
Crisp Dinner Rolls

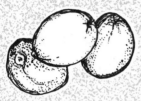

Au Shucks Oysters
Beef Braised with Mahogany Onions
Steamed Party Vegetables
Two Potato and Turnip Gratin
Lemon Poppy Seed Pound Cake
Onion Rye

Camembert Surprise
Carey LeGrange's Chicken and Smoked Sausage Gumbo
Boiled Rice
Cucumber Crescent Salad
Hot Chocolate Soufflé
or
Strawberry-Peach Crisp

Cocktail Party

Black Bean Pâté
Tenderloin of Pork with Southwestern Apple Chutney
Pretty Fancy Baked Brie
Smoked Tea Duck
Ginger and Curry Beef
Tangy Yogurt Cheese Ball
Crudités
Red Bell Pepper Dip
Tarragon Shrimp on Zucchini Rounds
Chocolate-Dipped Fruits

Dessert Buffet

Orange Caramel Cake
Almond Macaroons
Strawberry Mousse
Almond Tart
White Chocolate Banana Cream Pie
Mother's Chocolate Cream Fudge
Yogurt Pralines

Gift Ideas from the Kitchen

Chocolate Dipped Fruits
Lemon Butter
Caramels or Yogurt Pralines
Mother's Chocolate Cream Fudge
Almond Rice
Sweet Iced Christmas Bread
or
Gift Kuchen Bread
Kolachy (with red or green jelly for Christmas)

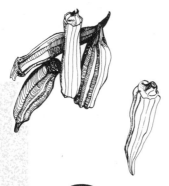

On the Side

"On the Side" turns its attention to colorful side dishes to round out the meal, something interesting to go with the main dish you've already decided on. It's help for someone who can't face steamed broccoli and rice again. By colorful I don't mean just green and red, but all the rich, warm, caramelized browns and blacks.

Vegetables are best cooked and served fresh, but there are any number of frozen products that are excellent and I certainly use them. I also cook vegetables ahead of time. I cook them until they are slightly underdone, then reheat them when I'm ready—they lose the first blush of perfection but they are easier to serve since they don't require waiting until the last minute to cook. A reheated vegetable is better than a frustrated cook.

I usually have my salad greens washed and in the crisper or a plastic bag lined with paper towel and pull them out as I need them, dressing them at the last minute.

Salads

Bob Lynn's Bread Salad

SERVES 6 TO 8

This dish isn't quite a salad or a bread. Softened chunks of grilled rolls dotted with currants and arugula make for a colorful and unusual combination somewhere in between those two categories. This recipe is reminiscent of hearty peasant food and is a comforting dish to eat; the garlic is wonderful! At different times I have added other leftovers to the bowl, such as roasted marinated red bell peppers and onions. Hoagie rolls differ from store to store. I prefer the ones that are similar to French rolls with a hard crust. You might think the final result looks a little wilted but keep eating—it's addictive! And the flavor improves with age; you can eat of this for days if you don't toss it with the arugula, which will collapse.

Bob Lynn is head recipe developer for the highly successful restaurant chain Houston's. We frequently share recipes. Bob is modest and says he got the idea from someone else, but fiddled with it. I figure that makes it his.

1 pound (6 to 9) French-style
   Hoagie rolls
1½ cups extra virgin olive oil
4 garlic cloves, minced
4 shallots, minced
¾ to 1 cup chicken stock or
   broth, fresh or canned
5 tablespoons apple cider
   vinegar
2 teaspoons red wine vinegar
5 tablespoons lemon juice
½ teaspoon Tabasco sauce

1 tablespoon Dijon mustard
1 cup dried currants, plumped
   in 2 teaspoons each of red
   wine vinegar and water
½ cup toasted pine nuts or
   roasted sunflower seeds
1 tablespoon kosher salt
2 teaspoons cracked black
   pepper
3 cups arugula or watercress,
   washed, stems removed, and
   coarsely chopped

Preheat a grill or broiler.

Slice the rolls in half lengthwise and brush with ¼ cup of the olive oil. Grill or broil the rolls lightly until they take on the smoke flavor and light grill marks appear. Tear the rolls into 1- to 2-inch chunks and put in a bowl.

Cook the garlic and shallots in ¼ cup of the olive oil until translucent. Do not let brown. Drizzle the bread chunks with the chicken stock. Place the vinegars, lemon juice, Tabasco, and mustard in a bowl or food processor. With a whisk or in the processor, slowly add the remaining 1 cup olive oil. Drizzle enough of the dressing over the bread to dampen it slightly but not soak. Toss.

Drain the currants and pat dry. Add them, the garlic and shallots, and the pine nuts to the bread and season with salt and the cracked black pepper. When ready to serve, toss the combination with the arugula or watercress and serve immediately. Serve the remaining dressing separately.

Beet Salad Vinaigrette

SERVES 6 TO 8

I generally mound this salad on frilly greens. It's delicious as well as stunningly colorful. However, I have seen it in restaurants beautifully molded into a small round. To mold it at home, use individual ramekins, packing them firmly with the salad, then chilling them for about 30 minutes. Unmold onto individual plates and garnish. Serve as a starter or a salad. You may substitute canned beets.

Sometimes viewers send me the best recipes. My card file says this recipe comes from Chef Thomas Valenti of Alison's on Dominick Street in New York City, and, alas, that is *all* I know.

6 medium beets, each about
   2 inches in diameter
5 tablespoons olive oil, divided
¼ pound tiny green beans,
   preferably French *haricots*
   verts, cut into ¾-inch lengths

1 teaspoon chopped shallot
Pinch kosher salt
½ teaspoon Dijon mustard
Freshly ground black pepper
3 tablespoons red wine vinegar
1 tablespoon lemon juice

Garnish
Chicory, *mâche*, watercress, or
   other salad greens tossed in
   Vinaigrette (page 209)

2 green onions, thinly sliced

Preheat oven to 400 degrees.

Line a baking pan with foil. Trim off as much of the beet roots and stems as possible without cutting into the beets, which will cause their color to run. Wash the beets thoroughly under running cold water, then dry. Rub them lightly with a little olive oil and arrange in a baking pan. Bake 45 minutes to 1 hour, or until a knife or skewer can easily be inserted into the centers. They should be firm but not resistant. Set aside to cool slightly.

Add the beans to boiling salted water. Bring back to the boil, reduce heat, and cook 5 to 7 minutes until cooked but still crisp. Rinse under cold water.

To prepare the dressing, place the shallot and salt in a food processor, blender, or bowl. Process or beat in the mustard, pepper, vinegar, and lemon juice until blended. Gradually beat in 4 tablespoons of the olive oil.

As soon as the beets are cool enough to handle, trim any remaining stems. Peel. Do not wash the beets as color will be lost. Grate, julienne, or cut the beets into ¾- by ¼-inch sticks. Add the beets to the dressing. Add the green beans when ready to serve to preserve their color. Toss until well coated. When ready to serve, mound the beets on top of the tossed salad greens and garnish with the green onions. The individual components may be prepared ahead several days, but reserve dressing salad until just before serving.

Asparagus Salad with Orange Vinaigrette

SERVES 10 TO 12

Asparagus adds elegance to a buffet table or luncheon plate. The orange flavor here is exciting. If you have the optional herbs, do be sure to use them as they give a real boost. Although the asparagus tastes even more wonderful when marinated overnight, it does lose some of its green color. If you wish your asparagus to be very green, wait until the last minute to pour the dressing over it.

¼ cup red wine vinegar
¼ cup orange juice
2 tablespoons grated orange peel, no white attached
2 garlic cloves, chopped
1 tablespoon finely chopped fresh ginger
1 tablespoon Dijon mustard
1 heaping tablespoon finely chopped tarragon

1 heaping teaspoon finely chopped lemon balm, lemon thyme, or lemon verbena (optional)
1 cup olive oil
Salt
Freshly ground black pepper
Sugar
3 pounds asparagus

In a medium bowl, whisk together the red wine vinegar, orange juice, orange peel, garlic, ginger, mustard, tarragon, and lemon balm.

(continued)

Slowly whisk in the olive oil until thick. Add salt, pepper, and sugar to taste. Peel the asparagus if larger than a pencil. Cut off any woody ends. Place in a large frying pan of boiling water, being sure that the water covers. (Cook in batches if necessary and bring the water back to the boil with each batch.) Boil 3 to 5 minutes until tender. Drain. May be done ahead to this point. Pour salad dressing over asparagus and serve hot or cold.

Elizabeth Burris's Broccoli Salad

SERVES 4 TO 6

This pretty salad is particularly special in winter with the green broccoli contrasting with the red onions, white sunflower seeds, and dark raisins. The mushrooms and bacon put it "over the top" for flavor and texture.

Elizabeth Burris is a student of mine from Rich's. She has a Spanish son-in-law whose food she relishes nearly as much as she does her own. We swap recipes all the time, as we like the same foods.

1½ pounds (1 large bunch)
   broccoli
½ red onion, chopped
1 cup sunflower seeds
½ cup raisins
1 cup sliced fresh mushrooms

1 cup mayonnaise
2 tablespoons red wine vinegar
¼ cup sugar (optional)
½ pound bacon, cooked crisp
   and crumbled

Clean and cut the broccoli into small pieces, using all of the broccoli except the end chunks. Mix together the broccoli, onion, sunflower seeds, raisins, and mushrooms. Make the dressing by combining the mayonnaise, vinegar, and sugar. Twenty minutes before serving, toss the salad with the bacon and the dressing.

Broccoli and Green Bean Salad

SERVES 4 TO 6

Crunchy broccoli and beans with olives and garlic remind me of the way Italians serve salads, usually at room temperature, which enhances the flavor of these everyday ingredients. You may add the broccoli stems as well. First peel and slice them lengthwise, then boil for 5 or 6 minutes.

1 bunch (1¼ to 1½ pounds) broccoli
1 pound green beans (2 cups), tipped and tailed
½ cup olive oil
⅓ to ½ cup fresh lemon juice
Salt
Freshly ground black pepper
3 ounces (15) pitted black Greek, Italian, or French-style olives, sliced or chopped

2 bunches green onions or scallions, including the green, to make 1 cup
2 large garlic cloves, chopped
3 heaping tablespoons finely chopped fresh mint, lemon balm, or parsley
½ teaspoon dried hot pepper flakes (optional)

Remove the florets from the broccoli and blanch them in a large saucepan of boiling water for 2 to 3 minutes. Remove, drain, and run under cold water to refresh and set the color. Repeat the procedure with the beans, cooking them 5 to 7 minutes, until crunchy, but tender enough to bend slightly. Place the broccoli and beans in a glass bowl or serving dish. Mix together the olive oil and lemon juice. Season to taste with salt and pepper. Toss with the broccoli and beans. Top with the olives, green onions, garlic, fresh herbs, and hot pepper flakes, if using. Serve at room temperature. Although the vegetables will discolor from the lemon juice, this salad may be made ahead 1 or 2 days. Bring to room temperature before serving.

Carrot Salad

SERVES 6

My friend Gail Wescott got this recipe from her friend Susan Pakasader who got it from her mother. As Gail says, "Potluck people love it!" Gail prefers medium-cut length canned carrots. Fresh carrots are better, but the canned will serve just fine.

½ cup vegetable oil
½ cup red wine vinegar
1 cup sugar
1 teaspoon dry mustard
1 (8-ounce) can tomato sauce
1 pound julienned cooked baby carrots, four (4-ounce) cans (medium-cut length) whole baby carrots, or two (10-ounce) packages frozen carrots

1 large green bell pepper, cored, seeded, and sliced
1 medium onion, sliced
Salt
Freshly ground black pepper

Mix together the oil, vinegar, sugar, dry mustard, and tomato sauce. Add the carrots, green pepper, and onion. Season to taste with salt and pepper. Chill. May be made ahead several days.

Cucumber Crescent Salad

SERVES 2

A cooked cucumber salad is very different from a crunchy fresh one. Since this may also be made ahead without the cucumber's weeping, it becomes even more attractive, particularly for entertaining or for a family meal when you don't know the hour everyone will come to the table.

2 cucumbers, peeled, halved,
  seeded
1 tablespoon olive oil
2 tablespoons apple cider
  vinegar
Salt
Freshly ground black pepper

Pinch sugar (optional)
½ cup sour cream
2 green onions, chopped
2 heaping tablespoons finely
  chopped fresh dill
Toasted sesame seeds (optional)

Slice the cucumbers into ½-inch crescents. Heat the olive oil in a frying pan. Add the cucumbers and cook until crisp-tender, about 4 minutes. Add the vinegar, salt, pepper, and the sugar; cook until almost all the liquid has evaporated. Remove from the heat. Cool slightly and stir in the sour cream, green onions, and dill. Cover and chill at least 2 hours or up to 2 days. Top with the sesame seeds, if desired.

Gazpacho Salad

SERVES 6

Just like Spain's colorful tomato-based soup, this salad is pretty, tasty, and healthful. Use as a starter or to accompany hot or cold meat dishes. It's very flexible.

5 green onions or scallions,
  sliced, including the green
5 tablespoons red wine vinegar
2 heaping tablespoons finely
  chopped fresh parsley
1 heaping tablespoon finely
  chopped fresh basil
2 garlic cloves, chopped
Salt

Freshly ground black pepper
⅓ cup vegetable oil or olive oil
3 tomatoes, cut into wedges
1 small cucumber, thinly sliced
1 green bell pepper, cored,
  seeded, and cut into strips
½ pound button mushrooms
3 cups rotini or other small
  pasta, cooked and drained

Combine the green onions, vinegar, parsley, basil, garlic, salt, pepper, and olive oil. Add the tomatoes, cucumber, green pepper, mushrooms, and pasta. Toss lightly and chill. May be made ahead several days. When ready to serve, place in a glass bowl or on lettuce leaves for a particularly attractive presentation.

Green Salad with Garlic Cheese Toast

SERVES 4

The arugula here adds a nutty flavor; the nasturtium leaves a bite. Both can be hard to find and may be omitted if need be. Just use another green. Should you have nasturtium flowers, by all means garnish the salad with them!

1 small head Boston or Bibb lettuce
1 bunch watercress, washed, dried, and torn or cut into bite-sized pieces
1 cup other greens such as arugula or nasturtium leaves, washed and dried
4 slices bread

¼ to ½ cup olive oil
Garlic cloves, peeled
½ cup Montrachet or other soft goat cheese, Camembert, or Boursin cheese, at room temperature
½ cup Vinaigrette (see following recipe)

Toss the greens together and keep them covered or in a plastic bag in the refrigerator until needed.

To make the garlic toast, preheat oven to 400 degrees. Brush the bread with the olive oil and bake for 5 minutes, or until golden brown. While still warm, rub the slices with the garlic cloves, and cut them into triangles. Spread the cheese on the toasts, and set aside. When ready to serve, toss the greens with the vinaigrette and put them in a serving bowl or divide among plates. Top with the cheese toasts.

Will's Three Lettuce Salad

SERVES 10 TO 12

Salads are served at nearly every lunch and dinner at my home, and I just don't have the lifestyle to wash and tear greens moments before serving. So I wash and break them up in advance and layer them in paper towels in a tight-closing container such as a plastic bag. All I have to do is pull out what I need.

Will Deller, my bookkeeper, who helps cook on the television show, loves serving this huge salad when he caters. The greens are a bit bitter, but the red wine vinegar, coupled with some salt and sugar, adds a sweetness. Like me, wash and dry the greens ahead of time and refrigerate them in plastic bags.

14 cups loosely packed greens (1 head Romaine, 1 head radicchio, 3 Belgium endives), washed, dried, and torn into bite-size pieces

2 bunches green onions, white and green parts, sliced
½ cup finely chopped fresh basil

Vinaigrette
2 tablespoons Dijon mustard
¼ cup red wine vinegar
½ cup olive or salad oil

2 tablespoons sugar (optional)
Salt
Freshly ground black pepper

In a large bowl, combine the torn Romaine, radicchio, and Belgium endives. Toss with the green onions and basil. To make the Dijon vinaigrette, mix together the mustard and vinegar. Whisk in the olive oil. Add the optional sugar, salt, and pepper to taste. Before serving, toss with enough of the vinaigrette to moisten the leaves. Season to taste with more salt and pepper.

Onion and Tomato Salad

SERVES 6 TO 8

There is nothing better than a ripe tomato salad except, of course, the marriage between juicy vine-ripened tomatoes and sweet onions like Georgia Vidalias or Washington Walla Wallas! In a pinch you may substitute here a sweet Bermuda or red onion, but it won't be as good.

1 to 2 medium white onions, preferably a Vidalia or Walla Walla, sliced
3 to 4 medium tomatoes, sliced
⅓ cup red wine vinegar
1 teaspoon Dijon mustard
⅔ cup olive oil or vegetable oil
Salt

Freshly ground black pepper
1 teaspoon sugar (optional)
Bibb lettuce, arugula, or radicchio (optional)
3 to 4 heaping tablespoons finely chopped basil, thyme, or oregano

Alternate layers of the onions and tomatoes on a platter. Mix together the vinegar, mustard, and oil. Add salt, pepper, and sugar to taste. When ready to serve, garnish with lettuce leaves, if desired. Drizzle the dressing over the onions and tomatoes and sprinkle the herbs on top.

Wilted Salad with Country Ham and Whole Garlic Cloves

SERVES 4 TO 6

Romaine and escarole are sturdy enough greens to stand up to the heating required of them in this salad. My friend Jean Van den Berg insists the best way to clean this type of lettuce and greens is to wash them in water in the sink, then place them in a clean old pillowcase, tie the case securely, and put it in the washing machine on the last spin cycle. The spin leaves the lettuce and greens so crisp and fresh that they will keep airtight for up to two weeks.

¼ to ½ cup vegetable oil or olive oil

30 large garlic cloves, peeled

½ pound Country Ham, cut into ¼-inch cubes (page 111)

1 large head escarole, washed and dried, torn or cut into bite-sized pieces

1 large head Romaine, washed and dried, torn or cut into bite-sized pieces

2 heaping tablespoons finely chopped thyme or basil (optional)

½ cup red wine vinegar

Freshly ground black pepper

Heat half the oil in a large frying pan. Add the garlic and cook over medium-low heat until golden brown and tender, about 30 minutes. Add more oil as needed. Add the country ham and toss briefly to coat and marry the flavors. Set aside until needed, up to 1 day. When ready to serve, reheat the oil, garlic, and ham mixture. When hot, add the lettuce and toss for 1 or 2 minutes, until well coated with the dressing and slightly wilted. Taste. Add the herbs, vinegar, and pepper as needed.

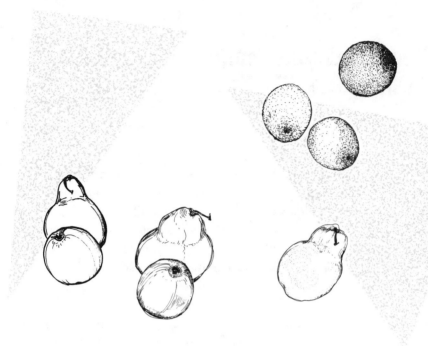

Orange and Fennel Salad

SERVES 6

The dark red flesh of blood oranges, if you can find them, makes a striking presentation here. Use 2 small blood oranges for each ¾ pound fennel in this recipe. If blood oranges are not available, any seedless orange is fine, too. Also, a pound of peeled and cooked large shrimp converts this into an unusual seafood salad.

1 or 2 bulbs fennel (total of 1½ pounds), core and fronds removed, bulbs cut into thin slices
2 or 3 seedless oranges, peeled and sliced

½ cup olive oil
Kosher salt
Freshly ground black pepper

Arrange a layer of fennel in the bottom of a glass serving bowl. Top with orange slices. Sprinkle with olive oil, coarse salt, and pepper. Continue making layers with the remaining fennel and orange slices.

Orange Salad

SERVES 6 TO 8

Fruit salads can be particularly refreshing, especially when greens are not readily available. This has a Spanish origin, as evidenced by the garlic and olive oil.

4 to 6 oranges, thinly sliced
   (may be peeled)
2 garlic cloves, chopped

3 tablespoons olive oil
2 teaspoons paprika

Arrange the orange slices on a platter. Combine the garlic with the olive oil and drizzle over the orange slices. Sprinkle with the paprika and let marinate ½ hour or longer. May be made ahead, and refrigerated, covered, overnight. Serve at room temperature.

Bill's Killer Pasta Salad

SERVES 4 TO 6 AS A MAIN COURSE;
8 TO 10 AS A SIDE DISH

Bill Baker is my friend Sharon Van den Berg Baker's husband. He's a great cook, and he fixed this for Sharon's Dad's eightieth birthday. Bill made so much of it we had to store it in garbage bags in the refrigerator. Inadvertently, someone threw it away! We only rescued it from the garbage can just in time for it to be served. It was a great hit.

    The salad may easily be multiplied four times. If multiplying, use a variety of bell peppers. Serve as a starter, main course, or side dish.

(continued)

This salad is a "killer" because it takes over a table with its beautiful colors and flavor.

The Dressing
1 tablespoon Dijon mustard
3 garlic cloves, chopped
¼ cup white wine vinegar
¾ cup olive oil
3 green onions, green and white
    parts, chopped, to make
    ¼ cup

Salt
Freshly ground black pepper

The Pasta
1 pound short pasta (rotelle,
    fusilli, or penne)

The Vegetables
¼ pound fresh snow peas,
    strings removed
Florets from 1 small bunch
    broccoli
2 small zucchini, cut into
    ¼-inch slices

1 large red bell pepper, seeded
    and cut into strips julienne
¼ cup freshly grated imported
    Parmesan cheese

To make the dressing, blend together in a bowl the mustard, garlic, and vinegar. Whisk in the olive oil. Add the green onions. Taste for seasoning and add salt and pepper.

Meanwhile, cook the pasta in boiling salted water 8 to 10 minutes. Drain. Rinse with cold water and drain again. Toss with half of the dressing and set aside. May be done several days ahead to this point, if necessary.

Up to 2 days before serving, steam the snow peas for 1 minute. Refresh in cold water. Drain well and set aside. Steam the broccoli florets and the zucchini slices separately for 3 minutes each. Drain well and set aside. Combine the sliced red pepper with the cooled and drained vegetables, and toss with the remaining dressing. Combine the vegetables with the pasta. Sprinkle with the Parmesan. Taste for seasoning and add more salt and pepper if needed. Refrigerate until ready to serve, at least 1 hour or up to 2 days, covered.

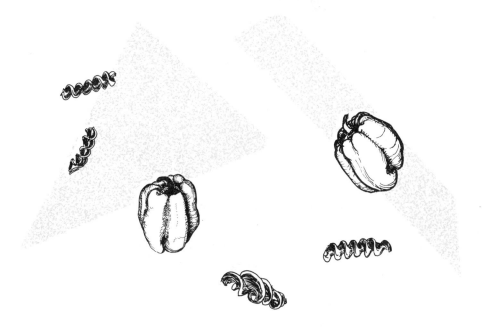

Roasted Pepper and Broccoli Salad

SERVES 4 TO 6

Technically this is a salad, but I serve it at room temperature as a side dish vegetable as well.

1 head broccoli, stems peeled and stems and florets sliced
1 tablespoon Dijon mustard
2 tablespoons red wine vinegar
6 tablespoons olive oil
½ teaspoon ground cumin seed
Salt

Freshly ground black pepper
1 large red bell pepper, roasted (page 99), cored, seeded, and cut into thin strips
1 cup finely chopped red onion
4 heaping tablespoons finely chopped fresh parsley

Bring a large quantity of water to the boil and add the broccoli stems and florets. Cook 2 or 3 minutes. Alternately, place the broccoli in a microwave container with a little water, and cook 2 or 3 minutes. Drain, refresh with cold water, and drain again.

Whisk together the mustard, vinegar, and oil. Add the cumin, salt, and pepper and blend well. Add the broccoli, red pepper, onion, and parsley. Toss well and serve. May be made ahead a couple of days. Serve at room temperature or chilled.

Hot German Potato Salad

SERVES 6 TO 8

I love the taste and crunch of bacon mixed with the sudden tartness and underlying sweetness of this potato salad. The bacon and potatoes here may also be cooked in the microwave, which I do in the summer. Not incidentally, this dish keeps very well on a picnic table as it contains no egg yolks or homemade mayonnaise.

4 medium or 1½ to 2 pounds new potatoes
6 slices bacon
1 onion, sliced
2 tablespoons flour
1 cup water
½ cup red wine vinegar
1 teaspoon finely chopped fresh parsley
Salt
Freshly ground black pepper
¼ cup sugar (optional)

Pierce the unpeeled potatoes through with a fork. Cook in a microwave oven with paper towels under the potatoes. Or, place in water, bring to the boil, and cook until tender but still firm. Peel if desired. Cut into bite-size pieces or slice if necessary.

Meanwhile, in a large skillet cook the bacon until crisp. Reserving the fat in the pan, remove the bacon and crumble. Add the onion and sauté until golden; remove and set aside. Add the flour to the fat, and cook over low heat until smooth. Add the water and vinegar to the flour mixture and bring to the boil, stirring until a smooth sauce forms. Add the potatoes, onions, parsley, and bacon. Stir gently so the potatoes hold their shape. Taste for seasoning, and add salt, pepper, and sugar. Serve warm. Or cover and let stand until ready to serve. May also be made ahead and served chilled.

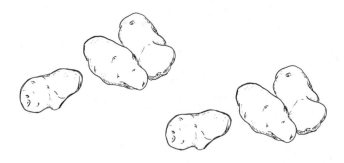

Rice Salad

SERVES 6 TO 8

The pimientos and pickles combine with the eggs to give color to this nutritious salad. One of the nice things about rice salads, in general, is that the rice may be cooked ahead, mixed with the other ingredients, and left to mellow.

3 cups Boiled Rice (page 262), cooled
½ cup finely chopped onion
½ cup finely chopped sweet or sour pickles
1 cup mayonnaise
1 teaspoon prepared mustard

¼ cup chopped pimientos or red bell peppers
4 large hard-cooked eggs, chopped
Salt
Freshly ground black pepper
6 to 8 lettuce leaves

Combine the rice, onion, pickles, mayonnaise, mustard, pimientos, and chopped eggs. Blend thoroughly. Season to taste with salt and pepper. Chill, covered. Serve on the lettuce leaves.

To Hard-cook Eggs

- **Prick a large egg with an egg pricker, if available. Place egg on large spoon and gently place in a pan of boiling water to cover. Lower heat to a simmer. Roll the egg carefully to center the yolk. Simmer, uncovered, for 11 minutes. Remove with a slotted spoon to a bowl of ice water. Crack on the large end and roll to crack sides. Peel from the top, and try to catch an air bubble as you peel.**

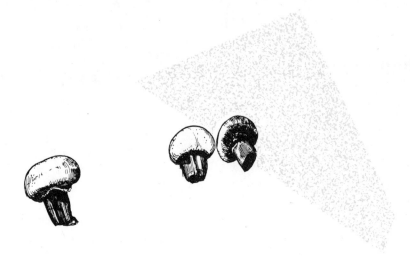

Spinach and Mushroom Salad

SERVES 4 TO 6

As classic and stylish as a black dress, this tried and true combination never goes out of style.

To Store Greens

- **I usually prepare all my salad ingredients and my dressing in advance, keeping them in separate covered containers or plastic bags until ready to serve.**

2 pounds fresh spinach, washed, dried, and torn or cut into bite-sized pieces
1 small red onion, sliced
½ pound mushrooms, cleaned and sliced
2 teaspoons Dijon mustard

⅓ cup red wine vinegar
⅔ cup vegetable oil or olive oil
2 garlic cloves, crushed
Salt
Freshly ground black pepper
6 slices bacon, crisply fried and crumbled

Place the spinach in a salad bowl or on a serving platter. Add the red onion and mushrooms. Whisk together the mustard and vinegar. Slowly whisk in the oil and add the garlic. Add salt and pepper to taste. Just before serving, toss the spinach, onions, and mushrooms with a portion of the dressing, adding more dressing as needed to coat the leaves. Sprinkle with the bacon. Serve immediately.

Two Japanese Spinach Salads

SERVES 4

Both variations of this salad below can be served either at room temperature or chilled.

To Drain Spinach
- **Here's a tip for draining blanched spinach thoroughly of its excess water. Place it between two sturdy (kitchen-type) plates facing the same way. Press the plates together over the sink. Remove the top plate. Your spinach should be well squeezed!**

1 pound fresh spinach, washed,
    stemmed, blanched, and
    squeezed dry

Dressing Number One

¼ cup soy sauce	2 tablespoons sugar
1 tablespoon dry sherry	⅓ cup sesame seeds

Dressing Number Two

2 tablespoons soy sauce	1 tablespoon sugar
2 tablespoons white vinegar	2 tablespoons toasted sesame
2 tablespoons vegetable oil	seeds

Make dressing number one: Combine the soy sauce, sherry, sugar, and sesame seeds. Toss the spinach with dressing and serve.

    For the variation, shape the squeezed spinach into 4 small mounds on salad plates. Combine the soy sauce, vinegar, oil, and sugar and pour the dressing over the spinach. Sprinkle with toasted sesame seeds.

Tabouli

SERVES 6 TO 8

This salad is a classic dish from the Middle East. Bulgur, parboiled dried and cracked wheat berries, is tossed with fresh mint and herbs, green onion, pepper, cumin, chick-peas, and cucumbers. The combination slides quietly into a dinner party but ends up stealing the show!

¾ cup medium-grain bulgur
½ to ¾ cup lemon juice
Grated peel, no white attached of 1 lemon
1½ teaspoons ground cumin seed
½ teaspoon red pepper flakes
4 garlic cloves, chopped
Salt
Freshly ground black pepper
4 cups finely chopped fresh parsley
½ cup finely chopped fresh mint

4 to 5 green onions or scallions, white and green parts, thinly sliced
1 carrot, grated
2 small cucumbers, peeled and chopped
1 cup canned chick-peas, drained and rinsed
3 tomatoes, seeded and chopped
1 red bell pepper, seeded and chopped
1 tablespoon olive oil (optional)
1 cup plain low-fat yogurt

Garnish
Romaine lettuce leaves

Place the bulgur in a bowl and add enough water to cover. Let sit 20 minutes. Squeeze out excess water. Toss with ½ cup of the lemon juice, the lemon peel, cumin, red pepper flakes, the garlic, and salt and pepper to taste. Let sit until soft, about 30 minutes. Add more of the remaining lemon juice if the bulgur is still too hard. Toss the bulgur with the parsley, mint, green onions, carrot, cucumber, chick-peas, tomatoes, red bell pepper, optional olive oil, and yogurt. Taste and adjust seasonings. Refrigerate, covered, until ready to serve. To serve, transfer the salad to a bowl or platter and garnish with the Romaine lettuce leaves.

The salad will keep in the refrigerator, without the lettuce leaves, for 2 or 3 days.

Wild Rice, Asparagus, and Pineapple Salad

SERVES 4 TO 6

This is particularly refreshing with lamb. If asparagus is out of season, snow peas may be substituted.

1 cup wild rice and long-grain
    rice, mixed
1 pound asparagus, diagonally
    cut into 2-inch pieces

Vinaigrette

⅔ cup olive oil
⅓ cup vinegar
Salt
Freshly ground black pepper
2 teaspoons Dijon mustard
3 to 4 slices fresh or canned
    pineapple, cut into 1½-inch
    pieces

2 to 3 heaping tablespoons
    finely chopped fresh mint or
    lemon balm (optional)
1 small head Bibb or butter
    lettuce (optional)

Rinse the rice under running cold water. Add the rice to 3 cups boiling water. Cover, and simmer until cracked and puffed, 50 to 55 minutes. Place the asparagus in boiling water to cover, and boil 3 to 5 minutes. Drain. Rinse with cold water to refresh and set color. Drain again.

Make the vinaigrette by mixing together the olive oil, vinegar, salt, pepper, and mustard. Combine the vinaigrette with the asparagus, the cooked rice, pineapple, and herbs. Serve warm or chill and serve cold on the lettuce. May be made several days in advance.

Tomato and Bread Salad

SERVES 6 TO 8

It is best not to use an egg bread in this recipe as it will get soggy rather than crumble. A Hoagie roll or French or Italian textured bread is preferred. If you don't have summer ripe tomatoes, make another recipe; they are a must! Peel the cucumbers if they are waxed; otherwise I rather like leaving the skins on for color.

10 thick slices French or Italian
    bread
6 large ripe firm tomatoes,
    peeled and thinly sliced
2 or 3 cucumbers, seeded and
    thinly sliced
2 large onions, thinly sliced
2 heaping tablespoons finely
    chopped fresh basil

1 or 2 garlic cloves, chopped
¼ to ⅓ cup olive oil
4 to 6 tablespoons wine vinegar
Salt
Sugar
Freshly ground black pepper

Soak the bread in cold water for about 5 minutes. Squeeze dry, then place in a salad bowl. Combine the tomatoes, cucumbers, onions, basil, and garlic with the bread. Toss with the olive oil and vinegar to taste and season with salt, a pinch of sugar, and plenty of pepper. Chill. May be made ahead up to 1 day.

Roberta's Tomatoes and Parsley

SERVES 4 TO 6

Once when visiting my friend Roberta Salma in California, she needed to stretch a meal for some extra guests who were friends of mine. "No problem" was the response, as she added this glorious tomato recipe and her Cucumber Side Dish (page 235) to dinner. As so often happens with simple, fresh dishes, they become the stars of the meal. The salt brings out the liquid in the tomatoes, making a wonderful tomato juice. The vinegar is unnecessary if the tomatoes are ripe.

2 pounds ripe tomatoes, cut into
    ½-inch cubes
1 teaspoon salt
Freshly ground black pepper

½ cup finely chopped fresh
    parsley
¼ cup red wine vinegar
    (optional)

Sprinkle the tomatoes well with the salt and pepper. Toss with the parsley. Cover and leave 1 hour or up to 2 days. Taste. Add vinegar if necessary.

Tomato and Fennel Salad

SERVES 6

I truly love this salad when tomatoes are lush and ripe and in season. Fennel is well worth seeking out in the grocery stores. When it is in short supply, which it sometimes is, I substitute arugula.

1 large bulb fennel or
    California anise, core and
    fronds removed, bulb cut
    into thin slices
4 medium tomatoes, cut into
    wedges and seeded
1 teaspoon Dijon mustard

3 tablespoons red wine vinegar
¾ cup olive oil or vegetable oil
Salt
Freshly ground black pepper
2 heaping tablespoons finely
    chopped fennel frond or
    cilantro

Combine the fennel and the tomatoes. Mix together the Dijon mustard, vinegar, and oil. Season to taste with salt and pepper. Pour the dressing over the fennel and tomatoes. Top with the chopped fennel.

Vegetables

Stuffed Artichokes

SERVES 4

These are very pretty as a starter. To eat, peel off the leaves first and pull the ends between your teeth to get to the stuffing. When finished with the leaves, remove the heart and eat it, too.

1 cup bread crumbs
1 cup freshly grated imported
    Parmesan cheese
3 green onions, chopped
2 teaspoons capers
4 garlic cloves, finely chopped

Finely chopped fresh parsley
Salt
Freshly ground black pepper
4 artichokes
½ cup vegetable oil

Combine the bread crumbs, Parmesan, green onions, capers, garlic, parsley, salt, and pepper in a food processor or by hand. Trim the tops and bottoms of the artichokes. Turn each upside down and press slightly against the counter to open the leaves. Scoop out the choke with a spoon. Fill the spaces among the leaves with the bread stuffing.

Put any remaining stuffing into the centers. Pour the oil over the stuffed artichokes. Steam the artichokes in a little water in a covered pot for 45 minutes, or until a leaf pulls off easily. Or microwave covered with plastic wrap on high power for 10 minutes. This may be done up to a day in advance. When ready to serve, run under the broiler until the stuffing is crisped and brown and the artichokes are heated through.

Mariella's Asparagus with Pine Nuts

SERVES 6 TO 8

Fantes is a wonderful gourmet cookware store in Philadelphia. The whole Fante family including Mariella seem to work there. When several of us came to town to attend Philadelphia's famous cooking event, "The Book and the Cook," the Fantes had a crowd for dinner. This was prepared by her mother at Mariella's home for one such gathering. I just love it, particularly since it was sitting at room temperature for several hours with no deleterious effect, making it an ideal fix-ahead dish.

Don't add the lemon juice until just before serving as it will change the color of the asparagus.

2 pounds asparagus
Salt
Freshly ground black pepper
½ cup butter

¼ cup fresh lemon juice
⅓ cup bread crumbs
⅓ cup pine nuts

Cut off the tough ends of the asparagus and peel the stalks if they are not pencil thin. Fill a frying pan or asparagus cooker with enough water to cover the asparagus and bring to the boil. Add the asparagus. Reduce the heat and simmer until done, about 2 to 3 minutes. Drain. Rinse with cold water to stop the cooking and to set the color. Drain. Place the asparagus in a buttered casserole and season with salt and pepper.

Melt the butter in a frying pan. Add half of the butter to the lemon juice and pour over the asparagus. Add the bread crumbs and pine nuts to the remaining butter in the pan and sauté until light brown. Top the asparagus with the mixture. Serve at room temperature. This dish may also be refrigerated, then reheated in a microwave or 350-degree oven if you prefer it hot.

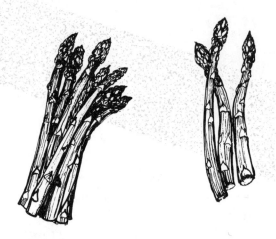

Asparagus Spears with Herbed Lemon Butter

SERVES 4 TO 6

When asparagus is in season (and cheap), I've been known to serve only it for dinner! And I only peel asparagus if the stalks are the width of my thumb or larger.

2 pounds asparagus
4 tablespoons butter (optional)
Salt
Freshly ground black pepper
Lemon juice

1 heaping tablespoon finely chopped fresh thyme, marjoram, basil, or peeled ginger

Cut off the tough ends of the asparagus. If necessary, peel the stalks from the bottom to the first of the offshoots. Fill a frying pan or an asparagus cooker with enough water to cover the asparagus and bring it to the boil. Add the asparagus. Reduce the heat, and simmer until done, about 3 to 5 minutes for small stalks, 5 to 8 minutes for large ones. Rinse with cold water to stop the cooking and set the color. Drain. May be made ahead to this point. When ready to serve, heat the butter, add the spears, and toss until heated through. Season with salt and pepper. Drizzle with the lemon juice and sprinkle with the herbs or ginger.

Durgin-Park's Boston Baked Beans

SERVES 10

When I was a young woman living in Cambridge, Massachusetts, a trip to "D.P.'s" was always a treat. Durgin-Park is a renowned Boston restaurant, located in an old warehouse that dates from pre-Revolutionary days. The restaurant is famous for its baked beans that are served in its special bean pot. The food at Durgin-Park is presented family style; one often finds oneself sitting with perfect strangers, and, by the meal's end, there is laughter and sharing and maybe a phone number exchanged. I've added brown sugar, ginger, and ketchup to perk this otherwise traditional dish up a bit.

I love this served with brown bread. Leftovers are great reheated for Sunday breakfast or a cold morning.

2 pounds pea beans (navy beans)
1 pound salt pork or bacon, with rind
3 medium onions, sliced
½ cup brown sugar

⅔ cup molasses
¼ cup Dijon mustard
2 tablespoons ground ginger
½ cup ketchup
Salt
Freshly ground black pepper

Cover the beans with water and soak overnight. Or place in a pan, cover with water, and bring the water to the boil. Remove from the heat and let sit 1 hour.

Preheat oven to 300 degrees. Drain the beans, place them in a pot or heavy casserole with enough water to cover, and boil for 10 minutes, until they burst. Cut the salt pork in half. Slice each half into ½-inch intervals up to the rind, leaving the rind intact. Put a piece of the pork on the bottom of a heavy pot. Add the onions, the beans and their liquid, the brown sugar, molasses, mustard, ginger, ketchup, and salt, and pepper to taste. Place the other half of the pork on top, fanned out. Cover. Bake 6 hours, checking every 2 hours, and adding more water as needed.

Butternut Squash and Cheddar Gratin

SERVES 6

This Cheddary gratin of winter squash and leeks is an unexpected pleasure on a holiday table as well as on the everyday one. As a substitute for butternut squash, use 2 or 3 split and seeded acorn squash, scooping out the insides. Serve the gratin in the pretty shells.

1 (2-pound) butternut squash, halved, and seeds scooped out	1 heaping teaspoon finely chopped fresh or dried thyme
Water	1 heaping teaspoon finely chopped fresh parsley
2 tablespoons butter	1½ cups grated Cheddar cheese
3 medium leeks, trimmed and cut into ¼-inch slices	Salt
½ cup bread crumbs	Freshly ground black pepper

Preheat oven to 375 degrees. Place the squash, cut sides down, in a shallow baking pan and add ½ inch boiling water. Cover tightly with aluminum foil and bake about 35 to 40 minutes until tender when pierced with a fork. (Butternut squash can also be cooked in the microwave for this recipe.)

Meanwhile, melt the butter in a large skillet. Add the leeks, and cook 5 to 8 minutes, until soft. Add the bread crumbs, thyme, and parsley.

Remove the skin from the baked squash and cut the flesh into 2-inch pieces. Add the squash to the skillet with 1 cup of the cheese and toss thoroughly. Season with salt and pepper. Place in a shallow buttered 1½- to 2-quart baking dish and bake 10 minutes until heated through and cheese is melted. Sprinkle with the remaining cheese.

Butternut Squash Stuffed with Zucchini

SERVES 2

Butternut squash is a particularly beautiful winter squash. It has a long neck with a large bowl at its bottom. When split, the tan skin forms a perfect cup for the light orange flesh that is filled here with green zucchini, giving a wonderful feeling of fall's gold and greens to the table. If you don't have fresh herbs, omit them. This makes a nice vegetarian lunch for two.

1 (2-pound) butternut squash, halved and seeds scooped out
2 tablespoons butter
1 small (4-ounce) onion, chopped
1 medium-large (12-ounce) zucchini, grated
1 garlic clove, chopped
2 tablespoons bread crumbs

1 tablespoon freshly grated imported Parmesan cheese
2 heaping teaspoons finely chopped fresh thyme (optional)
1 heaping teaspoon finely chopped fresh sage (optional)
Salt
Freshly ground black pepper

Preheat oven to 350 degrees.

Bake the squash in a pan for 45 minutes, or in a microwave for 8 to 10 minutes, until tender.

Meanwhile, melt the butter in a large skillet. Add the onion, grated zucchini, and the garlic and sauté over medium heat for 5 minutes. Add the bread crumbs, Parmesan, optional thyme and sage, and salt and pepper to taste. Scoop out a portion of the core from the neck of the squash to make a large cavity for the filling. Chop the scooped-out flesh and add to the zucchini mixture. Fill the squash cavity with the mixture. May be made ahead 1 day up to this point. Before serving, bake 10 to 15 minutes or 5 minutes in the microwave, until heated through.

Cauliflower Mornay

SERVES 4 TO 6

I love this on a winter's night, varying it occasionally to make a meal of it by adding a cup or so of chopped ham to the sauce.

1 cauliflower (about 1½ pounds)	1 teaspoon Dijon mustard
¼ cup butter, divided	¾ cup grated Cheddar cheese
2 tablespoons flour	Salt
1½ cups milk	Freshly ground black pepper
	⅓ cup bread crumbs

Preheat oven to 350 degrees.

To cook the cauliflower, cut off the thick or discolored parts of the stem. Cut an X with a sharp knife in the remaining stem. Remove all but the smallest green leaves. (If the cauliflower is large, remove the florets from the stem, discard the stem, and cook the florets in boiling water.) Place the cauliflower, stem side down, in a large pan of boiling water. Boil until tender, about 15 minutes. If microwaving, place in a microwave container, sprinkle with 2 tablespoons water, cover, and microwave until done, about 5 minutes.

To make the sauce, in a medium saucepan melt 2 tablespoons of the butter and stir in the flour. Add the milk and stir the mixture until it comes to the boil. Remove from the heat and add the mustard and ½ cup of the cheese. Stir until smooth and season to taste with salt and pepper. Place the well-drained cauliflower in a heatproof serving bowl, with the florets up. Sauté the bread crumbs in the remaining butter until brown. Top the cauliflower with the sauce, the remaining cheese, and the browned crumbs. The recipe may be made ahead to this point. When ready to serve, place the dish in the hot oven until the cauliflower is heated through, the cheese is melted, and the sauce is lightly brown and bubbling.

Creamed Cabbage

SERVES 3 OR 4

Cabbage is a favorite vegetable of mine. The flavor that comes from quickly sautéing it, then braising it in butter and cream is incredibly full and rich.

3 tablespoons butter	Salt
½ medium green cabbage, cored and cut into ¼-inch strips	Freshly ground black pepper
	1 teaspoon caraway seeds (optional)
½ cup heavy cream	

Melt the butter in a large heavy, non-iron frying pan over medium heat. Add the cabbage and sauté it for 5 minutes, tossing it to coat it with the butter. Pour in the cream. Season with salt and pepper. Bring quickly to the boil, cover the pan, and reduce the heat. Cook the cabbage over low heat for 15 minutes, or until tender but not soft. Sprinkle with caraway seeds before serving, if desired.

Sweet/Sour Cabbage

SERVES 8

This cabbage is amazingly sophisticated, with a lot of style. Serve it at an elegant grown-up dinner that features goose or duck on a wintery night. A word of warning: Avoid using a wooden spoon; it will turn red from the cabbage.

¼ cup butter, duck or goose fat, or bacon drippings
2 onions, sliced
1 bay leaf, crumbled
1 (3½-pound) red cabbage, thickly sliced
2 chicken or beef bouillon cubes, crumbled
½ cup red wine vinegar
1 cup red wine or non-alcoholic wine

2 Granny Smith or golden delicious apples, cored and chopped or grated
⅔ cup red currant jelly
Salt
Freshly ground black pepper
2 heaping teaspoons finely chopped fresh thyme

Heat the butter in a large casserole. Add the onions and bay leaf and cook until the onions are soft, about 5 minutes. Add the cabbage, bouillon cubes, wine vinegar, wine, and apples. Cover and cook 1 hour. Remove cover. Stir in jelly, salt and pepper, and thyme. Serve at once.

Chile Relleno Casserole

SERVES 8

Nearly a chili soufflé, with its cheese-stuffed chilies cushioned in an egg custard, this casserole is a wonderful side dish and can also serve as the main course for a light supper.

4 (7-ounce) cans whole mild
   green chilies
1 pound Monterey Jack cheese
5 eggs
1¼ cups milk
¼ cup flour

½ teaspoon salt
Freshly ground black pepper
2 heaping tablespoons finely
   chopped fresh cilantro
3 cups grated sharp Cheddar
   cheese

Preheat oven to 350 degrees.

Slit the chilies lengthwise down one side. Remove the seeds and drain. Slice the Monterey Jack into ¼-inch thick slices and stuff inside the chilies. Place the chilies in an ungreased 3-quart baking dish. Combine the eggs, milk, flour, salt, pepper, and cilantro and pour over the chilies. Sprinkle the top with the Cheddar and bake, uncovered, 45 minutes.

Speeded-up Oriental Ratatouille

SERVES 6 TO 8

Stunningly beautiful, easy to make, and a real winner with friends and family. These vegetables are traditionally associated with ratatouille but here are Orientally influenced.

2 eggplants, cut into cubes
Salt
3 tablespoons oil
2 garlic cloves, chopped
1 tablespoon finely chopped
    fresh ginger
3 green onions, chopped
2 bell peppers (red or green),
    cored, seeded, and cut into
    1-inch chunks

3 zucchini, sliced
2 tomatoes, cut into wedges, or
    ½ cup canned tomato sauce
½ cup sliced mushrooms
2 teaspoons Tabasco sauce
2 tablespoons soy sauce
2 tablespoons red wine vinegar
2 teaspoons sugar
½ cup chicken broth or stock,
    fresh or canned

Sprinkle the eggplant with salt, and let stand in a colander for 30 minutes to drain. Rinse and drain. Heat the oil in a large skillet or wok. Add the eggplant, and cook over high heat, tossing until soft and brown. Add the garlic, ginger, green onions, bell peppers, zucchini, tomatoes, and mushrooms. Cook over high heat, tossing, for 2 minutes. Add the Tabasco, soy sauce, vinegar, sugar, and chicken broth. Bring to the boil, and boil until the liquid is absorbed. Will last 2 to 3 days in the refrigerator.

Roberta's Cucumber Side Dish

SERVES 4 TO 6

Not quite a salad, not quite a sauce, this is a good accompaniment to casseroles and roasts alike. It's refreshing.

Roberta Salma, originally from Virginia, has been a friend of mine for more years than either of us can remember. Every now and then I manage to visit her in California and eat her wonderful food, an inventive California-Arab mixture due to the fact that her husband is Arabic.

3 cucumbers, 2 peeled,
  1 unpeeled, both diced
1½ cups plain yogurt
½ cup finely chopped fresh
  mint

1 tablespoon lemon juice
Salt
Freshly ground black pepper

Mix together the cucumbers, yogurt, mint, and lemon juice. Season to taste with salt and pepper. May be made in advance 1 to 2 days and kept, covered, in the refrigerator.

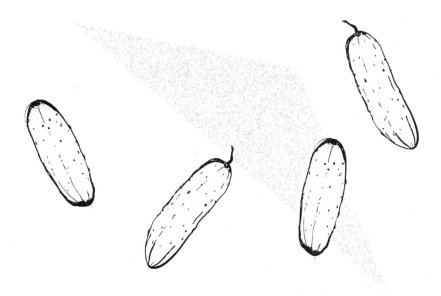

Fennel Gratin with Parmesan Cheese

SERVES 4

Fennel, a favorite vegetable in France and Italy, is much like celery in texture, but with a light anise flavor. Often it is sold under the name California anise. Who knows why? Be sure to ask for both when looking for it in the grocery store.

1 (1-pound) bulb fennel (12
   ounces after fronds are
   removed) or California
   anise, trimmed
3 tablespoons butter
3 tablespoons flour
2 cups milk

½ cup freshly grated imported
   Parmesan cheese
Pinch cayenne pepper
1 heaping tablespoon finely
   chopped fennel frond
Salt
Freshly ground black pepper

Quarter the fennel, and place it in a pan of boiling water. Return to the boil, and boil until nearly tender, about 10 to 12 minutes. Drain very well.

Meanwhile, in a saucepan melt the butter, add the flour, and stir briefly to make a *roux*. Add the milk, and bring to the boil, stirring. Add the cheese, cayenne, and fennel frond. Season to taste with salt and pepper. Place the blanched fennel in a buttered frameproof baking dish. Pour just enough of the sauce over the fennel to cover it, reserving extra sauce for another use. If making ahead, cover the dish. When ready to serve, remove the cover, and run the dish under a preheated broiler until the cheese is browned and the fennel is heated through. May be made 1 day ahead.

Charred Green Beans

SERVES 4 TO 6

When I first started learning how to cook, I inadvertently stumbled on this method of cooking green beans because I didn't know I had to boil them first. Fortunately, I loved the beans and so did my beau! I still love charred flavors, and the browned green beans are delicious, if not very attractive. I must tell you I use *all* the butter. I relish the beans greasy. My health-conscious staff, however, wants you to use less.

3 to 5 tablespoons butter
2 pounds green beans, tipped and tailed

Salt
Freshly ground black pepper

Place the butter in a large frying pan. When very hot, add the beans, and brown ever-so slightly. Reduce the heat, and continue cooking a few minutes more, stirring, until the beans are nearly soft. Season with salt and pepper.

Green Beans with Lemon and Onion

SERVES 6 TO 8

What makes this combination special is the way the lemon juice and onions spark the flavor of the beans. One of the many virtues of green beans is they may be cooked in advance and reheated.

3 pounds green beans, tipped
   and tailed
6 tablespoons butter
1 onion, finely chopped

1 lemon, juiced
Salt
Freshly ground black pepper

Bring a large pot of water to the boil. Add the beans. Return to the boil, and cook 5 to 7 minutes until crisp-cooked. Drain in a colander. Refresh under running cold water. The beans may be cooked ahead to this point.

    Meanwhile, melt the butter in a frying pan. Add the onion and cook until soft, about 5 minutes. Set aside. When ready to serve, reheat the onion butter. Add the beans and lemon juice and toss until heated through. Season with salt and pepper.

Green Beans with Red Peppers

SERVES 4

My very first job after I received my advanced certificate from the Cordon Bleu was as chef of a restaurant outside Polensa, Majorca. I was terribly inexperienced and scared. I learned many things from the kitchen staff, including this dish, and the fact that beans can be cooked ahead and reheated. To vary the recipe, I also roast the peppers (page 99).

1 pound green beans, tipped
    and tailed
2 tablespoons olive oil
2 garlic cloves, finely chopped
1 heaping tablespoon finely
    chopped fresh parsley

1 to 2 small red bell peppers,
    cored, seeded, and sliced
    thinly

Bring a large pot of water to the boil. Add the beans, return to the boil, and cook until nearly soft, about 7 to 10 minutes. Drain in a colander and refresh under running cold water.

In another pan, heat the oil, add the garlic, and cook until soft. Add the parsley. When ready to serve, reheat the butter mixture, add the beans, and stir-fry for a couple of minutes to coat and heat through. Add the bell peppers and cook several minutes more.

Green Beans with Tomatoes

SERVES 6 TO 8

Here is a make-ahead, colorful vegetable that reheats very well and is particularly pretty.

1½ pounds green beans, tipped
    and tailed
3 to 4 tablespoons butter
1 onion, finely chopped
1 to 2 garlic cloves, finely
    chopped
2 to 3 tomatoes, skinned,
    seeded, and cut into ½-inch
    cubes

1 small fresh hot pepper,
    seeded and chopped
1 to 2 tablespoons red wine
    vinegar
Salt
Freshly ground black pepper
½ to 1 teaspoon sugar

Bring a large pot of water to the boil. Add the beans and return to the boil. Cook 5 to 7 minutes until crisp-cooked. Drain in a colander and refresh under running cold water. The beans may be cooked ahead to this point.

Meanwhile, heat the butter in a frying pan. Add the onion, garlic, tomatoes, and hot pepper and cook until soft, about 5 minutes. Set aside. May be made ahead to this point several days. When ready to serve, reheat the tomato mixture. Add the beans and vinegar to taste, and toss together until headed through. Season with salt, pepper, and sugar, if needed.

Grilled Vegetables

SERVES 4

These beautiful still crunchy vegetables are a wonderful addition to any table! If fennel or California anise is not available, simply substitute the trimmed base of a whole celery, weighing about 12 ounces. Cut into 8 pieces as described below and add 2 teaspoons fennel seed.

1 red bell pepper
3 small new potatoes, washed but not peeled
2 onions
⅓ cup olive oil
1 (1-pound) bulb fennel (12 ounces after fronds are removed) or California anise

1 garlic clove, chopped
3 tablespoons red wine vinegar
½ cup freshly grated imported Parmesan cheese
Salt
Freshly ground black pepper
3 heaping tablespoons finely chopped fennel frond

Preheat the grill.

Place the pepper on the hot grill until blackened all over. Peel, seed (page 99), and cut into strips.

Quarter the new potatoes, place them in a small pan of boiling water, and cook 5 minutes, until nearly soft. Quarter the onions, toss in the olive oil, and place on the grill. Trim the base of the fennel to remove the discolored portion but leave the bulb attached at the base. Remove any tough outer layers. Cut off the fronds, reserving them. Cut the fennel in quarters, then each quarter in half, leaving a small section of the base attached to each piece. Toss in the oil and add to the grill. Drain the potatoes, toss in the oil, and add to the grill. Grill the vegetables until lightly charred all over. The inside of the onion and fennel should still be crisp.

In a bowl add the garlic and vinegar to the remaining oil. Add the pepper strips, potatoes, onions, fennel, and cheese and toss. Season to taste with salt and pepper and the chopped fennel frond. Serve at room temperature or chilled. May be made 2 days in advance and kept, covered, and chilled.

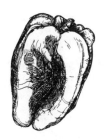

Baby Lima Beans or Broad Beans with Italian Sausage

SERVES 4 TO 6

Here is a nice side dish for Thanksgiving or other holiday meals, when meat eaters crave a little pork along with the turkey.

½ pound Italian bulk sausage, crumbled
1 onion, sliced
2 cups water
1 pound baby lima beans or broad beans

½ teaspoon ground cumin seed
1 fresh hot red pepper, seeded and chopped
Salt
Freshly ground black pepper

Place the sausage and onion in a heavy casserole or saucepan and sauté until light brown. Add the water and bring to the boil. Add the beans, cumin, and hot pepper and bring back to the boil. Cover, reduce heat, and simmer 20 minutes. Season well with salt and pepper.

- **This makes a good Sunday night supper accompanied by homemade cornbread (page 361). Simply break up the cornbread and pour this bean melange over it.**

Blue Cheese–Stuffed Mushrooms

MAKES 1 POUND MUSHROOM CAPS

There is an earthy richness to this dish. Use small button mushrooms for finger hors d'oeuvres; larger ones for a dinner party. Or experiment with *shiitake* mushrooms as a first course.

1 pound mushrooms, cleaned
1 tablespoon butter
1 medium onion, chopped
1 cup bread crumbs
2 tablespoons crumbled blue
   cheese or grated Cheddar
   cheese

Worcestershire sauce
Salt
Freshly ground black pepper

Preheat oven to 350 degrees.

Remove and chop the mushroom stems. Heat the butter in a sauté pan until singing, add the onions and chopped mushroom stems, and sauté until soft. Add the bread crumbs and blue cheese and mix well. Season with Worcestershire, salt, and pepper to taste. Stuff the mushroom caps. May be made ahead to this point. When ready to serve, bake the mushrooms for 10 minutes until heated through and the cheese is soft, or broil them for 5 minutes.

Okra and Chilies

SERVES 4 TO 6

Indians called okra "ladies' fingers" because the vegetable resembles long, slender fingers with beautiful nails. The okra is very pretty in this dish topped as it is with peanuts, and the chilies give a real boost to the flavor. This combination is a variation on an Indian one in which the okra is stir-fried instead of boiled. Good with curries and as an accompaniment to simple roast lamb.

4 tablespoons storebought
   chili oil
2 tablespoons chopped chili
   pepper
1 onion, chopped

1 pound okra, sliced
½ cup chopped peanuts
Salt
Freshly ground black pepper

Heat the oil in a large casserole, add the pepper and onion, and cook briefly. Stir in the okra, cover, and cook 5 minutes. Can be made ahead to this point, but be sure to cook the okra only 3 minutes or it will turn mushy when reheated. Add the peanuts and salt and pepper to taste. Heat through. Serve hot.

French-fried Onion Rings

SERVES 2 TO 4

If you have saved up all your calories to pig-out on truly wonderful onion rings, you could eat this whole batch yourself. Serve these when a group is gathered close to the stove, chattering, or when a game is on the television, and the cook's in the mood to serve something that will earn some attention. It's hard to cook onion rings in advance. The milk makes the rings crisper and sweeter by drawing out some of the bitter onion juice.

2 large Bermuda onions, peeled
   and cut into ¼-inch slices
1 cup milk
Shortening or oil for deep
   frying

1 cup flour
⅛ teaspoon salt

Separate the onion slices into rings. In a shallow dish cover the onions with the milk, and soak them for 30 minutes, turning several times.

Heat 2 or 3 inches of shortening to 365 degrees in a deep fryer or deep saucepan.

Place the flour and salt in a paper or plastic bag. Add a few of the onion rings at a time, and shake to coat. Place in the hot fat, and fry, a few at a time, about 2 or 3 minutes, or until golden brown.

(continued)

Turn once. Drain on paper towels. Repeat with the remaining onion rings. Salt lightly and serve immediately.

Steamed Party Vegetables

SERVES 16 TO 20 AS A VEGETABLE;
MORE AT A COCKTAIL PARTY

Vegetables are a very important addition to the party table, adding color and diversity as well as a little something extra to people who may be going out to dinner afterward. And, of course, along with a meat dish, vegetables like these can round out a meal for the person who is counting on dining at the party!

About Dried Tomatoes
*   **Dried tomatoes are to the tomato as raisins are to the grape. You can buy dried tomatoes packed in oil or dried. If you buy them dried, soften them briefly in a little water or vinaigrette before chopping.**

To serve fewer people, divide by 4 to serve 4.

4 pounds asparagus, peeled and
    trimmed as necessary
2½ pounds cauliflower florets
2½ pounds broccoli florets
18 garlic cloves, chopped
¾ cup red wine vinegar

2 tablespoons Dijon mustard
2¼ cups peanut and olive oil
Salt
Freshly ground black pepper
1 cup chopped dried tomatoes
    (optional)

Steam the asparagus, cauliflower, and broccoli separately until crisp. Whisk together the garlic, vinegar, mustard, and oil. Season with salt and pepper. Pour over the vegetables. Top with the dried tomatoes. The components may be made ahead several days. Dress vegetables at the last minute. Serve warm or slightly chilled.

Crunchy Garden Peas and Green Onions

SERVES 4

Southerners call garden peas "English peas." Although we traditionally cooked them a long time, now we cook them hardly at all to retain their vitamins.

5 to 6 tablespoons olive oil
2 cups shelled green garden
    peas (fresh or frozen and
    defrosted)
3 green onions or scallions,
    green and white parts,
    chopped
Salt

Freshly ground black pepper
3 heaping teaspoons finely
    chopped fresh basil
    (optional)
3 tablespoons freshly grated
    imported Parmesan cheese
    (optional)
Hot pepper flakes (optional)

Heat the olive oil in a large frying pan. Add the peas and green onions and sauté 2 or 3 minutes. Add salt and pepper to taste. Add the optional basil, cheese and/or the hot pepper flakes to taste. Cover the pan for 1 minute for young peas, longer for older ones. Serve hot.

Charred Peppers

SERVES 6 TO 8

Here is a great recipe for beginning cooks because the more you blacken the peppers, really char them, the better the dish!

Seasoning Sauce

1½ tablespoons light soy sauce
1 to 2 teaspoons Tabasco sauce
1 tablespoon red or rice wine
   vinegar
1 teaspoon sugar
2 tablespoons oil

7 red and green bell peppers,
   cored, seeded, and cut into
   1- by 2-inch chunks
1 tablespoon sesame seeds
   (optional)

Make the sauce: Mix together the soy sauce, Tabasco, vinegar, and sugar and stir until well combined.

Heat the oil in a large frying pan or wok. Add the peppers and stir-fry 4 to 5 minutes, pushing them down with a spoon or spatula to assist the charring. Add the sauce and toss and cook until all of it is absorbed. Sprinkle the sesame seeds on top. Serve at room temperature. May be made in advance up to 1 week and kept, covered, in the refrigerator.

Diet Mashed Potatoes

SERVES 6 TO 8

The lowest-calorie way to eat mashed potatoes is to mash them with some of their cooking broth, but the buttermilk here does add a real dimension, as do the herbs. Furthermore, buttermilk in comparison with heavy cream—and how marvelous that is with mashed potatoes, too—is significantly lower in fat. After all, what's life worth living if food doesn't taste good! Extra virgin olive oil is an acceptable if not spectacular substitute for the butter.

3 pounds potatoes
¼ to ½ cup butter or oil
1 cup buttermilk
Salt

Freshly ground black pepper
3 heaping tablespoons finely
   chopped fresh herbs
2 cups diced tomatoes (optional)

Peel the potatoes, cut them into quarters, and place in a pan with cold water to cover. Bring to the boil, reduce heat, cover, and simmer about 1 hour. Be sure the potatoes are thoroughly cooked. Drain, reserving the cooking liquid. Add the desired amount of butter to the pan and melt over low heat. Add the well-drained potatoes. With an electric mixer or whip, mash the potatoes until soft, incorporating the butter. Meanwhile, heat the buttermilk until bubbles form around the side. Pour into the potatoes. Add enough of the hot potato broth to bring the mashed potatoes to the desired consistency. Stir in the salt, pepper, herbs, and diced tomatoes, if desired.

Russ Parsons's Luxurious Diet Mashed Potatoes

SERVES 6 TO 8

These are not really serious diet potatoes. Russ just thinks they are since they're less fatty than those of his friend Michel Richard, who uses *equal* weights of butter and potatoes.

3 pounds potatoes
1 pound butter

Salt
Freshly ground black pepper

Peel the potatoes, cut them into quarters, and place in a pan with cold water to cover. Bring to the boil, reduce heat, cover, and simmer until done, about 1 hour. Be sure the potatoes are thoroughly cooked. Drain, reserving the cooking liquid. Add the butter to the pan and melt over low heat. Add the well-drained potatoes. With an electric mixer or whip, mash the potatoes until soft, incorporating the butter and still-hot reserved broth to get to the desired consistency. Season to taste with salt and pepper.

Garlic-Flavored Potato Cake

SERVES 6

Crispy and brown on the outside, tender and white inside, this potato cake is an impressive dish for very little effort. It is best served right away, but may be made ahead and reheated in the oven. For a different flavor, try rendered goose or duck fat in place of the butter or oil.

2½ pounds potatoes, peeled
3 or 4 garlic cloves, chopped
2 heaping tablespoons finely chopped fresh parsley
1 heaping tablespoon finely chopped fresh oregano

Salt
Freshly ground black pepper
4 or 5 tablespoons butter or olive oil

Preheat oven to 450 degrees.

With a sharp knife, food processor, or mandoline, cut the potatoes into julienne strips, similar in size to a long grate. Toss with the garlic, parsley, oregano, salt, and pepper. Heat the butter until sizzling in a heavy non-stick 9- or 10-inch pan with a heatproof handle.* Add the potatoes. Cover with buttered aluminum foil. Press down with the bottom of another pan or a heavy weight. Cook over medium heat until the bottom is brown, about 10 minutes. Then bake 20 to 25 minutes, until potatoes are tender and bottom is crisp. Place a heat-proof serving dish over the pan and flip the cake out onto plate.

*Most handles will take heat up to 300 degrees. If you are concerned your pan handle won't go into the oven, cover it with aluminum foil.

Italian Herbed Potatoes

SERVES 16

Imagine having a healthy potato dish on hand that your family loves more than potato chips, one that is ready to be eaten after school, or can be served at your most important dinner party! My friend Mary Krudup sold me on this one day when we were having lunch at another friend's house. Mary said she keeps these potatoes in a big covered jar and the family snacks on them all week. You may reduce the recipe by half or even quarter it. It keeps well in the refrigerator and reheats easily.

5 pounds new potatoes, cut into
    1½-inch cubes
¼ cup finely chopped fresh
    parsley
¼ cup finely chopped fresh
    basil
½ cup chopped scallions or
    green onion greens
3 heads garlic, chopped

½ teaspoon dry mustard
1 tablespoon sugar
1 tablespoon Worcestershire
    sauce
1 cup olive oil
½ cup red wine vinegar
Salt
Freshly ground black pepper

Place the potatoes in a large pan of boiling water to cover. Bring back to the boil, cover, and reduce heat. Simmer 30 minutes, or until done. Drain and put in a bowl. Sprinkle the parsley, basil, and scallions over the potatoes. Combine the garlic, mustard, sugar, Worcestershire, olive oil, and vinegar. Pour over the potatoes. Season to taste with salt and pepper. Combine, then let stand at least 4 hours or up to 1 week. Stir occasionally. Cover. Serve at room temperature, refrigerating if keeping more than a day. May also be served hot. Reheat quickly in a frying pan or the microwave.

Parsley and Chive Potatoes

SERVES 4 TO 6

Many herbed potatoes call for a much higher proportion of butter. In an effort to reduce fat but keep flavor high, I've boosted the herb and shallot measurements while reducing that of the butter.

2 pounds new potatoes, scrubbed and peeled
1 shallot, chopped
2 to 3 tablespoons butter
1 to 2 heaping tablespoons finely chopped fresh parsley
1 to 3 tablespoons lemon juice

1 to 2 heaping teaspoons finely chopped fresh tarragon (optional)
½ to 1 heaping tablespoon finely chopped fresh chives
Salt
Freshly ground black pepper

Place the potatoes in water to cover. Bring to the boil and cook until tender, about 20 to 30 minutes. Drain. Set aside. In a saucepan, sauté the shallot in the butter until tender. Add the parsley, lemon juice, tarragon, and chives to taste. Season with salt and pepper. When ready to serve, reheat the herb butter and add the potatoes, just to heat through.

Potatoes Ray

SERVES 4 TO 6

Many times I'm asked how I come up with new recipes. This combination is a good example. I showed Ray Overton, who is my assistant in testing recipes, an article with a recipe on potato-wrapped fish. Several months later he was ill and stayed home. The next day he came in and said he'd been thinking about that recipe and what about doing potatoes encasing a vegetable like broccoli. I suggested adding bacon, leeks, onions, and garlic. We decided to make a cheese sauce to bind it. First Ray tried baking it in a heatproof glass bowl, but I felt it needed to be crisp and brown outside, like the classic potato dish pommes Anna. So we retested it in a heavy non-stick frying pan with a handle that could go in the oven. Then we decided to call it "Potatoes Ray."

This looks like a cake; it's so beautiful, rounded and brown. What a surprise to find the color inside! It is important to slice the potatoes very thin lengthwise. I think they look like Schmoos, Al Capp's old cartoon critters. It is also imperative to use a non-stick pan and butter it well.

8 slices bacon

2 tablespoons reserved bacon fat or olive oil

2 leeks, whites only, sliced

2 onions, sliced

5 garlic cloves, chopped

1 potato, cut into ½-inch cubes

1 (1½-pound) head broccoli, cut into small florets and stalks cut into ¼-inch slices

¼ cup butter

4 tablespoons flour

1½ cups milk

1½ cups grated Cheddar cheese

Salt

Freshly ground black pepper

6 potatoes, cut lengthwise into ⅛- to ¼-inch-thick slices

Fry the bacon in a skillet or microwave until crisp, reserving 2 tablespoons of the fat. Crumble the bacon into small pieces. Set aside. Heat the fat in a large skillet. Add the leeks and onions and sauté until browned. Add the garlic and diced potatoes and cook until soft, about 10 minutes. Add the broccoli to the mixture. Sauté 3 minutes, or until crisp-tender. Add the crumbled bacon.

Melt the butter in a saucepan. Stir in the flour. Cook until a light nut brown. Add the milk all at once and bring the mixture to the boil, stirring until thick. Remove from the heat. Add the cheese, salt, and pepper to taste. Pour the sauce over the vegetables and toss lightly.

Butter well a 10-inch non-stick skillet with a heatproof handle. Line the bottom and sides with some of the sliced potatoes, overlapping them slightly. Pour the vegetable mixture onto the potatoes and top the mixture with the remaining potato slices, overlapping them slightly. Cover the potatoes with buttered foil and place a weight on top to compress the mixture. Cook over medium heat 15 minutes, until the potatoes on the bottom are brown. Remove the weight.

Preheat oven to 400 degrees. Place the foil-covered pan in the oven and bake the potato cake for 30 to 40 minutes, or until the potatoes are soft. Remove from the oven and cool 10 minutes. Uncover and invert onto a serving platter. Cut into wedges to serve.

Twice-Baked Potato Casserole with Mushrooms and Cream

SERVES 2 TO 4

Here is an elegant potato dish that can be made ahead. You may substitute wild mushrooms for the cultivated ones called for here. Soak 1 ounce in 1 cup hot water for 30 minutes. Squeeze dry and chop coarse. Toss for a few minutes in the butter. The mushrooms taste almost like ham in this dish.

2 pounds potatoes, scrubbed
    and pricked
2 tablespoons butter
¼ pound mushrooms, sliced

Salt
Freshly ground black pepper
¾ cup heavy cream

Preheat oven to 400 degrees.

Place the potatoes in the oven and bake until tender, 45 to 50 minutes. Meanwhile, in a small skillet heat the butter, add the mushrooms, and sauté 5 minutes.

Scoop out the cooked pulp of the potatoes and coarsely break it up in a bowl. Add the mushrooms, salt, and pepper. Spoon into a 1½-quart buttered gratin dish. When ready to cook, pour the cream over the top. Reduce the heat to 350 and bake until browned, about 30 minutes.

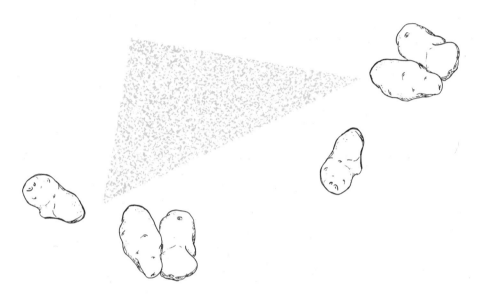

Pan-Browned Potatoes with Onions

SERVES 2

This is a simple way to add flavor to a meal. I can't seem to get enough slightly charred food!

4 to 6 tablespoons butter
2 potatoes, cut into quarters
2 onions, cut into quarters

Salt
Freshly ground black pepper

Melt the butter in a frying pan. Add the potatoes and onions and brown over high heat, letting them get as brown as you like. (I like mine charred.) Turn when brown and cook until done, 15 to 20 minutes. Season to taste with salt and pepper.

Red Cabbage and Apples

SERVES 6 TO 8

Somewhat tart, but with an underlying sweetness, this colorful combination is a welcome foil to rich main dishes like venison, lamb, and duck.

¼ pound bacon or salt pork, cubed and blanched
2 onions, sliced
1 (3½-pound) red cabbage, shredded or grated
2 Granny Smith apples, peeled and cut into wedges

½ cup apple cider vinegar
Sugar
Salt
Freshly ground black pepper
3 heaping tablespoons finely chopped fresh parsley

Fry the bacon in a large casserole until crisp. Remove with a slotted spoon, and set aside. Add the onions to the pan, and cook until soft. Add the cabbage, the apples, and the vinegar, and toss. Cover, and simmer 10 minutes. Remove cover, taste for seasoning, and add sugar if necessary. Season with salt and pepper. Garnish with the parsley and crumble the bacon over the top.

Spinach with Garlic and Pine Nuts

SERVES 4 TO 6

This bright green spinach, tossed with garlic, pine nuts, raisins, and anchovies is one of my favorites from my days as a chef in Majorca. When I don't want the expense of pine nuts, I substitute sunflower seeds.

2 pounds spinach, trimmed
3 tablespoons olive oil or butter
2 garlic cloves, chopped
3 tablespoons pine nuts or
   sunflower seeds
⅓ cup seedless raisins or
   currants
4 anchovy fillets, chopped
Salt
Freshly ground black pepper

Wash the spinach, and shake off most of the water, leaving a bit on. In a pan heat the olive oil. Add the garlic and cook briefly. Add the spinach, cover with a lid, and cook 2 to 3 minutes, until the spinach is soft. May be made ahead to this point. When ready to serve, put the pan over high heat. Add the pine nuts, raisins, and anchovy fillets. Season with salt and pepper, cover, and reheat for about 5 minutes, until cooked lightly and heated through.

Squash and Zucchini Casserole

SERVES 6 TO 8

When I'm being decadent and irresponsible about calories, I use sour cream in this bubbly casserole of green and gold. When I'm being responsible, I use yogurt.

2½ cups sour cream or plain
   yogurt
1 or 2 (¾ pound) summer
   squash, sliced ¼ inch thick
1 or 2 (¾ pound) zucchini,
   sliced ⅛ inch thick
2 heaping tablespoons finely
   chopped fresh parsley and
   basil, mixed
1 medium onion, sliced
1½ cups bread crumbs
½ cup grated Swiss cheese
½ cup freshly grated imported
   Parmesan cheese
Salt
Freshly ground black pepper
¼ cup butter

To remove excess water, place the sour cream or yogurt in a strainer lined with cheesecloth or Handi Wipes and set over a bowl to drain for several hours.

    Preheat oven to 400 degrees. Put the squash and zucchini slices on a baking sheet, and bake for 10 minutes. Remove from oven. Reduce oven temperature to 350 degrees.

Combine the squash, zucchini, fresh herbs, onion, and ½ the bread crumbs. Alternately layer the vegetable mixture, the cheeses, and the sour cream in a 3-quart buttered baking dish. Season with salt and pepper. Melt the butter and combine with the remaining bread crumbs. Sprinkle the buttered bread crumbs over the top of the casserole. Bake for 45 minutes to 1 hour, until browned and bubbly. May be made 1 or 2 days ahead. Freezes satisfactorily for leftovers.

Easy Squash and Corn Pudding

SERVES 6 TO 8

When we first tested this with fresh Silver Queen corn, it was so sweet you could eat it like candy. We decided it was the best corn pudding in the world, with its sweetness contrasting with the bacon and garlic in what is almost a soufflé. Canned corn will do in a pinch.

5 ears corn
3 slices bacon
3 garlic cloves, chopped
1 onion, chopped
1 pound squash, such as
   summer yellow or zucchini
   cut into ⅛-inch-thick rounds
2 egg yolks
2 eggs
½ cup milk

½ cup cream
Salt
Freshly ground black pepper
⅛ teaspoon freshly ground
   nutmeg
1 to 2 heaping teaspoons finely
   chopped fresh thyme
1 cup shredded Monterey Jack
   cheese

Preheat oven to 375 degrees.

Shuck the corn. Cut off the kernels and then scrape the ears, saving all the juices.

Meanwhile, fry the bacon. Drain on paper towels, and reserve the drippings. Add the garlic and onion to the drippings and sauté until soft. Add the squash slices and cook until soft and wilted, about 10 minutes.

In a large bowl, combine the yolks, the whole eggs, milk, cream, salt, pepper, nutmeg, and thyme. Whisk until smooth. Add the cheese and the corn and squash mixture. Stir until well blended. Pour into a 2½-quart buttered casserole. Set the casserole in a shallow pan and pour ½ inch of boiling water into the pan. Bake the casserole in the water bath for 45 to 50 minutes, or until the custard is set in the center.

Stuffed Squash

SERVES 8 TO 10

Stuffed summer squash, such as crookneck, is a great side dish for Sunday dinner or for an all-vegetable meal.

10 small-to-medium yellow
  summer squash
6 tablespoons butter, divided
2 onions, chopped
2 garlic cloves, chopped
⅓ cup bread crumbs
2 heaping tablespoons finely
  chopped fresh thyme
  (optional)

½ cup freshly grated imported
  Parmesan cheese
½ cup grated Swiss cheese
Salt
Freshly ground black pepper

Cut the squash in half. Spoon out the insides to make a boat of each half. Place the boats in boiling water to cover or in the microwave and cook until just tender. Drain inverted on paper towels. Chop the insides coarse.

Meanwhile, melt 5 tablespoons of the butter in a sauté pan. Add the onions and garlic and cook until soft. Add the chopped squash and cook briefly. Add the bread crumbs and the optional thyme. Cool slightly. Stir in the cheeses. Season to taste with salt and pepper. Stuff the boats with the crumb filling. May be made in advance 1 to

2 days to this point. Place the boats in a buttered ovenproof dish. Dot with the remaining butter. When ready to serve, reheat in 350-degree oven for 15 minutes, or until cheese is melted and the boats are heated through. Or reheat in the microwave.

Vickie Mooney's Sautéed Grated Sweet Potatoes

SERVES 4 TO 6

I love incredibly easy side dishes that add color and flavor. Try this for Thanksgiving or any time you need to cook ahead and reheat. Its awfully good!

Vickie Mooney is one of those friends of mine who has gone through fire for me. I love serving a recipe of hers at important times, like Thanksgiving, as well as at casual times because it makes me feel close to her.

4 sweet potatoes
6 tablespoons butter
1 to 2 tablespoons sugar

Salt
Freshly ground black pepper

Peel and grate the potatoes. Heat the butter in a large sauté pan. Add the potatoes and sauté 5 minutes. Add the sugar, salt, and pepper to taste. Serve hot. To make ahead, cook to this point. Place in a casserole. When ready to eat, reheat in a 350-degree oven for 10 minutes; or reheat in a microwave.

Two Potato and Turnip Gratin

SERVES 10 TO 12

Creamy gratins are popular Thanksgiving dishes at my house, always requested by family and guests alike. (when it's not really in to eat "a bit of this and a bit of that" so the calories even out). The number of root vegetables here makes it particularly tasty as well as pretty.

1½ pounds white turnips, peeled, sliced ¼ inch thick, and blanched in boiling water for 5 minutes

1½ pounds sweet potatoes, peeled and sliced ¼ inch thick

1½ pounds all-purpose potatoes, peeled and sliced ¼ inch thick

½ cup butter

1 to 2 heaping tablespoons finely chopped fresh tarragon

Salt

Freshly ground black pepper

1 cup freshly grated imported Parmesan cheese

1 cup bread crumbs

2 cups heavy cream

Preheat oven to 350 degrees.

Combine gently the blanched turnips, sweet potatoes, and white potatoes. Place a layer of the vegetables in a buttered 3-quart casserole, dot with butter, sprinkle generously with tarragon, salt, and pepper, and cover with Parmesan. Make another layer. Top with bread crumbs and pour the cream around the sides. Dot with the remaining butter. Bake 1 to 1½ hours, until vegetables are soft but not mushy.

Zucchini and Carrot Combo

SERVES 4

This is a fast and easy summer appetizer. It also works well for an hors d'oeuvre. The recipe multiplies up easily.

2 tablespoons oil
1½ teaspoons wine vinegar or
    lemon juice
Salt
Freshly ground black pepper
3 heaping tablespoons finely
    chopped fresh basil, thyme,
    oregano, parsley, or other
    mixed herbs (optional)

2 medium carrots, peeled and
    grated
1 medium zucchini, thickly
    sliced

Whisk together the oil, vinegar or lemon juice, salt, pepper, and optional mixed herbs. Toss the carrots lightly in the dressing. Mound the dressed carrots on the zucchini slices and chill. May be made up to 1 day ahead, covered tightly, and kept chilled.

Zucchini Strips with Moroccan Spices

SERVES 4 TO 6

The Moroccan spice mixture used here is called *chermoula*, and it catapults zucchini into another league of great cuisine! The squash will extrude its own juice, requiring no more oil, provided you keep the heat low as the mixture cooks.

2 pounds zucchini, washed,
    trimmed, and cut into
    8 lengthwise batons
Salt
6 tablespoons olive oil
1 large onion, chopped
3 large garlic cloves, finely
    chopped
¼ teaspoon ground hot pepper
2 teaspoons chopped red bell
    pepper

¾ teaspoon ground cumin seed
½ teaspoon freshly ground
    black pepper
2 heaping tablespoons finely
    chopped fresh parsley
1 to 2 heaping tablespoons
    finely chopped fresh cilantro
2 tablespoons lemon juice

Sprinkle the zucchini batons with salt and let sit ½ hour. Rinse and drain. In a skillet heat the oil and add the onion, garlic, and zucchini. Mix together the hot pepper, bell pepper, cumin, pepper, and salt to taste. Toss with the zucchini. Cover and cook over low heat until tender, 15 to 20 minutes. Sprinkle with the parsley, cilantro, and lemon juice.

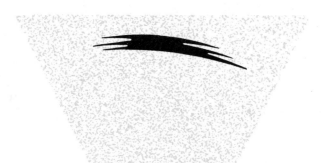

A Group of Grains and One Grass

Boiled Rice

To cook rice, you can always follow the package directions, but this easy method guarantees good results and tastes delicious. For drier rice, use 2 tablespoons less liquid. Rice is a perfect foil for additions. To the finished product, add 1 cup chopped pecans, or canned or frozen defrosted artichoke hearts, or chopped green onions or scallions, or fresh herbs.

1 cup uncooked long-grain
   white rice
2 cups water or beef or chicken
   bouillon

½ teaspoon salt
Freshly ground black pepper
1 tablespoon butter or olive oil
   (optional)

Place the rice and water or broth, salt, pepper, and optional fat in a 2- to 3-quart saucepan and bring to the boil. Stir once or twice. Lower heat to a simmer. Cover with a tight-fitting lid or heavy-duty foil and cook 15 minutes. If the rice is not quite tender or the liquid is not absorbed, replace the lid and cook 2 to 4 minutes longer. Season with salt and pepper. Fluff with a fork. May be made ahead and kept tightly covered, or frozen.

• **To reheat rice, place in a colander over boiling water, cover the colander with a lid or wax paper to prevent the rice from drying out. Take care the water does not boil into or soak the rice, but only steams it. The rice will stay fluffy as long as the water doesn't evaporate.**

Chinese Fried Rice

SERVES 4

Forsythia Chang, who is half Chinese and half Japanese, is one of Atlanta's top caterers and prefers to make this recipe for her family with leftover rice, which can be easily frozen, then quickly defrosted in the microwave.

The thrifty Chinese originally used this dish as a leftover, never for company. Over the years, however, it's become acceptable as a dish in its own right. Two cups chopped meat (bacon, ham, or shrimp), chopped green peppers, shelled and roasted peanuts, or chopped leftover vegetables may be added to the rice before cooking over the heat.

2 tablespoons peanut or vegetable oil	2 eggs, slightly beaten
	1 tablespoon soy sauce
2 cups coarsely chopped green onions or scallions	½ teaspoon salt
	Freshly ground black pepper (optional)
2 cups cold cooked rice	

In a frying pan, heat the oil and in it fry the green onions until brown. Add the cooked rice. Combine the eggs, soy sauce, and salt and pour into the rice. Stir over the heat, until the eggs are scrambled and cooked and the rice heated through. (Instead of scrambling the eggs, some people cook the eggs separately in a pan with a little hot oil. When done, they turn out the eggs, cut them in strips, and toss into the fried rice.) Season with salt and pepper. The rice may be made in advance to this point. Remove to a bowl and refrigerate. Just before serving, reheat in a skillet with a small amount of oil or in the microwave.

Red Beans and Rice

SERVES 4 TO 6

A winter day is perfect for this satisfying dish. Heap on hot sauce, sit in front of the fire, and think of New Orleans. The poor of many cultures have used versions of these two basic ingredients to survive, as beans and rice form a perfect protein. This dish is more than just good then; it's an important dietary compliment.

1 pound dried red beans (or kidney beans), soaked overnight in water to cover
½ pound salt pork, diced, or ham hock, diced
3 cups chopped onion
1 bunch green onions with tops, chopped
1 cup chopped green bell pepper
2 large garlic cloves, chopped
1 cup finely chopped fresh parsley
1 tablespoon salt

¾ teaspoon ground red pepper, sometimes called hot cayenne
1 teaspoon freshly ground black pepper
½ heaping teaspoon finely chopped fresh oregano
2 bay leaves, crumbled
3 or 4 generous dashes hot sauce
1 tablespoon Worcestershire sauce
1 recipe Boiled Rice (page 262)

Drain the beans, place them in 2 quarts of water with the salt pork, and bring to the boil. Reduce heat, and simmer, covered, for 45 minutes. Add the chopped onions, green onions, bell pepper, and garlic; and cook slowly for 2 to 3 hours, stirring occasionally. Test the beans after 2 hours. They should be tender not mushy. Add the parsley, salt, peppers, oregano, bay leaves, hot sauce, and Worcestershire. In a large pot combine with the cooked rice. May be made ahead and reheated over low heat or the microwave.

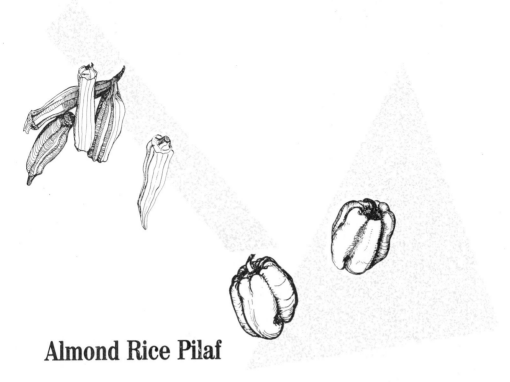

Almond Rice Pilaf

SERVES 4 TO 6

This is a wonderful side dish—full of texture and crunch. It also makes an interesting gift for a new mother or for a holiday, so I've given those directions first. Place the rice, raisins, onions, chicken stock cubes, salt and pepper in a plastic bag, write out the recipe directions, and tie it all up with a bow. Wrap the slivered almonds and butter separately and tape on if practical. Tuck directions inside.

1 cup brown rice
¼ cup raisins or currants
2 tablespoons dehydrated
   chopped onion
1 tablespoon butter (optional)

2 chicken stock cubes
2 to 2½ cups water
⅓ cup slivered toasted almonds
Salt
Freshly ground black pepper

Place the rice, raisins, onion, butter, stock cubes and water in a 2- to 3-quart saucepan. Bring to the boil, and stir once or twice. Reduce heat, cover, and simmer 45 to 50 minutes, or until rice is tender and liquid is absorbed. Remove from heat. Add almonds, season with salt and pepper, and fluff with a fork.

When not giving as a gift, omit the dehydrated onion and sauté a small chopped onion in the butter before proceeding with the recipe.

Brown Rice

SERVES 4 TO 6

Brown rice retains more of its nutrients than does white rice, which has had its bran and germ removed.

1 cup brown rice
2 to 2½ cups liquid (water,
   stock, or juice)

1 tablespoon butter
1 teaspoon salt (optional)

Place the rice, liquid, butter, and salt in a 2- to 3-quart saucepan. Bring to the boil, and stir once or twice. Reduce heat, cover, and simmer 45 to 50 minutes, or until rice is tender and liquid is absorbed. Fluff with a fork.

Couscous

SERVES 2 OR 3

One Christmas David and I took a Russian cruise ship from England to Africa. On arriving in Morocco, we rented a car and drove through a rare pelting rain to Marrakech. There I was enchanted with the couscous—the traditional dish of North Africa—with its separate, fluffy grains. We cupped it in our hands and ate it from our hands. Now I use the packaged kind, which is not as good, but infinitely easier than finding a *couscoussière*, lining it with cheesecloth, and cooking the fine grains for 30 minutes. Although ours was served at the end of the meal, I use couscous as a side dish when I'm in a hurry but want a bit of interest in the meal. Made from coarsely ground durum wheat (semolina), which has been pre-cooked, couscous can be prepared in minutes, and is one of the easiest side dishes—a well-kept secret in gourmet circles!

1¼ cups water or chicken broth
   or stock
2 tablespoons butter

1 cup couscous
Salt
Freshly ground black pepper

In a saucepan bring the water or broth to the boil. Add the butter, couscous, salt, and pepper. Stir. Cover. Remove the pan from the heat and let stand 5 minutes. Stir the couscous with a fork to fluff it up.

Vegetable Couscous Pilaf

SERVES 8

Almost any vegetable can be used to come up with this throw-together, last-minute side dish, but the red peppers and snow peas make it a world-class side dish.

3 tablespoons butter
6 green onions, thinly sliced
3 garlic cloves, chopped
1 red or green bell pepper,
   cored, seeded and chopped
   or julienned
¼ pound snow peas, julienned
¾ cup golden raisins
3 cups chicken stock or broth,
   boiling
1 heaping tablespoon finely
   chopped fresh basil

1 heaping tablespoon finely
   chopped fresh parsley
1 heaping teaspoon finely
   chopped fresh oregano
Salt
Freshly ground black pepper
2 cups couscous
2 medium tomatoes, seeded
   and cut into ½-inch cubes

In a large saucepan melt the butter. Add the green onions, garlic, red or green pepper, snow peas, and raisins. Sauté about 5 minutes until crisp-tender. Add the boiling stock and simmer 5 minutes. Remove from the heat and add the basil, parsley, oregano, salt, and pepper to taste. Stir in the couscous. Cover and let stand 6 to 8 minutes. Add the tomatoes and gently fluff with a fork.

Wild Rice

SERVES 8 TO 10

Wild rice is not really a rice, but a grass seed. It's very good nutri-tionally. One cup of uncooked wild rice makes 3 to 3½ cups of cooked rice. This recipe can easily be varied by using butter instead of olive oil, or by adding all or any of the following: sautéed mushrooms, onions, or sour cream to the finished rice.

2 cups wild rice
6 cups boiling water

1 tablespoon olive oil
Salt

To prepare the wild rice, wash it in a sieve under cold running water for 2 minutes. Put the rice in a heavy pan and add the boiling water and olive oil. Cover and over medium heat simmer the rice about 55 minutes until it is cracked and puffy. Drain and add salt to taste.

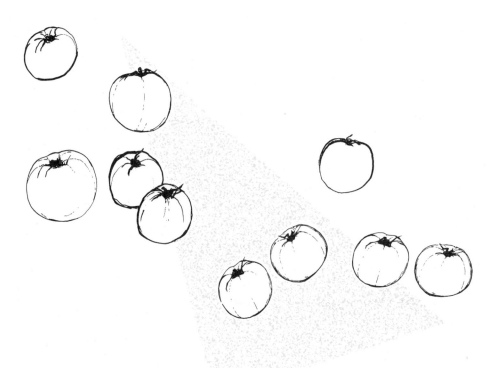

Wild Rice and Prune Dressing

SERVES 10 TO 12

I serve this dressing with turkey, wild or farm-raised duck or goose, and pork loin.

5 tablespoons butter, bacon drippings, or goose or duck fat (page 171)
3 onions, chopped
2½ cups wild rice
10 cups chicken broth or stock, fresh or canned
Salt
Freshly ground black pepper

2 cups corn bread crumbs
½ to 1 heaping tablespoon finely chopped fresh rosemary
½ to 1 heaping tablespoon finely chopped fresh thyme
1 cup chopped prunes, soaked in tea or Armagnac until soft

Preheat oven to 350 degrees.

Heat the butter in a large pan. Add the onions and wild rice, toss in the fat, and cook over low heat 5 minutes. Add the stock, salt, and pepper and bring to the boil. Cover, reduce the heat, and cook 50 minutes, or until the rice is done. Add the bread crumbs, rosemary, and thyme. Taste and add more salt and pepper if necessary. Add the prunes. Put the dressing in a buttered casserole. Bake for 30 minutes.

May be frozen and reheated.

Sweet
Inspirations

"Sweet Inspirations" are the icings on the cake, the extra touches of a meal. It is not crucial to make one's own bread or desserts every meal, but I do encourage both, because they put a meal over the top with very little effort.

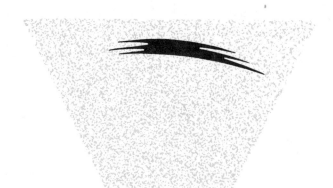

Cakes, Cookies, and Candy

Chocolate Marbled Angel Food Cake

MAKES 1 CAKE

Imagine a light angel food cake marbelized with chocolate—the best of all worlds! I've made two batters here, one plain to give height, one with chocolate, to provide the marbelizing effect. The chocolate part is slightly gooey, suggesting a sauce. If you grease the pan the cake won't be able to rise, so no grease and no non-stick pans!

2 tablespoons unsweetened
   cocoa powder
3 tablespoons boiling water
1 teaspoon almond extract
14 large egg whites, about
   1¾ cups

1 teaspoon cream of tartar
1¾ cups sugar
½ teaspoon salt
2 teaspoons vanilla
1¼ cups flour, sifted

Preheat oven to 350 degrees.

In a small bowl, combine the cocoa, water, and almond extract until blended. Set aside to cool.

Beat the egg whites with the cream of tartar until soft peaks form. Gently beat in the sugar, salt, and vanilla until the peaks retain their shape when the whisk is removed. Gradually fold in the flour until well blended. Remove 2 cups of the batter and combine it with the cocoa mixture.

Pour half of the light batter into an ungreased 10-inch tube pan with removable bottom. Pour the chocolate batter over the light. Finally, top with the remaining light batter. Gently swirl mixture with a knife to help remove any air bubbles and to create a marble pattern. Bake in the middle of the oven for 40 to 45 minutes until the cake is springy and begins to pull away from the sides of the pan. The cake will rise, crack on the top, and then fall slightly. This is normal. Remove from the oven and invert the pan over the neck of a bottle until the cake is completely cool, about 1 hour. Gently loosen the sides and remove the cake from pan. Place it on a serving plate. This cake can be served alone or with chocolate sauce. A serrated knife makes cutting the cake much easier.

The cake freezes wrapped well in plastic wrap.

Fudgy Brownies

MAKES 24

This recipe is now an ongoing memory of a memorial service to which the brownies were brought. Everyone who attended asked for the recipe, and my friend Bob Simonds sent it to me. I like that; life goes on in food. Easy to make, very chocolaty, these are good to keep on hand in the freezer.

1 cup unsalted butter
¾ cup unsweetened cocoa
    powder
2 cups sugar
4 eggs
1 cup all-purpose flour

2 teaspoons vanilla
½ teaspoon salt
1 (12-ounce) package
    semisweet-chocolate chips
1 cup chopped nuts (optional)

Preheat oven to 350 degrees. Grease a 13- × 9- × 2-inch pan.

Melt the butter over low heat; pour into a mixing bowl. Add the cocoa, and stir until well blended. Add the sugar, and mix well. Add the eggs, 1 at a time, beating well after each addition. Add the flour, vanilla, and salt and stir just until mixed together. Do not overbeat. Stir in the chocolate chips and nuts. Spread in the pan and bake 25 to 30 minutes. Let cool on a rack for 10 minutes. Cut into 24 squares.

The brownies freeze wrapped in plastic wrap.

Banana-Carrot Sheet Cake

MAKES 1 CAKE

You'll really like this easy carrot cake. The banana adds a new dimension to an old favorite. As a sheet cake this makes a particularly nice carry-along for pot luck suppers, funerals, or family occasions.

Before food processors, I had a job making carrot cakes for a restaurant and grudgingly grated carrots by hand to make 4 cakes a day. I kept the carrots in large fifty-pound sacks in the closet, where they stained the carpet. Never again! I use and highly recommend the food processor!

1 cup chopped pecans
1½ cups grated carrots (about 5 medium)
1½ cups mashed bananas (about 3 large)
¼ cup toasted coconut
3 cups all-purpose flour
1 teaspoon baking soda
1 teaspoon cinnamon
1 teaspoon salt
½ teaspoon ground cloves
½ teaspoon mace
1½ cups packed light brown sugar
1 cup unsalted butter, softened
3 eggs
1 tablespoon vanilla
¾ cup milk
Banana Cream Cheese Frosting (recipe follows) or ½ cup Confectioners' sugar

Preheat oven to 350 degrees. Grease and flour a 13- × 9- × 2-inch baking pan.

In a bowl mix together the pecans, carrots, bananas, and coconut. Sift together the flour, baking soda, cinnamon, salt, cloves, and mace. Set aside.

In a large bowl beat the brown sugar and butter until light and fluffy. Add the eggs and beat until smooth. Add the vanilla to the milk. Beat the milk mixture into the sugar mixture, ⅓ at a time, alternating with the dry ingredients, beginning and ending with the dry ingredients. Fold in the carrot/banana mixture until just incorporated. Pour into the prepared pan and bake in the middle of the oven 30 to 35 minutes, or until a toothpick inserted into center comes out clean. Cool the cake completely, and then frost with cream cheese frosting or dust with the sugar. Cut into 24 squares.

The cake, frosted or not, freezes wrapped in plastic wrap.

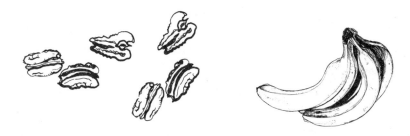

Banana Cream Cheese Frosting

MAKES 2½ CUPS

This is great both on Banana-Carrot Sheet Cake (recipe precedes) and Upside Down Gingerbread (page 286). Once I left this frosting in the refrigerator several weeks. It was still delicious, although slightly discolored. I just put it on hot gingerbread and used it like a sauce.

½ cup butter, at room temperature
12 ounces cream cheese, at room temperature
¼ cup sour cream

1 large banana, mashed
1 teaspoon vanilla
Dash freshly grated nutmeg
1 (16-ounce) package Confectioners' sugar

Beat the butter, cream cheese, and sour cream together in a large bowl until light. Add the banana, vanilla, nutmeg, and sugar, mixing well until fluffy. Spread over cooled cake if using as a frosting. Keep refrigerated until serving time.

The frosting freezes.

Lemon Poppy Seed Pound Cake

MAKES 1 LOAF CAKE

This is a special treat any time, although I love it for tea and have been known to eat it toasted for breakfast. Rose Levy Beranbaum, from whose book *The Cake Bible* I adapted this recipe, says, "This is perhaps my favorite way to eat pound cake!" Indeed, this one stays fresh for a long time because of the tangy syrup poured over.

The Cake

2¼ cups cake or soft winter wheat flour
1 cup plus 2 tablespoons sugar
1 teaspoon salt
1½ tablespoons grated or chopped, no white attached, lemon peel

4½ tablespoons poppy seeds
1¼ cups plus 1 tablespoon unsalted butter, soft at room temperature
5 large eggs, beaten to mix
1 tablespoon vanilla

The Syrup

¾ cup sugar
¾ cup lemon juice

Grease and flour a 9- × 5- × 3-inch loaf pan, line bottom with wax paper or parchment paper, grease the paper, and flour.

Preheat oven to 350 degrees.

Make the cake: Sift together the flour, sugar, and salt into a large mixing bowl. Add the lemon peel, poppy seeds, butter, ⅓ of the beaten eggs, and the vanilla and mix together on the low speed of an electric mixer until moist. Turn up the speed and beat for 1 minute. Add another ⅓ of the eggs, scraping down the sides of the bowl, and beat for 30 seconds. Scrape the sides of the bowl again and add the remaining eggs, beating for 20 seconds more. Turn into the prepared loaf pan. Bake 1 to 1¼ hours, or until a wooden toothpick inserted in the center comes out clean.

Meanwhile, make the syrup: In a small pan combine the sugar and lemon juice over low heat, stirring until the sugar is dissolved.

Remove the cake from the oven and place pan on a wire rack. Prick top with a toothpick or needle, and brush top generously with the room temperature or warm syrup, allowing lots of it to run down and soak into the sides and bottom of the cake. Cool slightly in the pan before removing cake to rack to finish cooling. Wrap tightly with freezer plastic wrap or foil and let rest a day before serving. Will keep nearly 1 week at room temperature or in the refrigerator.

The cake freezes well.

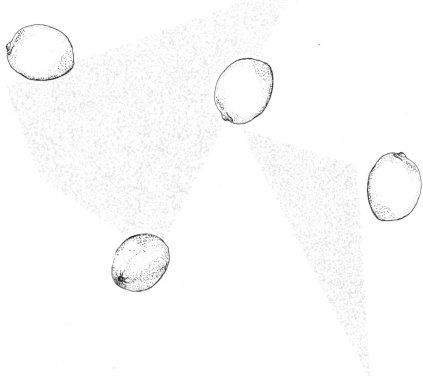

Orange Caramel Cake

MAKES ONE 2-LAYER 9-INCH CAKE

I usually make this cake ahead, then defrost and ice it on the day I plan to serve it. I've never known why Southerners say "ice" when Northerners say "frost," but it's a habit with me. The icing, Ray Overton's grandmother's recipe, is tricky to make but well worth it, requiring cooking to the soft-ball stage. The beating after that is really to prevent crystallization while the icing cools to spreading consistency. The measures for the icing are odd, but correct: less butter or less evaporated milk won't work. Finally, all the ingredients for making the layers should be at room temperature.

1 cup unsalted butter
3 cups sugar
6 eggs
2⅔ cups all-purpose flour
¼ teaspoon baking soda

1 teaspoon salt
1 (8-ounce) container sour cream
1 tablespoon vanilla or lemon extract

Ray's Orange Caramel Icing
2 cups packed light brown sugar
7 ounces evaporated milk
½ cup orange juice

9 tablespoons unsalted butter
¾ teaspoon salt
2 teaspoons vanilla
2 teaspoons grated orange peel

Preheat oven to 350 degrees. Grease and flour two 9-inch pans. Cut rounds of wax paper to fit the bottoms of the pans, grease and flour the rounds, and put them in the pans.

Beat the butter until light. Gradually beat in the sugar until the mixture is light and fluffy. Add the eggs, 1 at a time, beating well after each addition. Sift together the flour, baking soda, and salt. Mix ¼ of the flour mixture into the eggs, then ⅓ of the sour cream, and combine thoroughly. Repeat, alternating flour and sour cream, beginning and ending with the flour. Stir in the vanilla or lemon extract. Divide the batter between the prepared pans. Tap the pans lightly on the counter top several times to remove any air bubbles. Bake 25 to 35 minutes, until the cake springs back when touched. Remove the pans from the oven onto cake racks. Cool 10 minutes, then carefully remove the cakes from the pans. Remove the paper. You may freeze the layers at this point once they are thoroughly cooled. Wrap them in plastic wrap and then in foil.

Meanwhile, to make the icing, in a saucepan combine the brown sugar, milk, orange juice, butter, and salt. Bring to the boil and boil until the soft-ball stage, 238 to 239 degrees on a candy thermometer. Remove from the heat, and stir in the vanilla and orange peel. Beat on low speed with an electric mixer or stir by hand 10 to 12 minutes, until thick and creamy and nearly room temperature. The icing should be spreadable.

To ice, place long strips of wax paper on the cake plate to cover it. Place the bottom layer of the cake over the paper, strips extending beyond the cake. Reserve half the icing for the top and sides. Spread the bottom layer with a portion of the icing. Top with the remaining cake layer. Do not put too much icing in the middle or the cake will slide. Ice the top and sides. Let set and remove the strips.

Pavlova

SERVES 6 TO 8

Both Australia and New Zealand claim the honor of creating this airy, cream-filled fruit-bedazzled dessert, which has been named for the famous Russian ballerina Anna Pavlova (1885–1931).

3 egg whites
¾ cup sugar
1 tablespoon cornstarch
1½ teaspoons white vinegar or
    ¼ teaspoon cream of tartar
1 teaspoon vanilla
1 cup heavy cream, whipped
    until it holds firm peaks

3 cups sliced fresh tropical fruit
    in season—strawberries,
    bananas, kiwis, peaches,
    papayas, mangoes, or
    pineapple

Preheat oven to 250 degrees. Grease and flour a 9-inch pie plate or line a baking sheet with parchment and draw a 9-inch circle, using the plate as your guide.

Whip the egg whites until they hold stiff peaks. Beat in the sugar, 1 teaspoon at a time, until the mixture is stiff and shiny. Then, beat in the cornstarch, vinegar, and vanilla. Fill the plate with the meringue mixture, hollowing out the center slightly. Or, mound mixture in center of circle. Spread meringue out to cover circle, then make a depression in the center. Bake for 1¼ to 1½ hours, or until the meringue is very lightly browned. Cool slightly, then unmold and cool completely. (It may collapse slightly.) Just before serving, add sugar to taste to the whipped cream, add half the fruit, and fill the center of the Pavlova with it. Pile the remaining fruit on top.

Pumpkin Cheesecake

SERVES 16

Candied ginger, found in the spice section of the grocery store, gives this crust a little tang.

Lillian Marshall, former Food Editor of the *Courier-Journal/ Louisville Times*, sent me this lovely recipe. It can be made in a good food processor or by hand. This cake freezes so well, I frequently use it as the dessert for large parties or take it to covered dish suppers.

1 (6-ounce) package zwieback
    or graham crackers, crushed
    into 1½ cups fine crumbs
½ cup butter, melted
2 cups plus 2 tablespoons sugar,
    divided
1 (2-ounce) jar candied ginger,
    minced finely
4 (8-ounce) packages cream
    cheese

¼ cup flour
Grated peel of 1 lemon, no
    white attached
2 cups (16-ounce can) solid
    pack pumpkin (not pumpkin
    pie filling)
6 eggs, beaten
2 cups sour cream
⅓ cup honey

Preheat oven to 400 degrees.

Mix the zwieback crumbs with the melted butter, ⅓ cup of the sugar, and the ginger. Reserve ⅓ cup of this mixture. Press the crumbs firmly on the bottom and about a third of the way up the sides of a 9-inch springform pan. In a food processor or by hand blend the cream cheese, the remaining 1⅔ cups sugar, the flour, lemon peel, pumpkin, eggs, and ¼ cup sour cream together well; and pour gently into the pan. Bake for 15 minutes. Reduce heat to 225 degrees and bake 1½ hours. Remove the pan from the oven and spread the remaining sour cream combined with the remaining 2 tablespoons sugar on top. Sprinkle the reserved crumbs over the sour cream. Return the pan to the oven, and bake 10 minutes. Cool completely in the pan on a rack. Refrigerate overnight and remove the cake from the pan the next day. Drizzle the honey over the top before taking the cake to the table. The recipe can be halved, but use a 9-inch pie plate and reduce the second baking time to only 1 hour.

Quick Yeast Galette

SERVES 8

I wish I could remember where this recipe came from! Over the years I've adapted it, using it when "people time" is short in the kitchen. This is a very popular, delicious dessert. I would urge you to use bread flour as any other flour will not create the desired result.

1 package active dry yeast
½ cup sugar
6 tablespoons water (105 to 115 degrees)
½ cup unsalted butter, softened
1 egg

1 teaspoon grated lemon peel
½ teaspoon salt
1¾ cups bread flour
Sliced fresh peaches or berries (optional)

Dissolve the yeast and 2 tablespoons of the sugar in warm water. Either in a food processor or by hand, beat together the yeast mixture, ¼ cup of the butter, the egg, lemon peel, and salt. Gradually add enough flour to make a soft dough. Turn the dough out onto a floured board and knead it until it is no longer sticky, 10 to 15 minutes by hand, or 1 minute in the food processor. Place in a greased bowl or plastic bag and turn. Cover and let rise in a warm place until doubled in size, about ¾ to 1 hour. Punch the dough down and turn out onto a floured surface. Knead lightly. Roll out into a 15-inch round and place on a greased 14-inch pizza pan. Form a rim around the edge. Spread all over with the remaining ¼ cup soft butter and sprinkle with the 6 tablespoons sugar. Let stand in a warm place 20 minutes. Preheat oven to 500 degrees.

Bake in the middle of the oven for 6 minutes, or until golden brown. Serve hot, cut into pie-shaped wedges and serve with the peaches as a garnish if desired.

3-Layer Chocolate Cake with Margaret Ann's Buttercream

MAKES ONE 9-INCH CAKE

This is a decadent cake. The use of margerine in addition to butter in the buttercream makes it especially easy to work with.

1½ cups water
1 cup unsweetened non-
    alkalized cocoa
5 large eggs
1 tablespoon vanilla
3½ cups cake flour

2 cups sugar
1 teaspoon baking soda
1 teaspoon salt
1½ cups unsalted butter,
    softened

Margaret Ann's Buttercream
6 egg whites
1½ cups sugar
1 pound 2 ounces butter,
    softened

¼ pound margarine, softened
3 ounces bittersweet or
    semisweet chocolate, melted
    and cooled

Preheat oven to 350 degrees. Grease and flour three 9-inch cake pans. Cut rounds of wax paper to fit the pans, grease and flour the rounds, and put in the pans.

Boil the water and whisk into the cocoa. Mix until smooth. Set aside to cool.

Combine eggs, about ½ cup of the cocoa mixture, and the vanilla. In a mixer bowl, combine flour, sugar, baking soda, and salt and mix together on low speed for 30 seconds to blend. Add butter and remainder of cocoa-water mixture. Blend on low speed to incorporate liquids, then beat on medium speed for 1½ minutes.

Gradually beat the egg mixture in 3 batches into the flour mixture, scraping down the sides of the bowl as necessary. Pour the batter into the prepared pans, filling each about ½ full. Bake 20 to 30 minutes, or until cake springs back when lightly touched in the center. Let the cakes cool in the pans on a rack for 10 minutes. Turn out of pans, gently remove the paper liners, and turn upright. Let cool completely.

Make the buttercream: Combine the egg whites and sugar in a mixer bowl and set bowl in a larger one of warm water. Stir until sugar has dissolved. Remove bowl from warm water and beat at high speed on mixer until mixture forms stiff peaks. Gradually beat in softened butter and margarine, 1 to 2 tablespoons at a time, at medium-high speed. Mixture may look slightly curdled before you have added all the fat, but should smooth out as you continue to beat and all the fat is incorporated. Add the melted chocolate and mix until well combined. Makes enough buttercream to fill, frost, and decorate 3 layers. Spread the buttercream among the layers. Frost top and sides, piping decoratively as desired.

Buttercream freezes well but must be brought completely to room temperature before using. You may want to beat it a minute or two to fluff it up.

Upside Down Gingerbread

MAKES ONE 9-INCH CAKE

I'm a "gingerbread freak" and I love upside down cakes the way some people love chocolate. I think with this one it's the brown sugar and nut topping.

The Topping
¼ cup unsalted butter
½ cup packed dark brown sugar
1 (16-ounce) can pear halves,
  drained

6 to 8 pecan or walnut halves

The Gingerbread
1 cup flour
½ teaspoon baking soda
¼ teaspoon salt
2 teaspoons cinnamon
1 teaspoon ground ginger
¼ teaspoon ground nutmeg

¼ teaspoon ground cloves
1 egg, beaten to mix
½ cup dark brown sugar
6 tablespoons molasses
½ cup buttermilk
¼ cup shortening, melted

The Yogurt Sauce (optional)
½ cup heavy cream
1 cup plain yogurt

Preheat oven to 350 degrees.

To make the topping, in a saucepan melt the butter, add the sugar, and stir 1 or 2 minutes over low heat to make a smooth syrup. Spoon into a 8-inch round or 8-inch square cake pan. Arrange the pears in the pan, cut side down. Put the nuts in the gaps.

To make the gingerbread, in a large bowl sift the flour with the baking soda, salt, cinnamon, ginger, nutmeg, and cloves. Mix together the egg, sugar, molasses, buttermilk, and cooled shortening. Make a well in the flour, add the molasses mixture, and beat hard for 1 minute, or until the batter is very smooth. Pour the batter over the topping. Bake 40 to 45 minutes, or until a skewer inserted in the center comes out clean. Turn the gingerbread out onto a platter while still warm, and serve with the yogurt sauce. Meanwhile, make the yogurt sauce. Whip the heavy cream until it holds a soft shape. Fold in the yogurt.

Another Sauce

- **You could substitute plain whipped cream or cream cheese mixed with cream if you prefer. For cream cheese sauce, beat ¾ cup light cream into 3 ounces cream cheese to form a smooth sauce that pours easily. If you like, sweeten with a little sugar.**

Almond Macaroons

MAKES 24

In the great debate between almond and coconut macaroons, I cast my vote for the almond ones. If you don't have a pastry bag, take a heavy freezer plastic bag, snip off the end, and use that to pipe the mixture.

6½ ounces (1½ cups) ground blanched almonds
¾ cup sugar

2 egg whites
½ teaspoon vanilla

Preheat oven to 350 degrees. Line a baking sheet with wax paper.

Stir together the almonds and sugar. Beat the egg whites until they nearly form a peak. Then, beat them into the almonds to make a paste just stiff enough to pipe. Beat in the vanilla. Using a pastry bag with a large plain tip, pipe 2-inch rounds onto the wax paper. Bake until the macaroons begin to brown, 15 to 20 minutes. Carefully pour a little water on the baking sheet under the paper to loosen.

The macaroons freeze in an airtight container.

Chinese Fortune Cookies

MAKES 5 DOZEN COOKIES

Throw out any preconceived ideas of how these should look and concentrate on how they taste. They are light, crisp, wonderful. I think it is so much fun to make up the messages that go inside. It's a sweet way to communicate! If the cookies harden before you have a chance to fold them and enclose the messages, return the cookies to the oven for a moment and they will resoften.

5 egg whites
1½ cups sugar
¼ teaspoon salt
1 cup unsalted butter, melted
    and cooled slightly

1 cup all-purpose flour
½ teaspoon almond extract
5 dozen messages

Preheat oven to 375 degrees.

Place the egg whites in a bowl. Add the sugar and salt and stir until the sugar has dissolved and the mixture is thick and shiny. Gradually beat the butter into the egg white mixture. Stir in the flour and add the almond extract. Using a measuring spoon, drop by teaspoonfuls, well apart, onto a greased or non-stick baking sheet. Bake 1 sheet at a time for 7 or 8 minutes, or until the edges are lightly browned. Working quickly, place a message in the center of each cookie, and fold in half while still warm. Place the still-warm folded cookies in cool muffin tins to shape. Cool completely before storing.

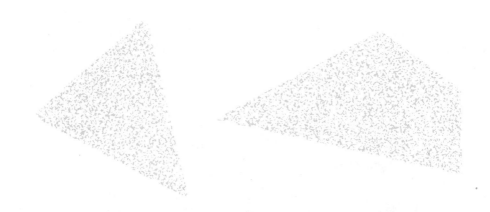

Crisp Florentines

Florentines are frequently sandwiched with melted chocolate. These crisp cookies are a wonderful treat. They may also be shaped into cylinders to use as cornucopias for fresh berries. If you desire a perfect round rather than a lacy edge, remove the cookie sheet from the oven after 5 minutes, and, using a cookie cutter, push the edges of each cookie inside the cutter. Return to oven for 5 to 6 minutes until lightly browned. Lastly, it's easier to chop the candied fruits if sprinkled with the flour before chopping!

3 tablespoons unsalted butter
½ cup heavy cream
½ cup sugar
⅛ teaspoon salt
6 tablespoons blanched almonds, pecans, or hazelnuts, finely chopped

¾ cup candied storebought or homemade orange peel, chopped into ¼-inch pieces (page 298)
¼ cup candied cherries, quartered or chopped into ¼-inch pieces
⅓ cup flour

Preheat oven to 350 degrees.

In a saucepan heat the butter, cream, sugar, and salt together until the mixture comes to the boil. Remove from the heat. Stir in the nuts, candied peel, cherries, and flour. Drop by teaspoonfuls, 2 inches apart, onto a well-greased cookie sheet. Bake for 10 minutes, or until lightly brown around the edges. Let cool slightly on the cookie sheet, enough to prevent tearing, then remove and let cool on a wire rack until crisp.

The cookies freeze in layers separated by wax paper in an airtight container.

Double Chocolate, Chocolate Chip Sandwich Cookies

MAKES 20 SMALL OR 9 LARGE SANDWICHES

These two-layer cookies make a very rich, special dessert, and warrant a knife and fork for fine dining.

- **In addition to making a chocolate filling, this recipe for *ganache* could be used warmed, as a poured icing over a cake or roulade; at room temperature, as a dipped coating for candies and fruits; and chilled, as a center for truffles.**

¼ cup unsalted butter
1 (1-ounce) square unsweetened chocolate
¾ cup all-purpose flour
¼ teaspoon baking powder
¼ teaspoon baking soda
1 teaspoon salt
3 tablespoons packed light brown sugar

3 tablespoons sugar
½ teaspoon vanilla
¼ cup sour cream or buttermilk
1 large egg, lightly beaten
¼ cup finely chopped pecans or walnuts
½ cup semisweet chocolate mini-chips or chocolate chunks

Chocolate Ganache Filling
¾ cup semisweet or milk chocolate chips or chunks
¼ cup unsalted butter

¼ cup plus 1 tablespoon heavy cream

Preheat oven to 375 degrees.

In a small pan over low heat melt the butter and chocolate together.

Meanwhile, mix the flour, baking powder, baking soda, and salt together. Cool the chocolate and pour into the bowl of a mixer. Beat in both sugars, the vanilla, sour cream or buttermilk, and egg. Add the flour mixture, nuts, and chocolate chips and mix well. Grease cookie sheets. For 3-inch round cookies, drop the batter by teaspoonfuls onto the cookie sheet, leaving about 2 inches in between each cookie. Bake at 375 degrees for 8 to 10 minutes. Do not let edges brown. For 4½-inch round cookies, drop the batter by tablespoons, leaving about 2 inches between each cookie. Baking time will be 12 to 15 minutes. Use a spatula to transfer the cookies to racks to cool.

To make the ganache filling, melt the chocolate and butter in a small pan over low heat or in the microwave. Gradually whisk in the cream. Let stand at room temperature, stirring occasionally, for ½ hour or longer, until barely thickened. Or place the bowl in ice water if you are in a hurry, but don't let the filling harden.

Turn half the cookies upside down on a large piece of wax paper. Spread a tablespoonful on each of the turned cookies. Quickly cover with the remaining cookies, right sides up, and press gently down to spread the filling to the edges. Let stand at room temperature or chill briefly until the filling is set.

Drop Sugar Cookies

MAKES ABOUT 6 DOZEN COOKIES

This simple little cookie is child's play to make, but still an all-time favorite. Buttery and delicious. May be decorated with sprinkles, cinnamon sugar, or as you desire.

4 cups all-purpose flour
1 tablespoon baking powder
½ teaspoon salt
1 teaspoon ground cardamom
    or freshly grated nutmeg
1½ cups unsalted butter,
    softened

1½ cups sugar
2 eggs
2 tablespoons milk
2 teaspoons vanilla
Sprinkles (optional)

Preheat oven to 350 degrees.
    Mix the flour, baking powder, salt, cardamom, and nutmeg and

set aside. In a bowl beat the butter and sugar until light and fluffy. Beat in the eggs, milk, and vanilla. Stir in the flour mixture just until blended. Drop by level tablespoonfuls onto 2 lightly greased baking sheets. Flatten slightly with a fork. Decorate with sprinkles, if desired. Bake 12 to 15 minutes, or until edges are lightly browned. Cool on a wire rack.

The cookies freeze in an airtight container.

Nearly Brownie Cookies

MAKES 50 TO 60 COOKIES

Some people call these crisp-on-the-outside, chewy-on-the-inside, brownie-like small cookies mulattoes. They are so good it doesn't matter what you call them—but I hereby put the name to rest!

8 ounces semisweet chocolate	¾ cup sugar
3 tablespoons butter	½ teaspoon vanilla
¼ cup all-purpose flour	1 cup (6-ounces) semisweet
¼ teaspoon baking powder	chocolate bits
⅛ teaspoon salt	2¼ cups (8 ounces) pecans,
2 eggs	chopped coarse

Preheat oven to 350 degrees. Line cookie sheets with parchment paper or aluminum foil.

Melt the semisweet chocolate and the butter in a small pan over low heat, stirring until smooth, or in the microwave.

Sift together the flour, baking powder, and salt. In a bowl beat the eggs, sugar, and vanilla at high speed until well combined. Slowly beat in the cooled chocolate, then the dry ingredients, until just blended but smooth. Stir in the chocolate bits and the nuts. Drop by heaping teaspoonfuls, 1 inch apart, onto prepared cookie sheets. Bake 10 to 12 minutes, taking care to not overbake. Remove from oven and cool on a rack. May be made ahead several days or frozen.

Caramels

MAKES EIGHTY-ONE 1-INCH PIECES

There's no need to spend all that money on candy at the movies—make your own caramels for a very special treat.

1 cup sugar
1 cup butter
1 cup dark corn syrup

1 (14-ounce) can condensed milk
1 teaspoon vanilla

In a saucepan bring the sugar, butter, and syrup to the boil, stirring. Boil 4 minutes without stirring. Remove the pan from the heat and add the milk. Mix well. Return the pan to the heat and cook at a medium-low boil for 30 minutes, or until mixture reaches 238 degrees on a candy thermometer. Stir constantly. Remove from the heat and stir in the vanilla. Pour into a buttered 9-inch square pan. Cool in pan for 2 hours. Cut with a very sharp serrated knife into 1-inch pieces, and wrap each piece in wax paper.

Mother's Chocolate Cream Fudge

MAKES SIXTEEN 1½-INCH SQUARES

This is a perfect old-fashioned fudge, ever so slightly grainy, as it should be. It will be gone before you know it. Mother told me she got this recipe from a 1930 cookbook her mother gave her and that it is the recipe my sister and I made when we were little girls. Everyone who eats it has a story to tell about someone special who made this for them when they were young. The original recipe called for nutmeats—an old-time term for chopped nuts. The corn syrup prevents it from crystallization and graininess.

3 cups sugar
¼ cup corn syrup
3 (1-ounce) squares
    unsweetened chocolate
¼ teaspoon salt

1 cup evaporated milk
1 teaspoon vanilla
½ cup roughly chopped pecans
    or walnuts

Butter an 8-inch square pan. Mix together the sugar, corn syrup, chocolate, salt, and milk in a heavy pan. Bring to the boil, and boil to the soft-ball stage, 238 degrees on a candy thermometer. Or drop a little of the liquid into cold water to see if it forms a soft ball. Cool until lukewarm, add the vanilla and nuts, and beat until creamy. Pour into prepared pan. When cool, cut into 1½-inch squares.

The fudge freezes, wrapped in plastic wrap and aluminum foil.

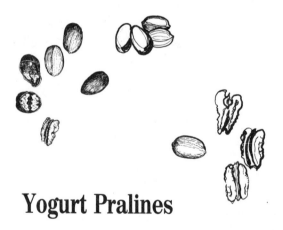

Yogurt Pralines

MAKES TWENTY-FOUR 1½-INCH CANDIES

A candy thermometer is a real asset when making this low-cal version of a Southern favorite. It's not the yogurt that makes these lower in calories than usual pralines; it is the reduced amounts of butter and sugar. There are still 162 calories per praline—worth it! Be sure to make these pralines in a large enough saucepan (about 5 quarts) as the mixture bubbles and increases in volume a great deal. And work quickly when dropping the candy onto wax paper; otherwise you will lose some of the creamy consistency and the mixture will become grainy and unmanageable.

1¾ cups sugar	2 tablespoons corn syrup
½ teaspoon baking soda	1½ teaspoons vanilla
¾ cup plain low-fat yogurt, drained	2 tablespoons unsalted butter
	1½ cups pecan halves

Mix the sugar and baking soda together in a heavy 5-quart (12-inch) saucepan. Blend in the yogurt and the corn syrup. Cook over low heat for about 5 minutes until the sugar is dissolved. Bring to the boil, reduce heat to low, and simmer about 10 minutes until the foamy mixture no longer increases in volume. Stir to combine caramel mixture. Simmer 15 to 20 minutes more, without stirring, until the syrup reaches 238 degrees on a candy thermometer, or forms a soft ball when a drop is put in cold water. Remove the pan from heat. Stir in the vanilla and butter until well incorporated. Add the pecans and stir until well distributed and mixture becomes thick and creamy. Allow candy to cool. Whip until mixture becomes opaque and creamy. Drop by tablespoonfuls onto wax paper. Cool. Store in airtight containers.

Fruit Finales

Chocolate-Dipped Fruits

MAKES 1⅓ CUPS SAUCE FOR 3 CUPS FRUIT

Everyone loves chocolate-dipped fruits—both as party food and as snacks. The chocolate makes you feel that you've had something decadent and it is just enough to make you feel good but not guilty. I use dried apricots, pineapple, and prunes as alternatives to fresh strawberries. The recipe may be halved.

8 ounces semisweet chocolate
¼ cup butter
¼ cup light corn syrup

3 cups assorted dried fruits or fresh strawberries

Heat the chocolate, butter, and corn syrup either in a heavy pan over very low heat or in the microwave until melted; stir until smooth. Remove from the heat, and beat with a wooden spoon until cool but still pourable. (If in a rush, cool over ice.) Dip the fruit halfway into the chocolate. Place on wax paper and refrigerate overnight. Remove from the paper. Store in one layer in a tightly covered container in the refrigerator.

Unbelievably Easy, Indestructible Raspberry-Peach Mousse

SERVES 10

This is a ridiculously easy mousse for the raves it gets! The frozen raspberries and peaches help set the gelatin mixture. Arrange the ingredients so you can work quickly; the gelatin sets rapidly. By the time the fruit is broken up and separated, the mousse is firm enough to keep the fruit from sinking. This is especially attractive chilled and served in stemmed glasses. Avoid using a deep mold as the heavy fruit may crack the mousse.

Once we multiplied this recipe by three to serve a crowd. The last portion set up on us in lumps, so we melted it in the microwave, stirred it over ice until cold, and put it back in the mold. It worked fine! Now that's indestructible.

2 (3-ounce) packages peach-
    flavored gelatin (Jell-O)
2 cups water
1 cup sour cream
1 pint frozen peach ice cream

2 (10-ounce) packages frozen
    whole raspberries with juice
½ (16-ounce) package frozen
    sliced peaches
1 tablespoon lemon juice

For Decoration
2 cups heavy cream
1½ teaspoons vanilla extract

½ cup sugar

Set out 10 stemmed glasses or oil a 2-quart mold or clean and dry a large glass bowl.

Place the gelatin in a large bowl. Bring the water to the boil. Add it to the gelatin, stirring well to dissolve. Whisk in the sour cream until smooth. Cut the still-frozen ice cream into 12 pieces and quickly add them to the mixture, stirring until melted and smooth. Toss the frozen raspberries and the peaches with the lemon juice and add to the mixture. Stir until cold. Quickly pour the mousse into the stemmed glasses, the oiled mold, or the large glass bowl. Refrigerate for at least 3 hours or up to 3 days. Serve in the glasses or deep bowl, or unmold if necessary.

To unmold, oil a serving plate. Tilt the mousse in its mold and pull it gently away from the sides to catch an air bubble. Place the oiled plate over the mold, then invert. Give a quick shake and remove the mold. Never use hot water to unmold a cream dessert.

Whip the cream with the vanilla and the sugar. Decorate the mousse using a pastry bag or plastic bag and a star tip.

Julia Child's Orange Blueberry Bowl

SERVES 8

I use a large glass bowl for this striking, intensely colored strata of fresh fruit. The extra candied peel can be used for many other recipes, such as the Crisp Florentines (page 289). Storebought orange peel is hard to find. The peel is a side benefit of the flavored sugar syrup. The peel may be kept, refrigerated, for some time, so I usually make several batches at one time when navel oranges are at their prime.

The candied orange peel puts this dessert "over the top." This lovely recipe is so similar to one of Julia Child's in *Julia Child & More Company* we decided to name it after her. She and her books are always inspirations, and leave lasting impressions.

5 or 6 large thin skinned navel
   oranges
2½ cups sugar
2 tablespoons corn syrup

¾ cups water
1 pint blueberries, fresh or
   frozen

Remove the orange part of the peel of the oranges, and scrape off all the white. Cut the peel into very fine (⅛-inch) julienne strips. Drop in boiling water, lower heat, and simmer 10 to 15 minutes, until tender. Drain.

Meanwhile, combine 2 cups of the sugar, the corn syrup, and the water in a heavy pan. Cook over low heat until the sugar is dissolved, then bring to a boil. Boil over high heat for a few minutes until the bubbles are very big and the syrup has reached the soft-ball stage, 238 degrees on a candy thermometer. (The syrup will form a soft ball when dropped in cold water.) Add the drained peel to the syrup, return to the boil, and boil slowly for several minutes until the syrup has thickened again. Remove the peel, cool on a rack, and place in an airtight container. Let the syrup cool. The syrup may be stored indefinitely in the refrigerator. If it is too thick or even hard when it cools, add a half cup of water, return it to the boil, and boil a few minutes until it liquifies. Cool.

A few hours or up to a day before serving, slice the scraped oranges. Place them with their juice in a plastic bag or covered bowl. Add enough syrup to cover and refrigerate them. Defrost the blueberries if necessary. Toss them with several tablespoons of sugar if necessary, cover, and refrigerate. Up to 4 hours before serving, arrange a layer or two of orange slices in the bottom of a glass bowl. Spoon a little of the orange peel syrup over them. Sprinkle a layer of the berries on top of the oranges. Repeat. Top with a generous portion of the candied orange peel. Cover and refrigerate until serving time. Save the rest of the syrup and peel for another time.

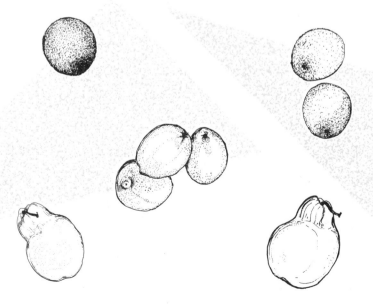

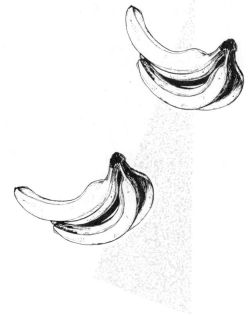

Iceberg Bananas

SERVES 4

Not only are these refreshing, tasty, and very easy to make, but they are great to do when the bananas are turning brown and you don't have time to eat them. I frequently peel bananas, wrap them in plastic wrap, and leave them several weeks before I use them. Sometimes I just want a little something sweet at night and this fills the bill. Other times it's a good finish for lunch. The yogurt does not coat and freeze the same way the cream does, but it's fine.

4 bananas
½ cup sugar
2 teaspoons cinnamon

1 cup heavy cream or plain
low-fat yogurt

Peel the bananas and wrap them tightly in plastic wrap. Freeze at least 4 hours. Mix the sugar and cinnamon and set aside. When ready to serve, slice the bananas by hand or in a food processor with the slicing blade. Place them in individual serving bowls or shallow glasses. Sprinkle with the cinnamon sugar, and slowly pour the heavy cream over the bananas, coating each piece. The cream freezes almost instantly when it hits the bananas. Serve immediately.

Red-Glazed Poached Pears

SERVES 4 TO 6

The secret to perfectly poached pears is in having the right pan. It should be small enough so the pears can be covered by a modest amount of wine or juice and so that they do not bob onto their sides, yet be large enough so that they don't touch. Always buy a few more pears than you need to be sure the pan is filled properly. (If you can't get the pears to stay still any other way, use toothpicks to join them.) They are a beautiful red when done, with the darker red of the reduced syrup glistening over them. Different pears will cook in varying amounts of time. D'Anjous take 1½ hours; Boscs, about 1¼ hours.

4 to 6 pears
3 to 6 cups dry red wine or
    cranberry juice
1 stick cinnamon

1 cup sugar (optional)
½ cup heavy whipping cream,
    whipped

Peel the pears, leaving the stems on. Cut the bottom of each pear flat, so it will stand upright. Place the pears in a straight-sided, narrow, heavy pan, standing up, without touching one another or the sides of the pan, leaving only very little extra room. Pour in enough wine to completely immerse the pears. Add the cinnamon stick. Bring to the boil. Reduce heat to a simmer. Cover and poach until the pears are tender. Carefully remove the pears and place them upright on a serving platter or dish. Remove the cinnamon stick.

Taste the wine and add sugar if necessary. When the sugar is dissolved, bring the wine to the boil, and boil until well reduced, very thick and glossy. (You may want to transfer the wine to a large skillet to speed up the reduction.) Drizzle the pears with the glaze. It will cling to them with a dark red luster. Serve hot or chilled. May be made several days in advance if serving cold.

To garnish with the cream, use a traditional pastry bag or cut a small slit in the corner of a plastic bag. Place the whipped cream inside the bag and push out the cream in ribbons onto each pear. Pipe around the pears, then pull a fork through it to make a pattern.

Strawberry Mousse

SERVES 4 TO 6

It is rare to see one of these beautiful, quivering soft desserts any more as so many people are afraid to make them.

To Make a Gelatin Mousse

- **Powdered gelatin is softened in liquid, causing it to swell up like a small sponge, before being melted over low heat to a liquid.**
- **The beaten egg mixture and whipped cream should be the same texture when folded together.**
- **It is best to get the cream whipped ahead of time, so that it doesn't have to be done when the gelatin is added, increasing the risk of the gelatin setting prematurely.**
- **Cream-based gelatin mixtures should not be unmolded with the help of hot water. Instead gently pull the mousse away from the edges with your fingers to create an air pocket.**

1 pint strawberries, hulled	1 egg yolk
1 lemon, juiced	6 tablespoons sugar
½ cup water	¾ cup heavy cream, whipped
2 envelopes gelatin	until it holds soft peaks
2 eggs	

For Decoration

½ cup heavy cream, stiffly whipped	4 to 6 strawberries

Lightly oil a 1-quart ring mold, charlotte mold, or bowl. Purée the strawberries in a food processor or blender. They should yield at least 1 cup purée. Set aside. Place the lemon juice, water, and gelatin in a very small, heatproof pan, 1-cup metal measure, or microwave dish and let stand 5 minutes, or until spongy.

Mix the eggs, egg yolk, and sugar in a heatproof bowl. Beat them with an electric mixer or a whisk over nearly boiling water until the mixture is thick and light in color and the whisk leaves a light trail. Remove from the heat and continue to beat until the mixture is cool.

Dissolve the gelatin over low heat or in the microwave, making sure all the granules are dissolved. Stir the liquid gelatin into the egg yolk mixture. Add the purée. Place the entire mixture over a pan of ice water and stir with a rubber spatula until the mixture is at the point of setting. Fold in the softly whipped cream. Pour the mousse into the prepared mold. Cover and chill until set, 3 to 4 hours or overnight.

Lightly oil a serving plate. Tilt the mousse in its mold and pull it gently away from the sides to catch an air bubble. Place the oiled plate over the mold, then invert. Give a quick shake and remove the mold. Put the stiffly whipped cream into a pastry bag or plastic bag fitted with a star tip and decorate with rosettes of cream. Place the strawberries on top. May be made up to 1 day in advance.

Strawberry and Orange Dessert

SERVES 2 TO 4

I serve Almond Macaroons (page 287) with this simple dessert. Strawberries and oranges seem to be more and more available all year round, but they also seem to need some attention to up their flavor and sweetness.

1 pint ripe strawberries, hulled and halved

1 medium navel orange, peeled, halved, and sliced thinly

2 tablespoons orange juice

2 tablespoons sweet vermouth (optional) or grape juice

3 teaspoons sugar (to taste)

Put the strawberries and oranges in a bowl and mix well. Mix together the orange juice and sweet vermouth if using and drizzle over the fruit mixture. Stir to mix. Check to see if the berries are sweet enough for your taste; if not, add sugar. Cover the bowl and chill in the refrigerator for 2 hours before serving. Stir gently several times to blend the flavors.

Summer Pudding

SERVES 6 TO 8

Summer pudding is a dense, richly colored, English cold pudding. I usually make it when there is an abundance of fruit for a low price at the height of the season. It's very easy to prepare.

4 cups raspberries or blueberries
1 cup sugar
2 tablespoons finely chopped
  crystallized ginger, plus
  additional for topping

16 to 20 slices white bread
2 cups whipped cream or
  Crème Fraîche (page 306)

Place the fruit, sugar, and ginger in a heavy saucepan. Bring to the boil, reduce the heat, and simmer slowly over low heat until the fruit is soft and has released its juices. Remove the crusts from the bread and tightly line a 1½-quart bowl with it. Add the fruit, reserving some of the juices. Cover the fruit with a layer of bread. Place a plate on top of the bread in the bowl. Put a 2- to 3-pound weight on the plate. Refrigerate overnight. Remove the weight and plate, and run a knife around the edges to loosen. Invert the pudding onto a serving plate. Pour the remaining juices over the pudding and top with the additional crystallized ginger. Serve with cream or crème fraîche.

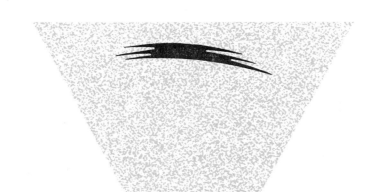

Miscellaneous Decadence

Caramel Sauce

MAKES 2 CUPS

Caramel can be tricky because any sugar granules that remain can cause the boiling syrup to crystallize. Be sure the sugar syrup is clear and all the sugar has dissolved before the mixture boils. Avoid stirring after the sugar is dissolved, and, when you do stir, always use a clean wooden spoon. Brush the sides of the pan with a wet pastry brush whenever granules form to keep the sides free of granules. Keep a large pan of cold water by the side of the stove, and insert the pan of caramel if it starts to turn brown too rapidly. For a rich change, use 1 cup heavy cream in place of the second half-cup water.

1 cup sugar
1 cup water, divided

In a heavy saucepan, dissolve the sugar in ½ cup of the water over low heat, without boiling. Brush down the sides of the pan with a clean, wet pastry brush. When all the sugar has dissolved, bring the syrup to the boil and cook steadily to a rich brown, caramel color. It changes color quickly towards the end! Remove from the heat and place the pan in a large pan of cold water to stop the cooking. Cover the hand holding the pan with a cloth and quickly pour in ½ cup warm water. Return to the heat and bring mixture back to the boil, stirring, to dissolve the caramel; pour into a sauceboat and let cool. Pour over oranges, cooked pears, or serve with cream puffs! Keeps indefinitely in the refrigerator.

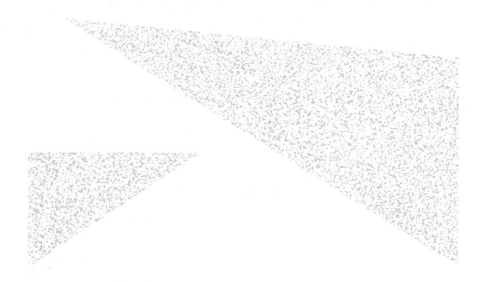

Crème Fraîche

MAKES 4 CUPS

2 cups sour cream
2 cups heavy whipping cream

Whisk together the sour cream and cream. Leave at room temperature for a few hours or overnight, until thick. Cover and refrigerate until needed.

Ginger Ice Cream

MAKES 2 QUARTS

Homemade ice creams are a favorite of mine. I offer this rich, smooth, creamy recipe in hopes the objections to lightly cooked custards will be worked out to everyone's satisfaction. Heavy cream is higher in butter fat than whipped cream, so it makes a richer ice cream. Be sure to use a large pan to boil the milk, so it doesn't boil over. Do not boil the custard or it will curdle. Usually it thickens by the time the eggs are at 180 degrees. The foam should subside by the time the custard is done.

4 cups milk
10 egg yolks
1½ cups sugar
5 tablespoons chopped candied
    ginger

1½ cups heavy cream, whipped
    until it holds soft peaks

In a large saucepan bring the milk to the boil. In another saucepan, beat the egg yolks with the sugar until thick and light. Quickly whisk in all the hot milk without whisking too much foam and return to the heat. Heat gently, stirring constantly with a wooden spoon, until the custard thickens slightly and the mixture is at 180 degrees on a candy thermometer. If you draw your finger across the back of the spoon, it will leave a clear trail.

Remove the custard from the heat and strain it into a bowl. Stir in the chopped candied ginger, and let custard cool. Pour into an ice cream churn freezer. After about 5 minutes or when the ice cream is partially set, add the lightly whipped cream and continue freezing in the churn freezer until fully set. Remove the dasher, taste the ice cream; stir in the ginger at the bottom of the freezer if desired. Replace lid, cover lid with aluminum foil, wrap the churn in towels, and let the ice cream set ½ hour in the freezer to cure.

Hot Chocolate Soufflé

SERVES 4 TO 6

Soufflés are not difficult to make or magical, but they seem that way to the uninitiated. Guests are always thrilled by them. The trick is to avoid overcooking them as the bubbles will burst and the soufflé will fall. An undercooked soufflé, on the other hand, may be removed from the oven and served, then placed back in the oven if need be. It is important to have serving plates ready and the guests eagerly awaiting the soufflé.

To Make a Soufflé

- **A soufflé base may be made a day or two in advance, and baked when ready to serve. Refrigerate if keeping more than an hour, and try to bring it back to room temperature before baking. If made ahead more than a few hours, use one more egg white to assure volume. Placing the soufflé dish in a hot metal pan in the oven will give the rise a boost. Be sure to remove the top rack from the oven so the soufflé may rise.**

Just after I received my Advanced Certificate from the London Cordon Bleu, I went to Majorca, Spain, where I was asked to be chef of a restaurant. Like a fool, I accepted. I'd never worked in a restaurant and didn't even have a cookbook with me. One of the owners had a cookbook by Michael Field, so I adapted this recipe from one of his for chocolate soufflé and became known for it throughout the island! Over the years I've changed the recipe and added the sauce.

2½ tablespoons unsalted butter, at room temperature
5½ tablespoons sugar, divided between the base and the whites
1 tablespoon cornstarch

½ cup milk
½ cup semisweet chocolate bits
4 egg yolks
6 egg whites
Confectioners' sugar

Chocolate Sauce
½ cup heavy cream
3 heaping tablespoons semisweet chocolate bits

Preheat oven to 350 degrees. Butter a 1½-quart soufflé dish and coat it with some of the sugar. Make a paper collar, and butter and sugar it, too.

Place the cornstarch in a heavy pan. Slowly add the milk, stirring until smooth. Bring to the boil, stirring. Off the heat, add the chocolate to the cornstarch mixture with 2 tablespoons butter and 3 tablespoons of the sugar. Stir until the butter and chocolate are melted, putting back over low heat if necessary. Remove from the heat, and stir in the egg yolks, 1 at a time. May be prepared ahead to this point and covered with plastic wrap.

Whisk the egg whites until soft peaks form. Fold in 2 tablespoons sugar, and beat to stiff, shiny peaks. Stir 3 or 4 tablespoons of the egg white mixture into the soufflé base to lighten it, then fold this mixture into the egg whites.

Pour the mixture into the prepared soufflé dish. Smooth the surface with a spatula. May be prepared ahead to this point. Refrigerate if holding more than 1 hour. Bring back to room temperature before cooking.

One half hour before serving, place the soufflé on a metal pan in the lower third of the hot oven. Bake for 25 minutes for a soft center, or 30 to 35 minutes for a firmer one. Serve at once sprinkled with the Confectioners' sugar and accompanied by the sauce.

As the soufflé bakes, prepare the sauce by heating the cream in a heavy pan or in the microwave. When hot, add the chocolate and cook until the chocolate is melted and smooth. Set aside until needed. Will keep in the refrigerator 1 or 2 weeks, covered. Reheat over low heat or in the microwave if necessary.

Parisian Soufflé Omelet

SERVES 2 TO 4

My first day in Paris I ate this puffy, nearly soufflé omelet, filled with wild strawberries. I was overwhelmed and thrilled. It was the perfect end to a perfect meal in a beautiful park restaurant a block from the Champs Elysées.

Neither a soufflé nor an omelet, this is light as a soufflé, looks like an omelet, and tastes delicious with just simple jam inside. It takes just minutes to make and is very easy for something so special! Fill it with your choice of sweets. Use an 8-inch omelet pan and 2 or 3 metal skewers.

- **If you want an alternate sweet filling for the omelet, use fresh sliced strawberries or fresh peaches mixed with 1 tablespoon of warmed red currant jelly. For a savory filling, omit the sugar in the base and substitute ½ cup grated Cheddar cheese, or ½ cup goat cheese, or sautéed mushrooms, or a crisp fresh vegetable of your choice.**

4 egg yolks
1 tablespoon sugar
2 tablespoons cream
4 egg whites
1 tablespoon butter

¼ cup raspberry or strawberry jam, melted
2 tablespoons Confectioners' sugar for sprinkling

Preheat oven to 400 degrees.

In a bowl beat the egg yolks with the sugar until thick and light. Stir in the cream. In another bowl beat the egg whites to hold stiff peaks. Fold the yolk mixture into the whites with a rubber spatula or metal spoon. Heat the butter in an 8-inch omelet pan until foaming, then add the omelet base. Cook over moderate heat 45 to 60 seconds to brown the bottom. Do not stir. Put the pan in the preheated oven and bake until the top is set, about 5 minutes. Spread the omelet quickly with the warmed, melted jam, slide onto a warm platter, and fold the omelet in half with a metal spatula. Heat the metal skewers in the flame of a gas burner or under the broiler until red hot. Sprinkle the omelet with the Confectioners' sugar and with the hot skewers mark a lattice-type pattern across the top. This gives a traditional finish and a pleasant taste of caramel. Serve at once.

Lime Butter

MAKES 1 CUP

Lime butter is rich, fattening, sinful, and wonderful with a lovely taste of lime. Its high acid content allows it to keep indefinitely in the refrigerator. Thin with whipping cream or use as is to fill puff pastry or cream puffs. It also makes an excellent hostess gift, jarred with a bow on top.

1 cup sugar
½ cup unsalted butter
3 eggs, beaten to mix together
2 tablespoons flour

3 limes, juiced and peel, no white attached, grated (you should have 3 tablespoons rind and ½ cup juice)

Place the sugar, butter, eggs, flour, lime juice, and grated peel in a heavy saucepan. Cook, stirring, over low heat without boiling, until thick. Remove from the heat and cool. Use as a sauce or icing. Will keep indefinitely covered in the refrigerator.

Pastries and Pies and Tarts

Croquembouche

MAKES 1 CROQUEMBOUCHE

A tall dazzling cone of cream puffs, this is typically served at weddings in France, as it was at my daughter Audrey's.

This seems like a terribly daunting recipe, but each of its parts can be done on different days. Cream puffs freeze very well, unfilled. The final filling and forming of the cone needs to be done the same day as it is to be served; otherwise, there is a danger of humidity melting the caramel. It is easiest to make the dough in a large, heavy pan—just don't use an iron skillet that might convey a rusty flavor.

You may want to consider making your *croquembouche* with unfilled puffs several days in advance and freezing it, then having another recipe of puffs, which you freeze, defrost, fill, and serve the day of the event, leaving the *croquembouche* "just for show." I frequently do this, as puffs filled way in advance are slightly soggy and hard to serve. Also, making the *croquembouche* close to the time of serving is something of a pressure.

Cream Puffs

1 cup unsalted butter
2 cups bread or all-purpose
    flour
1 teaspoon salt

1½ teaspoons sugar
2 cups water
7 or 8 eggs

Glaze

1 egg, beaten, mixed with
    1 teaspoon water

Pastry Cream

2 cups milk
6 egg yolks
½ cup sugar

⅓ cup flour, sifted
1 tablespoon vanilla

Caramel

2 cups sugar
1 cup water
2 tablespoons light corn syrup

Preheat oven to 375 degrees. Grease and flour a baking sheet.

To make the cream puffs, melt the butter in a heavy broad-bottomed frying pan, 10 to 12 inches in diameter. Mix together the flour, salt, and sugar. Remove the pan from the heat and stir in the flour mixture. Add the water and stir briefly; don't worry if it's lumpy. Return the pan to the heat and stir constantly until the mixture comes together in a paste. "Dry" over high heat 4 to 5 minutes by stirring until the flour is cooked and the dough does not stick to your fingers. Be careful not to burn the mixture. The bottom of the pan should have a light crust of dried dough and the dough should look like buttered mashed potatoes.

Remove the dough from the pan and place in a food processor or a mixing bowl. Add 7 of the eggs, 1 at a time, processing or beating well after each addition. Process until shiny and smooth. Test the mixture. It should drop from a spoon like thick mayonnaise. If the dough is too thick, add some of the remaining egg and test again.

With a pastry bag or plastic bag fitted with a small round tip pipe small rounds onto the baking sheet(s). Or, drop the batter by spoonfuls, using 2 spoons to make uniform-sized puffs. Give the puffs room to expand during baking. Slightly flatten tops with tines of a fork dipped in water so puffs will be uniform in shape and stack easily when assembling. Brush them with the egg glaze, being careful not to drip any on the baking sheet. Place the baking sheet on the second rack from the top of the oven. Bake until the puffs are puffed, golden, and firm, 25 to 30 minutes. Remove to a rack and prick a hole in the bottom of each with a plain pastry tip. The puffs may be refrigerated in an airtight container, or wrapped well and frozen.

To make the pastry cream, in a saucepan bring the milk to the boil. Beat the egg yolks with the sugar until light, being careful not to incorporate too many air bubbles into the mixture. Stir in the flour. Whisk the boiling milk into the egg mixture. Return mixture to the pan and stir over gentle heat until boiling. Stir constantly to prevent lumps. The cream will thicken and then it will thin slightly. Keep cooking to this point to insure that the flour is cooked. Stir in the vanilla (or other flavorings such as orange or rum). Strain the pastry cream through a fine sieve into a bowl. Let cool with a piece of plastic wrap on the surface to prevent a skin from forming. Once cooled, the pastry cream can be stored, covered, in the refrigerator for 1 to 2 days.

To make the caramel, heat the sugar with the water and corn syrup in a heavy pan until the sugar dissolves. Make sure the sugar is dissolved before the mixture comes to the boil. Bring to the boil and boil rapidly until the syrup is a light golden caramel. Stop the cooking by dipping the bottom of the pan in cold water.

Place the pastry cream in a pastry bag or plastic bag fitted with a small tip. Make a small hole in the side of the puff and squeeze in some of the pastry cream. Using tongs, dip the side of a puff in the still warm and liquid caramel, taking care as the hot caramel can burn you, and set on a large, round doily or serving plate, forming a ring. Each puff should touch the one next to it; the caramel will act as "glue." Continue building rings, one on top of the other, now dipping the bottom and one side in the caramel. Each ring should be slightly smaller than the previous one, so that the croquembouche eventually forms a cone at least 18 inches high. If there are any cream puffs left at the end, they can be dropped inside before the last hole is closed up, or served on the side filled with pastry cream.

To spin caramel around the cone, take a whisk that has had the round top cut off and dip the prongs into the caramel. Pull the whisk up out of the caramel to form long strands of sugar and gently wrap or "spin" them around the cone, repeating until a web of spun sugar is formed.

Beignets

MAKES 2½ DOZEN BEIGNETS

These light French doughnuts are crisp and brown on the outside and soft within and should be eaten hot, sprinkled with sugar. These are made from cream puff paste (*pâte à choux*) and are a bit different from *beignets* usually made from pastry dough. These cannot be made ahead and should be served freshly made.

It is important to have the fat hot. And remember not to fill any pan more than half way when deep-fat frying. Long frying time is needed to allow beignets to expand and thoroughly cook.

Shortening or oil for deep frying	1½ tablespoons sugar
½ cup butter	1 cup water
1 cup all-purpose flour	4 eggs, at room temperature
¼ teaspoon salt	1½ teaspoons vanilla
	Confectioners' sugar

Heat 2 or 3 inches of shortening to 365 degrees in a deep fryer or deep saucepan.

For the *pâte à choux* base, melt the butter in a heavy frying pan, 7 to 10 inches in diameter. Remove from the heat and stir in the flour, salt, and sugar, making a *roux*. Add the water and stir briefly; don't worry if it's lumpy. Return the pan to the heat and stir constantly until the mixture comes together in a paste. "Dry" over high heat 4 or 5 minutes by stirring until the flour is cooked and the dough does not stick to your fingers. Be careful not to burn the mixture. The bottom of the pan should have a light crust of dried dough and the dough should look like buttered mashed potatoes.

Remove the dough from the pan and place in a food processor or a mixing bowl. Add 3 of the eggs, 1 at a time, processing or beating well after each addition. Process until shiny and smooth. Test the mixture. It should drop from a spoon like thick mayonnaise. If the dough is too thick, add some of the remaining egg and test again. Beat in the vanilla.

Drop the dough by teaspoonfuls, a few at a time, into the heated shortening. Fry 7 or 8 minutes, or until evenly brown. Turn as needed for even browning. Remove with a slotted metal spoon, drain on paper towels, and roll in Confectioners' sugar. Continue to make beignets with the remaining dough in the same manner. Serve warm.

Rugelach

MAKES 48

In college I dated a wonderful young man, Alan Cohen. He took me to a holiday party at an Israeli student's apartment where rugelach were served. It was one of those nights that divided time as I learned about the diversity of life and the richness of cultures other than the Southern traditions I had grown up with. I was grateful to find this recipe, which I have adapted, in *The Jewish Holiday Kitchen* by Joan Nathan.

1 cup unsalted butter, softened   2 cups all-purpose flour
8 ounces cream cheese,
   softened

Filling
¾ cup sugar, divided   1 cup finely chopped nuts
½ cup seedless raisins   ½ cup unsalted butter, melted
1 teaspoon ground cinnamon   (optional)

In a food processor or mixer, beat the butter and cream cheese together until light. Beat in the flour, a little at a time. Divide the dough into 4 portions, wrap each in plastic wrap, and refrigerate at least 1 hour.

To make the filling, combine ½ cup of the sugar, the raisins, cinnamon, and chopped nuts on a piece of wax paper. Divide.

Preheat oven to 350 degrees.

On a piece of wax paper, roll out 1 portion of the dough into a circle ¹⁄₁₆ inch thick. Dust the dough with flour if it sticks. Using a knife or pastry wheel, cut the dough into 16 triangles. Sprinkle or spread ½ tablespoon of the filling over each triangle of dough. Beginning at the wide edge of each triangle, roll the dough up toward the point. Place on an ungreased cookie sheet, and carefully sprinkle each with ¼ teaspoon of the remaining sugar. Make pastries with the remaining dough and filling. Bake for 25 to 30 minutes, or until golden. Brush with melted butter after 15 minutes, if desired.

Kolochy

MAKES 30 TO 40 PIECES

These dainty jam-filled tarts, I learned from my student Gayle Robbins, are wonderful for a tea party or as a little taste with coffee after a heavy meal. I vary the jam as it peeks through and different-colored ones are pretty on the plate. These pastries are similar in a way to Rugelach.

½ cup unsalted butter, softened	1 cup sifted flour
3 ounces cream cheese, softened	⅓ cup jam or jelly
	Confectioners' sugar

Preheat oven to 375 degrees.

Mix the butter and cream cheese with a mixer or in a food processor taking care not to overprocess. Add the flour and mix just to combine. Chill dough 30 minutes. Roll out the dough very thin on a floured board or pastry cloth. Cut into 2-inch rounds with a cookie cutter. Dot the center of each round with ¼ teaspoon of jam or jelly. Fold 2 opposite edges to the center and press firmly together. Place on an ungreased cookie sheet and bake for 15 minutes. Transfer the pastries to wax paper generously dusted with Confectioners' sugar and sift more of the sugar over the kolochy while they are still hot.

One-Crust/Two-Crust Pie Dough

MAKES ENOUGH DOUGH FOR ONE 9-INCH CRUST

There is nothing more revered than a good pie. Probably, that's why it's associated with good mothering and patriotism when we speak of motherhood and apple pie. Over the years, this reverence has led to a most appalling intimidation. Grown people, competent in other aspects of their lives, will express fear of making a pie crust.

In fact, a good pie crust is easy to make. Not only that, it is cheap! But it takes a little thinking about, and perhaps a little practice. Ideally, when you make your first pie crust, you could approach it as if you were hitting a tennis ball for the first time. You could dedicate a cool Saturday morning when you had no other pressures, and could practice, making one crust after the other, until you got the one of your dreams. I've done this with pie crusts, finding a variety that have different qualities and require different techniques. When I'm testing pie crust, I just bake a tiny piece of it on a cookie sheet, then taste and crumble it. I think, Is this flaky enough? Is it tender? Is it crumbly? Is it fast to make? Is it easy? Is it tasty? Is it light? Then I write up the recipe. Here's one I like.

1¼ cups all-purpose flour	8 tablespoons shortening
½ teaspoon salt	3 to 6 tablespoons ice water

Mix the flour and salt together in a bowl. Cut in the shortening with a pastry blender or fork until the mixture resembles cornmeal. Divide the dough into thirds. To one portion of the mixture add some of the ice water, a little at a time. Set aside. Repeat, adding water until the remaining two portions are moist. Gather all the dough into a smooth ball and flatten into a round. Wrap well with plastic wrap and chill.

Flour a board, wax paper, or pie cloth and use a floured or stockinged rolling pin to roll out the dough. Place the dough round in the center of the floured surface. Starting in the center of the dough, roll to, but not over, the top edge of the dough. Go back to the center, and roll down to, but not over, the bottom edge. Pick up the dough and turn it a quarter circle. This will keep it round and prevent it from sticking.

Continue rolling, repeating the quarter turns until you have a round ⅛ inch thick and 1½ inches larger than your pan. Fold into quarters.

Place the pastry in a pie pan with the tip of the triangle in the center and unfold. Trim the pastry 1 inch larger than the pie pan and fold the overhanging pastry under itself. To decorate, press the tines of a fork around the edge. To make a fluted pattern, use both of your thumbs to pinch the dough all around the rim so that the edge of the dough stands up. Place in the freezer or chill in the refrigerator for 30 minutes before baking.

To prebake: Preheat oven to 425 degrees. Prick the pastry all over with a fork. Crumple a piece of wax paper, then spread it out to the edges of the pie pan. Weight the paper with raw rice or dried peas. Bake for 20 minutes. Carefully remove the rice or peas and paper. (The rice or peas may be used again the next time you prebake a pie crust.) Fill the prebaked shell with a filling and bake according to filling directions. If the filling requires no cooking, bake the pie shell 10 minutes more before filling.

Two-Crust Pie Directions

- **If making a 2-crust pie, double the ingredients and make the bottom crust larger than the top crust. Dampen the rim of the bottom crust before putting on the top one, then seal the two together. Be very careful not to stretch either dough so that they stay together when baked.**

To make a leaf edging, with the tip of a sharp knife cut out 1½-inch oval leaf shapes from leftover pastry scraps. Lightly mark veins on leaves. Press the edge of the crust flat to the rim of the pie plate; brush with water. Place leaves in zigzag pattern around the edge. Press them gently, but firmly, to adhere. If desired, glaze the edging by brushing it with the white of 1 large egg, lightly beaten.

Rapid Puff Pastry

MAKES 1½ POUNDS
(SIXTEEN 3- BY 4-INCH *FEUILLETÉES*)

Although this pastry is quicker to make than the traditional puff pastry, it is still a challenge for the novice cook. I call it rapid because the butter is cut in pieces making it easier than the classic paste, which requires the butter be incorporated in a thick layer. The dough is rolled, folded, and turned to make nearly 700 flaky layers after 6 "turns." Don't try to make the dough the day of serving; it's best done when you have plenty of time. You will need a cool room and surface, as well as patience. The major expense is the butter, but this flaky multilayered dough is well worth it! I always keep 4-inch squares or rectangles in my freezer. I bake them as I need them, filling them with creamed chicken or beef stew, whipped cream and strawberries, or caramel sauce.

It is important to weigh the flour for puff pastry as flours measure differently according to the type of flour and the climate.

½ pound bread flour
¼ pound all-purpose flour or
   cake flour

½ teaspoon salt
¾ pound unsalted butter, cold
¾ cup ice water

Sift the flours and salt together into a large bowl. Cut the butter into ½-inch squares and combine with the flour, using a knife or an electric mixer until the flour coats the butter and the butter pieces are the size of large lima beans. Don't cut in too much; if the butter pieces are too small, the pastry won't rise. Add the ice water quickly and stir until the mixture just holds together. The dough will have a rough texture at this point.

Lightly dust your work surface with flour. Turn out the dough. Dust the dough and a rolling pin with flour. Brush off any excess. Push or roll the dough out into a rough rectangle 15 inches long and about 5 inches wide. Pick up the dough to be sure it isn't sticking. Again dust the surface with flour and place the dough back on it. Don't worry if the dough is crumbly. Fold over in thirds as you would a business letter. First fold the bottom up one-third the way from the top, then fold the top down to cover it. Turn the dough so that the long open side is to your right. Sprinkle the work surface again with flour. Then roll the folded dough out again to 15 inches long and 5 inches wide. Fold and turn as directed above. Repeat the rolling, folding, and turning 2 more times. Any time the dough becomes too warm to work, wrap it in plastic wrap and refrigerate. After the fourth fold and turn, wrap the dough in plastic wrap and let rest in the refrigerator at least 1 hour, or up to 2 days.

Remove the dough from the refrigerator and let sit at room temperature until it is easy to roll, but not soft. Give the dough 2 more rolls, folds, and turns, then divide in half. Roll out 1 piece ¼ inch thick. Refrigerate the other half.

Preheat oven to 400 degrees.

To test how thick to roll out the dough, cut two 3- by 4-inch rectangles (called *feuilletées*) from the rolled-out dough. On a floured surface, roll one rectangle into a large, thinner piece, ⅛ inch thick. Chill if necessary. Place both pieces on a cookie sheet and bake. After 20 minutes, lower the oven to 350 degrees. Continue baking the pieces until they are lightly browned. Measure the height of the pastry. If the ⅛-inch rectangle has risen to 1 or more inches high, then roll the rest of the dough to ⅛ inch thick. If the rectangle has risen less than 2 inches high, roll the rest of the dough ¼ inch thick before cutting into *feuilletées* 3- by 4-inches each.

Puff pastry may be refrigerated or frozen before or after rolling, then defrosted overnight. When baking shaped dough, place in the hot oven when it is very cold, preferably from the freezer. Bake the shapes as you did the test pieces. Fill the rectangles with Lime Butter (page 311). Three tablespoons fill one very nicely. Top with whipped cream.

Sublime Tart Dough

MAKES ONE 8- OR 9-INCH PIE SHELL;
OR, FORTY-EIGHT 1-INCH TARTLETTES
OR TWENTY-FOUR 2-INCH TARTLETTES

This is an easy, tender pie dough, geared especially to dessert tarts. It must be doubled for a two-crust pie. Do not use it prebaked when the filling you are using needs to cook more than 20 minutes, as the high ratio of sugar will cause the crust to darken too much. Candy Sheehan adapted this from her teacher and mentor, Simone (Simca) Beck, whom we both regard fondly and with admiration.

1 cup all-purpose flour
¼ teaspoon salt
1 tablespoon sugar
½ teaspoon baking powder

5 tablespoons cold unsalted
  butter
3 tablespoons heavy cream
1 egg yolk

Mix together in a bowl the flour, salt, sugar, and baking powder. With a knife or food processor, cut in the butter until the mixture resembles oatmeal. Beat together the cream and egg yolk and add to the flour. Mix to make a smooth ball and flatten into a round. Wrap well with plastic wrap and chill.

Flour a board, wax paper, or pie cloth and use a floured or stock-inged rolling pin to roll out the dough. Place the dough round in the center of the floured surface. Starting in the center of the dough, roll to, but not over, the top edge of the dough. Go back to the center, and roll down to, but not over, the bottom edge. Pick up the dough and turn it a quarter circle. This will keep it round and prevent it from sticking. Repeat your rolling and the quarter turns until you have a round ⅛ inch thick and 1½ inches larger than your pan. Fold the round into quarters.

Place the pastry in a pie pan with the tip of the triangle in the center, and unfold. Press well into the bottom edge being careful not to stretch the dough. Trim the pastry 1 inch larger than the pie pan, and fold the overhanging pastry under itself. To decorate, press the tines of a fork around the edge. To make a fluted pattern, use both of your thumbs to pinch the dough all around the rim so that the edge of the dough stands up. Place in the freezer or in the refrigerator for 30 minutes before baking.

To prebake, preheat oven to 425 degrees. Prick the pastry all over with a fork. Crumple a piece of wax paper, then spread it out to the edges of the pie pan. Fill the paper with raw rice or dried peas. Bake for 20 minutes. Carefully remove the rice or peas and paper. (The rice or peas may be used again the next time you prebake a pie crust.) Fill the crust with a filling and bake according to filling directions. If the filling requires no cooking, bake the pie shell 10 minutes more before filling.

The dough freezes wrapped in plastic wrap.

Almond Tart

MAKES 1 TART

The almond filling here puffs up, making a delightful contrast with the sweet crust beneath. Sometimes I top this with fresh strawberries or raspberries and brush them with a glaze of warmed strained strawberry or raspberry preserves.

2 cups finely ground almonds
½ cup sugar
½ teaspoon almond extract
3 eggs, beaten
1 lemon, juiced

1 prebaked 8- or 9-inch
  Sublime Tart Dough crust
  (recipe precedes) or small
  tarts, prebaked

Preheat oven to 375 degrees.

Mix the almonds, sugar, almond extract, eggs, and lemon juice until the mixture forms a firm paste. Pour into the prebaked pie shell and bake 20 to 25 minutes.

Cool Mint-Raspberry Pie

MAKES ONE 9-INCH PIE

I'm very fond of this unusual combination; the fresh mint is particularly tasty with the raspberries. Use your imagination designing the steam vents for the top crust. Sometimes I crisscross fork marks, other times I make decorative slits.

1½ cups sugar
3 tablespoons cornstarch
½ teaspoon salt
5 cups fresh raspberries
2 heaping tablespoons finely
    chopped fresh mint

1 recipe unbaked One-Crust/
    Two-Crust Pie Dough (page
    318), doubled
2 tablespoons unsalted butter

Glaze
1 egg white, mixed with
    1 teaspoon water

Preheat oven to 375 degrees.

Combine the sugar, cornstarch, and salt in a bowl. Toss the berries and mint gently in the mixture. Spoon into the unbaked pie crust. Dot with the butter. Moisten pastry edge with water.

Roll the top crust 1 inch larger than the bottom crust and place over the filling, pressing the edges together to seal. Flute and cut slits or designs in the top crust or prick the top with fork. Chill ½ hour if necessary. Brush crust with the glaze and bake pie for 40 to 50 minutes. Serve slightly warm or at room temperature.

Dave's Grape-Pudding Tart

SERVES 4 TO 6

My student, Dave Norman, developed this recipe years ago, using a French *clafouti* as a starting point. It is a custardy kind of cake or cakey kind of custard. The dessert may be frozen, but turns a bit watery when defrosted—acceptable, but not as wonderful as it is when served without freezing. Cherries or sliced peaches are also wonderful in this.

3 cups seedless green grapes
1 cup sugar
2 egg yolks
1 egg
½ cup butter

1 cup flour
2 teaspoons rum flavoring or
    2 tablespoons rum
¼ teaspoon almond extract
1 cup milk

Preheat oven to 400 degrees

Sprinkle the grapes with half the sugar, and let stand 30 minutes. For the batter, in a bowl beat together the remaining sugar and egg yolks. Then beat in the egg. While beating, gradually add the butter, then the flour. Finally, add the rum flavoring, almond extract, and milk and beat until very smooth. May be done in the food processor.

Pour ⅓ of the batter into a heavily buttered 8- or 9-inch baking dish or pie pan. Spoon the grapes and their juice over the batter. Pour the remaining batter over the grapes. Bake the tart on the lower rack of the oven for 40 minutes, or until a toothpick comes out clean. The texture should be soft and nearly custardy. Cool slightly and serve from the pan in wedges or squares. May be done several days in advance. Serve warm, reheated, or at room temperature.

Down East Apple Pie

MAKES 1 PIE

A fan of the TV show sent me this recipe but left off her name and the bottom half of the recipe, so we've done the crust in an unusual way. If you would prefer dividing the dough into two rounds and making a two-crust pie, that is fine, too. You may substitute crushed or whole berries, canned or frozen. I prefer the frozen. Either way, add half the sugar to start. Taste and add more if necessary.

The Dough
2½ cups all-purpose flour
¾ teaspoon salt

1 cup vegetable shortening
8 to 10 tablespoons ice water

The Cranberry Base
2 cups cranberries
½ cup sugar, or to taste
½ cup orange juice
½ cup water

Grated peel, no white attached,
   of 1 orange
Pinch of freshly grated nutmeg

The Apple Filling
5 to 6 Granny Smith apples,
   peeled, cored, and sliced
⅓ cup flour
1 cup sugar
2 teaspoons cinnamon

½ teaspoon freshly grated
   nutmeg
Pinch salt
¼ cup unsalted butter

The Glaze
¼ cup milk

2 tablespoons sugar

To make the dough, place the flour and salt in a bowl and cut in the shortening. Add the water, 1 tablespoon at a time, stirring quickly. When mixture is moist enough to stick together, form into a ball, flatten slightly, and chill the dough in a dampened cloth in the refrigerator for about 1 hour.

    To make the base, combine the cranberries, sugar, orange juice, water, orange peel, and nutmeg in a medium saucepan and cook over low heat until mixture is reduced by a third, to about 1¾ cups. Cool.

To make the filling, toss the apples with the flour, sugar, cinnamon, nutmeg, and salt.

Preheat oven to 375 degrees.

Roll the chilled dough into an 18-inch round. Center over a 9-inch glass deep pie dish, gently easing the dough over the sides. Drape the rest of the dough carefully outside the pan so that it extends 3 inches over rim. Pour the cranberry base in the bottom, and top with the apple filling. Dot with the butter. Fold the dough over the top, pleating as necessary to cover the filling. Brush with the milk and sprinkle with the sugar to make the glaze. Bake on a cookie sheet to catch the drippings for 50 to 60 minutes.

Free-Form Brown Sugar Apple Tart

MAKES 1 TART

When the apples are at their peak, there is nothing better than a free-form tart of crisp, thinly rolled pastry, topped with a swirl of apples and brown sugar, and burnished with a glaze of strained jam. You can substitute pears for the apples—also pretty good!

1 recipe One-Crust/Two-Crust
    Pie Dough (page 318)
2 or 3 Golden Delicious or
    Granny Smith apples,
    peeled, cored, and sliced

¼ to ½ cup dark brown sugar
¼ cup raisins or currants,
    plumped in water

Glaze
1 to 2 tablespoons lemon juice
½ cup apricot jam

1 recipe Caramel Sauce
    (optional, page 305)

Preheat oven to 375 degrees.

Roll the dough to about ⅛ inch thick on a floured surface and place on a cookie sheet. Cut out the design of your choice, either by hand or with a pattern. A traditional shape is a 10-inch circle or a rectangle, but alternate shapes include a Christmas tree, Christmas ball, turkey, apple, or pear. Cut a ½-inch-wide strip of dough to use as a rim. Brush the outer ½-inch edge of the dough with water. Put the strip of dough on the moistened part and press lightly to seal. Leave the edge as it is, or decorate it. Roll any scraps out into a rose, bow, or cut out into shapes. Chill. Fill the form with crumpled wax paper and rice or beans, and bake for 20 minutes. Remove the rice or beans and paper.

Arrange the apples in the form, overlapping them slightly to account for shrinkage. To make a spiral pattern, overlap apple slices, starting from the outside rim, always with the rounded edges towards the outside rim, and spiraling to the center. Sprinkle with brown sugar to taste. Sprinkle the raisins down the center to look like apple seeds. Bake 20 to 30 minutes, or until the fruit is soft.

To make the glaze, mix the lemon juice and jam, bring to the boil, and strain. Brush the hot glaze on the apples. Cool the tart on a wire rack. Serve it lukewarm or at room temperature. Serve with optional caramel cream sauce.

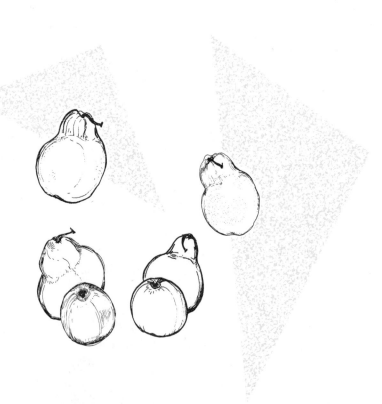

Gingered Pumpkin Pie

MAKES 1 (DEEP DISH) PIE

Although classic pumpkin pie is a favorite of mine, so too is this zippy combination, layered with candied ginger and almonds.

½ cup finely chopped almonds
½ cup chopped candied ginger
1 cup firmly packed light brown
  sugar, divided
3 tablespoons unsalted butter,
  softened
2 teaspoons all-purpose flour
¼ teaspoon almond extract
1 (9-inch) deep dish pie shell,
  unbaked
4 ounces cream cheese
2 eggs

2 cups fresh, cooked until soft,
  or canned solid pack
  pumpkin (not pumpkin pie
  filling)
½ cup heavy cream
⅓ cup sour cream
1 tablespoon maple syrup
1 teaspoon cinnamon
½ teaspoon freshly grated
  nutmeg
½ teaspoon salt
½ teaspoon vanilla

Preheat oven to 425 degrees.

Combine the almonds, ginger, ½ cup of the brown sugar, butter, flour, and almond extract. Toss with fork until well blended. Spoon into the unbaked pie shell. Press firmly onto the bottom and part way up the sides of the shell. Chill.

Beat the remaining ½ cup brown sugar and cream cheese until fluffy. Beat in the eggs, pumpkin, cream, sour cream, and maple syrup. Add the cinnamon, nutmeg, salt, and vanilla. Beat well to combine. Spoon over the chilled almond-ginger layer. Bake for 15 minutes. Reduce the temperature to 350 degrees and bake for 50 to 60 minutes. Cover the edge of crust with foil, if necessary, to prevent overbrowning. Cool to room temperature before serving.

Strawberry-Peach Crisp

SERVES 6 TO 8

In an era of oats and whole-wheat flour, we've become accustomed to them even in simple desserts. I like the mix of the fruits and an addition of vanilla ice cream melting on top of the crisp hot from the oven.

2 cups sliced strawberries
2 cups sliced peaches
1 tablespoon lemon juice
¾ cup sugar

¼ cup whole-wheat flour
½ teaspoon cinnamon
Pinch freshly grated nutmeg

Topping
1 cup whole-wheat flour
¾ cup light brown sugar
½ cup quick oats

½ cup unsalted butter, melted
½ teaspoon cinnamon

Preheat oven to 375 degrees.

Mix the strawberries, peaches, lemon juice, sugar, whole-wheat flour, cinnamon, and nutmeg in an 8-inch square baking dish.

Make the topping by tossing together the whole-wheat flour, sugar, oats, butter, and cinnamon. Sprinkle the topping mixture over the strawberry-peach filling.

Bake for 35 minutes, or until the topping is golden brown and crisp. Serve with ice cream or whipped cream.

Treacle and Blueberry Tart

MAKES ONE 8-INCH TART

Treacle is the affectionate word I learned for syrup, or even molasses, in England. It's even mentioned in *Alice in Wonderland*.

If using a shallow crust baked in a flan ring, halve the recipe below.

1 recipe (8-inch) One-Crust/
    Two-Crust Pie Dough (page
    318) or Sublime Tart Dough
    (page 322), lightly prebaked
10 tablespoons golden syrup (or
    2 tablespoons dark corn
    syrup and 8 tablespoons
    light corn syrup)

1½ cups fresh or frozen
    blueberries or raspberries
¼ cup unsalted butter, at room
    temperature
4 tablespoons heavy cream
2 teaspoons grated, no white
    attached, lemon peel
3 eggs, lightly beaten

Preheat oven to 375 degrees.

Brush the prebaked crust with 2 tablespoons of the syrup. Drain the berries if frozen and put in the shell. Warm the remaining syrup in the microwave or over low heat. Add the butter. When melted, mix in the cream, lemon peel, and beaten eggs. Pour the mixture over the berries in the crust. Bake 25 to 30 minutes until the filling is set and light brown. Serve warm or at room temperature.

White Chocolate Banana Cream Pie

MAKES ONE 9-INCH (DEEP DISH) PIE

This is a tremendous hit at a dinner party or informal meal. It combines the comfort of banana custard with the luscious excess of white chocolate.

Graham Cracker Crust

1½ cups graham cracker crumbs	2 teaspoons sugar
	½ cup melted butter

Filling

2 medium bananas, cut into ½-inch slices	3 cups milk
¾ cup sugar	4 egg yolks
6 tablespoons cornstarch	¼ cup butter
¼ teaspoon salt	2 teaspoons vanilla
	6 ounces white chocolate

Meringue

5 egg whites	8 tablespoons sugar

Preheat oven to 350 degrees.

To make the graham cracker crust, toss together the crumbs, sugar, and butter. Press into a 9-inch deep pie plate. Bake 15 minutes. Let cool.

For the filling, place the banana slices in the crust. Place the sugar, cornstarch, and salt in a very heavy saucepan. Stir together until there are no lumps. Mix together the milk and egg yolks and stir into the sugar-cornstarch mixture until smooth, whisking if necessary. Place the pan over medium heat. Stir constantly until the custard comes to the boil, taking care to scrape the bottom and sides. Reduce the heat to a gentle boil and cook, stirring, until thick, about 3 minutes. Avoid scorching. Remove from the heat and beat in the butter and vanilla. Strain out any brown lumps. Taste to be sure it is not scorched. Pour the custard over the bananas. Cool 20 minutes at room temperature, covered with plastic wrap to prevent a skin from forming. Cut half the chocolate into 1-inch pieces and dot over the custard. Make chocolate curls, shave, sliver, or grate the remaining chocolate, and set aside. (To shave white chocolate, chill slightly, then shave thin with a very sharp knife or potato peeler.)

To Make Chocolate Curls
* **Melt the chocolate over a double boiler with 1 teaspoon vegetable oil. When smooth, spread evenly on a cold marble slab or cookie sheet. When chocolate just begins to harden but is still malleable, take a spatula and with the edge gently push chocolate to remove and curl from slab. Place curls on a cookie sheet and freeze until ready to use.**

Meanwhile, make the meringue by beating the egg whites until they form firm peaks. Fold in the sugar and beat again, if necessary, to peaks. Spread the meringue over the custard, all the way to the crust. Bake 12 to 15 minutes, until the meringue is golden brown. Cool to room temperature. Top with the chocolate curls or shaved chocolate. Refrigerate, if necessary, but serve at room temperature.

Winter Fruit Christmas Ball Tart

MAKES 1 TART

I have a lot of fun with this tart. Sometimes I shape the dough into a giant Christmas tree. Other times I cut out a design such as a Christmas ball and top the baked dough and custard with pieces of strawberries, bananas, grapes, kiwis, and star fruits, creating fantasy designs to duplicate Christmas tree ornaments. Use a straw to make a hole in the dough for a ribbon or string. The custard has a tartness that is pleasing, especially with fruit.

1 recipe One-Crust/Two-Crust
    Pie Dough (page 318)

Cream Cheese Custard

2 large eggs
¼ cup sugar
1 teaspoon cornstarch
3 tablespoons lemon juice
2 (3-ounce) packages cream
    cheese, at room temperature
¾ cup sour cream, at room
    temperature

¼ cup milk
4 cups seeded green grapes,
    kiwis, berries, and sliced
    starfruit
Light brown sugar (optional)

Preheat oven to 350 degrees.

Roll out the pie dough as thinly as possible, about ⅛ inch thick, and shape as desired. (See free-form tart directions, pages 327 to 328.) Bake 15 to 20 minutes until pale brown. Place the baked crust, still on the baking sheet, on a wire rack to cool.

Make the cream cheese custard by beating the eggs to mix. Place them in a heavy saucepan, add the sugar, and mix well. Dissolve the cornstarch in the lemon juice, and add to the eggs. Beat the cream cheese until soft. Add to the egg mixture and stir over heat until the mixture thickens and comes just to the boil. Remove from the heat and whisk in the sour cream and milk until nearly smooth. Don't worry if it is lumpy. Chill until ready to use.

When the tart shell is cool, fill it with the chilled cream cheese custard. If you find it isn't sweet enough because the fruit you are using needs more sweetening, depending on the time of year, feel free to sprinkle granulated brown sugar over the fruit. Shortly before serving, arrange the fruit decoratively, over the custard, to simulate a Christmas tree ball. Place string or ribbon in the hole. Carefully move to a serving plate.

Breads

Homemade bread changes the mood of any occasion, frequently stealing the show from more expensive ingredients. Why this magic occurs, I don't know. Surely the aroma of homemade biscuits can't be equaled in the finest of restaurants, and that is part of the pleasure.

Everyone has a favorite method for making bread. I make most of mine in a standard-size food processor. It kneads one loaf using 2½ to 3½ cups of flour. For a larger recipe, I divide the dough and process it in batches, then knead it all together at the end by hand. I use the steel blade, although many people prefer the white plastic blade.

After all the ingredients are added (with the exception of nuts and fruits, which might be chopped too fine), I process the dough up to 1 minute, checking it to be sure it is soft and yet springs back when lightly touched. If it is too hard and stiff, I add more liquid; too soft and sticky, more flour.

Breadmaking is a very flexible endeavor, and the main thing to remember is to proceed by feel rather than by recipe. Flour absorbs moisture from the air and so the weather often affects the amount needed.

Yeast is very variable, too. There are several kinds on the market: active dry, which may be dissolved in 105 to 115 degree water, or placed with the dry ingredients and hotter (125 degree) water added; RapidRise, where liquid up to 140 degrees is added and only one rise is necessary; and cake yeast, which is rarely seen. It comes in a block like butter, one ounce of which equals one package active dry. Cake yeast needs to be mixed with a little sugar. Recipes may be adapted according to the type of yeast available by changing to follow package directions.

I usually allow my bread to double in an oiled plastic bag, but an oiled bowl covered with plastic wrap or a tea towel is fine, too.

Yeast Breads and Rolls

Brioche

MAKES 10

Brioche is a sweet, richly flavored, tender-textured bread. In fact, it is more like a cake than a bread. Perhaps this is the bread Marie Antoinette was speaking of when she said "Let them eat cake." Brioche is very easy to make, but needs the time to rise overnight in the refrigerator to develop its rich unique flavor and cake-like texture. The dough is neither liquid nor is it a typical yeast dough when ready. It is wet—a glossy, shiny mass that will adhere to the sides of the bowl as well as the spoon used to test it, forming long strands. It will hold together in one mass when moved, much like very thick mayonnaise. This dough may be baked in the traditional individual, fluted brioche tins or muffin pans; it also may be baked in a loaf pan. If the brioche browns too rapidly, cover the top loosely with foil. Leftover brioche tastes wonderful when oven-toasted and buttered. I have added a Quick Brioche recipe as well.

(continued)

1 package active dry yeast
⅓ cup sugar
¼ cup warm water (105 to 115 degrees)

2⅓ cups bread flour
¾ cup butter, cool but not hard-chilled
3 eggs

Glaze
1 egg yolk, beaten, mixed with 2 tablespoons water

Grease and flour 10 small fluted ⅓-cup brioche tins or one 3-cup brioche pan.

Dissolve the yeast and a pinch of the sugar in the warm water. In food processor or mixer, combine the flour and the remaining sugar. Beat in the cool butter. Add the yeast mixture. Beat in the eggs, 1 at a time. Continue to beat until the dough is shiny and glossy, and forms long slick strings that have an adhesive quality. If the food processor turns off automatically, the dough is ready. Place it into an oiled plastic bag or oiled bowl and turn to coat. Seal or cover and let rise in a warm place, until tripled.

Punch down and let rise again covered, in the refrigerator for 6 hours or overnight. For a Quick Brioche, see below. Take two thirds of the now spongy dough and, working quickly, form it into 10 balls to fill the brioche tins by two thirds. Cut a ½-inch-deep cross in the center of each ball. With the remaining dough, form small pear-shaped knobs. Fit the pointed ends of the knobs into the center holes, pressing them firmly in place. Let rise, uncovered, in a warm place until the dough has doubled.

Preheat oven to 375 degrees. Brush the dough with the egg glaze. Bake on middle rack of oven until nicely browned, about 15 to 20 minutes. Cool slightly before removing from tins and cool on a rack. Keep in an airtight container. The brioche freeze.

Quick Brioche
• **For Quick Brioche, cover the kneaded dough in the greased bowl with plastic wrap and chill in the refrigerator for 1 hour. Grease the brioche tins. When the dough is chilled, knead it with floured hands. It should not require any more flour. Shape as described above. Brush all over with the glaze. Let double 15 to 20 minutes and bake at 375-degrees, about 10 minutes, or until brown.**

French Bread

MAKES 2 LOAVES

This is a simple, traditional bread. For an even lighter crumb, allow the dough to rise two times before shaping. The cornmeal gives it a touch of flavor and acts like a ball bearing, preventing sticking. The water makes it crisp.

This bread may be frozen, but since it is really only flour and water, it readily takes on other tastes. The loaf stales quickly but makes great toast and rusks.

2½ to 3½ cups bread flour
1 package rapid rise yeast
1 teaspoon salt

1½ teaspoons sugar
1 cup hot water (120 degrees)
1 tablespoon cornmeal

Glaze
1 egg, beaten, mixed with 1
    tablespoon water

In a food processor or mixer, combine 2½ cups of the flour, the yeast, salt, and sugar. Add the hot water. Process or knead to make a soft dough, adding more of the remaining flour if needed. Allow 1 minute in a food processor; 5 to 10 minutes in a mixer. Place in an oiled plastic bag or oiled bowl and turn to coat. Cover or seal and let rise until doubled. Punch down. Shape into 2 long loaves. Place on a baking sheet sprinkled with the cornmeal. Let double again.

Preheat oven to 400 degrees. Slash the tops of the loaves with a sharp knife. Brush with the egg glaze. Place on the middle rack of the oven with a small cake pan of boiling water on the bottom rack. Bake 20 to 25 minutes until crisp and the bottoms sound hollow when tapped.

Sweet Iced Christmas Bread

MAKES 1 LOAF

This festive bread is nice for serving on Christmas day as friends and family drop by. Making a starter gives the bread a full flavor, but if you are in a hurry omit this process. I frequently double the recipe and give a loaf as a gift.

3 to 4 cups bread or unbleached flour
1 cup warm milk (105 to 115 degrees)
1 package active dry yeast
¼ cup sugar
1 egg, at room temperature
½ teaspoon salt

½ cup butter, at room temperature
½ cup glacéed cherries
½ cup chopped mixed candied fruit
½ cup chopped dates
½ cup coarsely chopped walnuts or pecans

Glaze
1 egg, beaten, mixed with 1 teaspoon milk or water

Decoration
7 halves of glacéed cherries
7 walnut or pecan halves

Icing
½ cup Confectioners' sugar
½ tablespoon water

½ teaspoon vegetable oil
¼ teaspoon almond extract

In a food processor or mixer, mix 1 cup of the flour, the warm milk, yeast, and sugar. If time allows, cover the bowl with plastic wrap and leave the dough at room temperature to ferment and bubble for 2 hours. Add the egg, salt, and butter. Add the remaining flour, ½ cup at a time, to make a soft dough. Knead the dough in the food processor, mixer, or on a floured board by hand until elastic and smooth as a baby's bottom. Mix the cherries, candied fruit, dates, and nuts together and fold and knead ⅓ of the fruit mixture at a time into the dough until well mixed. Place in an oiled plastic bag or oiled bowl and turn to coat. Seal or cover and let rise in a warm place until doubled, about ¾ to 1 hour. Punch down. Knead briefly. Grease a 9- × 5-inch loaf pan. Form the dough into an oval approximately the length of the pan, and place in pan. Let rise again until doubled.

Preheat oven to 350 degrees. Brush the loaf with the glaze and decorate with several of the cherries and nuts. Bake in the middle of the oven about 40 to 50 minutes until it turns a nice brown. Cover with foil if the loaf browns too rapidly. Cool on a wire rack.

To make the icing, mix the Confectioners' sugar, water, oil, and almond extract. Brush cooled bread with icing, top with the remaining candied cherries and nuts.

The bread freezes, wrapped in plastic wrap and foil.

Gift Christmas Kuchen

MAKES 1 LARGE OR 2 SMALL LOAVES

Put a bright ribbon around this German Christmas bread for a delightful gift. It has a lovely light holiday flavor—of spices and citrus peels, and smells heavenly when baking! This idea came from a wonderful book, Bernard Clayton's *New Complete Book of Breads.*

1 package active dry yeast
¼ cup sugar
¼ cup warm water (105 to 115 degrees)
⅔ cup butter, at room temperature, divided
1½ teaspoons grated peel, no white attached, of 1 lemon,
1 tablespoon grated peel, no white attached, of 1 orange

½ teaspoon ground mace
1½ tablespoons ground coriander or anise seed
2 eggs, at room temperature
3 to 4 cups bread flour
1 teaspoon salt
½ cup warm milk (105 to 115 degrees)

Dissolve the yeast and 1 teaspoon of the sugar in the warm water. In a food processor or mixer beat ½ cup of the butter with the remaining sugar. Add the lemon and orange peels, mace, and coriander. Beat in the eggs, then 1 cup of the flour, the dissolved yeast, salt, and warm milk. Add enough of the flour, ½ cup at a time, to make a soft dough. Process or knead the dough until elastic and smooth as a baby's bottom. Place in an oiled plastic bag or oiled bowl and turn to coat. Seal or cover with plastic wrap and let rise at room temperature until doubled, about 1 hour.

Turn out the dough on a floured surface, punch down, and cut into 1 or 2 pieces, depending on the number wanted. Shape each piece into a rectangular loaf and place on a greased baking sheet. Melt the remaining butter. Brush the tops of the loaves lightly with the butter. Make paper ribbon strips the width of your gift ribbons and tie the bread loosely with the paper strips, placing the ends underneath to secure the strips, leaving enough room for the bread to rise. (The paper will leave marks for the position of the gift ribbons.) Let rise in a warm place until doubled, 30 to 40 minutes.

Preheat oven to 350 degrees. Bake loaves about 25 minutes for 2 small loaves to 45 minutes for 1 large loaf, until brown. Remove and place on a rack. Cool. Remove the paper strips and replace with bright ribbons.

Curried Wreath Bread

MAKES 1 ROUND LOAF

This pretty pale-yellow bread tastes mellow to start, but imparts a tanginess on your tongue. I use a medium-hot curry powder. You may prefer an even hotter one.

2½ to 3 cups bread flour

1½ teaspoons sugar

1 tablespoon curry powder

1 teaspoon salt

1 package active dry yeast

3 tablespoons butter, sliced or at
room temperature

1 cup hot water (120 degrees)

Glaze

1 egg, beaten, mixed with 1
tablespoon water

Mint Butter

1 cup butter, softened

3 tablespoons chopped fresh
mint

In a bowl or food processor, mix 2½ cups of the flour, the sugar, curry powder, salt, yeast, and butter. Add the hot water. Knead by hand or process to make a soft dough, adding more of the remaining flour as needed. Dough should be elastic and smooth as a baby's bottom. Place in an oiled plastic bag or oiled bowl and turn to coat. Seal or cover and let rise until doubled. Punch down. Shape into a round and place on a greased baking sheet. Make a hole the size of a small can through the middle of the dough. Oil a tube or an empty can and place in the hole while the dough rises and bakes. Cut a circle ¼ inch deep in the dough 1 inch from the can. With the tip of a damp knife make slashes from the circle to the edge, scalloping the edges to form the petals of a flower. Let double again.

Preheat oven to 350 degrees. Brush with the egg glaze and bake 25 to 30 minutes, until the bottom sounds hollow when tapped. Remove can. Cool on a rack.

In a bowl, cream the butter and stir in the mint. Serve the butter with the bread.

The bread freezes, wrapped in plastic wrap and foil.

Dark Bread

MAKES 1 ROUND LOAF

This hearty bread takes a bit longer to rise than does a white bread because of the cereal in it. The extra time is worth it. You may also make a refrigerator dough of it by placing the dough in the refrigerator in a plastic bag or covered bowl for several hours or overnight. When ready to bake, remove the dough from the refrigerator, shape, and let double, then bake. If you have trouble finding the rye flour, try your health food store.

2 packages active dry yeast
¼ cup dark molasses
¼ cup warm water (105 to 115 degrees)
1 teaspoon salt
1 cup buttermilk

1 cup light rye flour
1 cup wheat and barley cereal such as Grape-Nuts
2 teaspoons unsweetened cocoa powder
2 to 3 cups bread flour

Glaze
½ tablespoon molasses

1 tablespoon hot water

Dissolve the yeast and molasses in the warm water. In a food processor, mixer, or by hand, combine the salt, buttermilk, rye flour, cereal, cocoa, and yeast mixture. Add 1 cup of the bread flour and mix. Add remaining flour, ½ cup at a time and knead or process to make a soft but lightly sticky dough (due to the molasses). The dough should still feel supple and tender. Place in an oiled plastic bag or oiled bowl and turn to coat. Seal or cover and let rise in a warm place until doubled, about 1 to 1½ hours. Punch down. Shape into a round. Place on a greased baking sheet. Let double again.

To make the glaze, dissolve the molasses in the water.

Preheat oven to 375 degrees. Brush the loaf with the glaze.

Make cross hatches with a sharp knife on the top of the loaf to decorate. Bake in the middle of the oven 45 to 50 minutes. Remove from baking sheet and cool on a rack.

The bread freezes, wrapped in plastic wrap and foil.

Fennel-Raisin Round

MAKES 1 MEDIUM ROUND LOAF

This bread is earthy and textured, and I love it by itself, as a snack, or as an accompaniment to other foods at a party. For a gathering I double the recipe for one large or two regular loaves. If doubling, bake 15 minutes longer.

1 package active dry yeast
¼ cup warm water (105 to 115
    degrees)
2½ to 3½ cups bread flour
1 tablespoon sugar
2 teaspoons salt
¼ cup butter

½ cup warm milk (105 to 115
    degrees)
1 egg, lightly beaten
1 tablespoon fennel seed
⅓ cup pine nuts
⅓ cup black raisins or currants

Glaze
1 egg, beaten, mixed with 1
    teaspoon water

Dissolve the yeast in the warm water.

In a food processor or mixer, combine 2½ cups of the flour, the sugar, salt, and butter. Add the warm milk and the yeast mixture. Add the egg. Knead to make a soft dough, adding more of the remaining flour if needed. Using the metal blade in a food processor, allow 1 minute, or 5 to 10 minutes in a mixer using the dough hook. Do not overknead. By hand, knead in the fennel seed, pine nuts, and raisins. Place in an oiled plastic bag or oiled bowl and turn to coat. Seal or cover and let rise until doubled, about 1 hour. Punch down. Shape into a round. Let double again.

Preheat oven to 350 degrees. Slash the top with a sharp knife. Brush with the egg glaze. Bake ½ hour, or until the bottom sounds hollow when tapped. Cool on a rack.

The bread freezes, wrapped in plastic wrap and foil.

Onion Rye

Here is a bread with personality! Strong and gutsy, it will dominate any meal or party. Rye flour can sometimes be difficult to find. Try your local health food store if your grocer does not have it.

1 package active dry yeast
1½ teaspoons sugar
½ cup warm water (105 to 115 degrees)
2½ to 3 cups bread flour
2 teaspoons salt
1 cup rye flour
¾ cup milk or buttermilk, at room temperature

1 egg
2 tablespoons butter, softened, or vegetable oil
1 tablespoon Dijon mustard
¾ cup chopped onion
1 tablespoon caraway seeds
1 tablespoon sesame seeds

Glaze
1 egg, beaten, mixed with 1 tablespoon water

Dissolve the yeast and sugar in the warm water. In a food processor or mixer, combine 1 cup of the bread flour, salt, ½ cup of the rye flour, the milk, egg, butter, Dijon mustard, onion, and caraway and sesame seeds. Add the yeast mixture. Beat in the rest of the rye and any of the remaining flour necessary to make a soft but firm dough. (It will still be slightly sticky.) Place in an oiled plastic bag or oiled bowl. Seal or cover and let rise until doubled (or refrigerate overnight). Punch down and shape into an oval. Place on a greased baking sheet. Let double.

Preheat oven to 350 degrees. Brush the loaf with the egg glaze. Bake until the bottom sounds hollow when tapped, about 45 to 50 minutes. Remove from baking sheet and cool on a rack.

The bread freezes, wrapped in plastic wrap and foil.

Pepper Bread

MAKES 1 ROUND LOAF

There's zing to this speckled and pretty bread.

2½ to 3½ cups bread flour
1½ teaspoons sugar
2 teaspoons ground coriander
    seed
2 teaspoons coarsely ground
    black pepper

1 teaspoon salt
1 package active dry yeast
3 tablespoons butter, sliced or at
    room temperature
1 cup hot water (120 degrees)

Glaze
1 egg, beaten, mixed with 1
    tablespoon water

In a bowl or food processor, combine 2½ cups of the flour, the sugar, coriander, pepper, salt, yeast, and butter. Add the hot water. Process or knead to make a soft dough, adding more of the remaining flour as needed. The dough should be elastic and smooth as a baby's bottom. Place in an oiled plastic bag or oiled bowl and turn to coat. Seal or cover and let rise until doubled. Punch down. Shape into a round and place on a greased baking sheet. Let double again.

Preheat oven to 350 degrees. Brush the loaf with the egg glaze. Bake in the middle of the oven for 25 to 30 minutes until the bottom sounds hollow when tapped. Cool on a rack.

The bread freezes, wrapped in plastic wrap or foil.

Cinnamon Wheat Bread

MAKES 1 LOAF

If I wanted to make a healthy non-sweet bread the aroma of which filled the house, making everyone who walked in feel loved, this would be it!

1 package active dry yeast
¼ cup firmly packed dark
    brown sugar
¼ cup warm water (105 to
    115 degrees)
¾ cup boiling water
½ cup rolled oats, quick or old-
    fashioned

¼ cup crushed coriander seed
    or toasted sesame seeds
¼ cup butter
1 teaspoon salt
½ cup whole wheat flour
2 to 2½ cups unbleached all-
    purpose flour
1 tablespoon cinnamon

Dissolve the yeast and brown sugar in the warm water. Combine the boiling water and rolled oats. Stir the coriander into the oat mixture and let cool slightly. In a food processor or mixer, combine yeast mixture, butter, salt, and cooled oat mixture. Add the whole wheat flour and beat in the all-purpose flour to make a stiff dough. Place in an oiled plastic bag or oiled bowl and turn to coat. Seal or cover and let rise 15 minutes.

Turn out onto a lightly floured board and knead for 10 minutes, until elastic and smooth as a baby's bottom. Let rise until doubled, about 1 hour. Punch dough down. Make a 8- × 12-inch rectangle. Sprinkle with the cinnamon. Starting with a short side, roll up tightly. Seal seam and ends. Grease an 8½- × 4½-inch loaf pan. Place dough in the pan. Let rise until doubled, about 45 minutes to 1 hour.

Preheat oven to 375 degrees. Bake 30 to 35 minutes, until loaf is golden and sounds hollow when tapped. Remove immediately from pan to cool on wire rack.

The loaf freezes, wrapped in plastic wrap and foil.

Sunday Bagels

MAKES 1 DOZEN

Boiling, then baking the bagel dough gives you a nice crust with a soft, chewy inside. Make these the day of serving or make them a day ahead and reheat or freeze them.

Although bagels can be eaten any way, my favorite way is split, buttered, and toasted for a late breakfast.

1 package active dry yeast
2 tablespoons sugar
1 cup warm water (105 to 115 degrees)

3 to 4 cups bread flour, unsifted
Cornmeal
2 teaspoons salt
2 tablespoons vegetable oil

Glaze
1 egg white, beaten, mixed with
    1 tablespoon cold water

Topping
Poppy seeds, sesame seeds, or
    coarse sea salt (optional)

Dissolve the yeast and sugar in the warm water in a medium mixing bowl or food processor bowl. Add the salt, vegetable oil, and 1 cup of the bread flour. Add the remaining flour, 1 cup at a time. Divide the dough into 12 equal pieces. Roll each piece of dough into a smooth cylinder, about 8 to 9 inches long, tapered at the ends. Dampen the ends lightly with water, Overlap the ends by ½ inch and press together to form a circle. Place the formed bagels on a baking sheet. Cover loosely and allow to rise in a warm, draft-free place for 30 minutes.

Preheat oven to 400 degrees. About 20 minutes into the rising stage, bring a large pot of water to the boil. Drop 4 bagels into the water, 1 at a time. The bagels may float on the surface of the water, sink, and then immediately rise and float. Reduce the heat to a simmer. Simmer 2 minutes, then turn the bagels and simmer 2 minutes more, 4 minutes in all. Remove the bagels with a slotted spoon or wire skimmer. Place on the cornmeal-lined baking sheet. Repeat the poaching process with the remaining 8 bagels. Place the baking sheet in the upper portion of the oven and bake the bagels for 10 minutes. Brush the top of each bagel lightly with the egg glaze and add a topping. Return to the oven and continue baking 20 minutes longer, until the bagels are crisp and golden brown. Remove from baking sheet and cool on a rack.

Other Bagel Toppings

- **fennel seeds or caraway seeds**
- **garlic or onion salt**
- **Parmesan cheese**
- **toasted chopped pecans, peanuts, walnuts, or almonds**

Crisp Dinner Rolls

MAKES 12 TO 16 ROLLS

What makes these rolls so incredibly flavorful, and time-consuming, is the four risings, as the dough attracts wild yeast from the air. I make them on a rainy day when I don't want to go out; I half-snooze and half-wake fooling with the dough off and on during the day. What renders the rolls crisp is the boiling water as they bake.

You may reduce the amount of time involved by omitting the first and second risings. You will lose flavor and texture, but gain time.

2½ to 3½ cups bread flour
1 teaspoon salt
2 packages active dry yeast

1½ teaspoons sugar
1 cup warm water (105 to 115 degrees)

Glaze
1 egg, beaten, mixed with 1 teaspoon water

Place 2½ cups of the flour and the salt in a food processor, mixer, or kitchen bowl. Dissolve the yeast and sugar in the warm water. Add to the flour and process or knead until incorporated and a soft dough forms, adding more of the remaining flour as needed. The dough should be elastic and smooth as a baby's bottom. Place in an oiled plastic bag or oiled bowl and turn to coat. Seal or cover and let rise, about 1 hour. Punch down. Cover again and let rise 15 minutes. Pull off pieces of dough that are the size of a large egg and weigh about 3 ounces. Shape into rolls. Place on a greased baking sheet, 1 inch apart, cover with plastic wrap, and let double, about 45 minutes to 1 hour. For the fourth rise, flatten the rolls. Then roll into an oblong 5 inches long and 1 inch wide, tapered at the ends. Place, seam side down, on the baking sheet. Cover with plastic wrap and let double again.

Preheat oven to 450 degrees. Place a pan of boiling water on the bottom oven rack.

With a razor blade or knife slash the rolls ½ inch deep. Brush with the glaze. Bake 20 minutes. Remove from the pan and cool on a rack. Serve with Herb Butter (page 364) if desired.

The rolls freeze, packed in an airtight plastic bag.

Basil Crescent Rolls

MAKES 24 ROLLS

Filled with an herb butter, these pretty rolls are a special addition to any meal or as a snack. You can speed up the rising of the bread by heating the milk. The kneaded dough is slightly stickier than a regular dough as each piece is rolled out into a thin circle on a floured board, which adds more flour. If you don't have fresh basil, you may substitute oregano, thyme, and/or marjoram. But if your herbs are not fresh, move on to another recipe.

1 package active dry yeast
2 tablespoons sugar
¼ cup warm water (105 to 115 degrees)
½ cup milk or buttermilk

¼ cup butter, melted
1 teaspoon salt
2 eggs, beaten
½ cup whole wheat flour
2 to 3½ cups bread flour

Herb Butter
1 tablespoon chopped fresh basil
⅓ cup butter, at room temperature

⅓ cup freshly grated imported Parmesan cheese

Glaze
1 egg, beaten, mixed with 1 teaspoon water

In a mixer bowl or food processor, dissolve the yeast and 1 tablespoon of the sugar in the warm water. Add the remaining sugar, the milk, butter, salt, eggs, and whole wheat flour and beat until blended. Add the bread flour, ½ cup at a time, to make a smooth but still loose and slightly sticky dough. Place in an oiled plastic bag or oiled bowl and let rise in a warm place until doubled.

Punch dough down and divide into 3 pieces. On a floured board, roll out each piece, 1 at a time, to make a circle 10 inches in diameter. Mix the basil, butter, and Parmesan cheese. Spread ⅓ of the herb butter over each circle, then cut each circle into 8 triangles. Roll up from the long side of the triangle to the point. Pull the ends in to make a crescent shape. Place on greased baking sheets. Let rise until doubled, about 15 minutes.

Preheat oven to 375 degrees. Brush the rolls with the glaze. Bake on top rack of the oven about 15 minutes or until golden.

The rolls freeze, wrapped in plastic wrap and foil.

Currant Oat Wheat Rolls

MAKES 16 TO 20 ROLLS

Some memories last forever. Once I took these on a rainy day right out of the oven over to my friend Dudley's when he was just home from a trip. He split the warm roll in half, buttered it, and said, "Ah, this would be great with honey." So he ate his drizzled with honey, as we sipped hot tea with sliced oranges.

I love the delicious little currants in these rolls, but they can be hard to find. Dark raisins are a good substitute. The dough may be made in the food processor or mixer, with the currants kneaded in by hand at the end of the kneading; it is, however, a heavy dough and a half-recipe would work more easily if using a machine.

2 packages active dry yeast
1 tablespoon sugar
2½ cups warm water (105 to 115 degrees)
2 cups currants, plumped in 1 cup boiling water, drained
⅓ cup dark molasses

¼ cup oil
1 tablespoon salt
1 cup rolled oats, quick or old-fashioned
3 cups whole wheat flour
3½ to 5 cups bread flour

Glaze
1 egg, beaten, mixed with
    1 teaspoon water

In a large bowl, dissolve the yeast and sugar in the warm water. Stir in the currants, molasses, oil, salt, oats, and whole wheat flour. Gradually stir in enough of the bread flour to make a stiff dough. The molasses will make it feel tacky, but it should not stick to your hands. Knead to make a soft dough elastic and smooth as a baby's bottom. Place in an oiled plastic bag or oiled bowl and turn to coat. Partially seal the bag or cover the bowl with plastic wrap or a damp towel. Let rise in a warm place for 1 hour, or until doubled. Punch down, turn onto a floured board, and knead briefly. Shape into 16 to 20 rolls and place on greased baking sheets. Let rise in a warm place until doubled.

Preheat oven to 350 degrees. Brush the rolls with the glaze. Bake 25 to 30 minutes, or until rolls are golden and sound hollow when tapped. Let cool on wire racks. Serve as rolls, or slice and use for sandwiches or toast.

The rolls freeze, wrapped in an airtight plastic bag.

Orange Rolls

MAKES 18 ROLLS

Turn a cloudy day into a bright one with these light and easy-to-make brunch or luncheon breads. A lovely aroma, reminiscent of tiny orange blossoms, fills the kitchen as the dough bakes. And the orange butter enhances the delicate orange flavor of the rolls.

1 package active dry yeast
3 tablespoons sugar
½ cup warm water (105 to 115 degrees)
1 teaspoon salt
Grated peel, no white attached, of 1 orange

¼ teaspoon orange extract
3 tablespoons vegetable oil
1 egg white
2 to 3 cups bread flour

Orange Butter
1 tablespoon undiluted orange juice concentrate
¼ cup butter, softened

1 cup Confectioners' sugar
Grated peel, no white attached, of 1 orange

Dissolve the yeast and 1 tablespoon of the sugar in the warm water. Place the salt, orange peel, the remaining 2 tablespoons of the sugar, orange extract, oil, and egg white in a food processor or mixer. Add 1 cup of the flour, then the remaining flour, ½ cup at a time. Process or knead by hand to make a soft dough elastic and smooth as a baby's bottom. Place in an oiled plastic bag or oiled bowl and turn to coat. Seal or cover and let rise until doubled. Punch down. Grease the muffin tins and put in pieces of dough big enough to half-fill the muffin tins. Let double again.

Preheat oven to 350 degrees. Bake the rolls 12 to 15 minutes. Remove from tins and cool on wire racks.

To make the orange butter, beat the orange juice concentrate, butter, sugar, and orange peel together until light. Serve with the hot rolls.

The rolls freeze in an airtight plastic bag.

Spiral Olive Rolls

MAKES 10 ROLLS

One of these rolls is almost like having a mini pizza, with a lot of flavor packed into a beautiful, colorful spiral. Each roll is crisp on the outside, tender on the inside, with a burst of taste.

Dried tomatoes come in a variety of forms. If packed in oil, drain and chop them. (You may use the oil as part of the oil in the recipe.) If using vacuum-packed dried tomatoes, place them in boiling water for 30 seconds, drain, and chop. The oil-packed dried tomatoes make a redder filling than do the vacuum-packed ones, which start out dark and stay that way.

2½ to 3½ cups bread flour
1½ teaspoons sugar
1 teaspoon salt
1 package active dry yeast
5 tablespoons olive oil
¾ cup hot water (120 degrees)
¼ cup butter, softened
½ cup freshly grated imported Parmesan cheese

1¼ cups chopped ripe olives
4 tablespoons chopped dried tomatoes
1 tablespoon Dijon mustard
1 tablespoon chopped fresh basil
1 tablespoon chopped fresh rosemary

Place 2½ cups of the flour, the sugar, salt, yeast, and olive oil in a bowl or food processor. Add the hot water. Process or knead by hand to make a soft dough, adding more of the remaining flour as needed.

(continued)

The dough should be elastic and smooth as a baby's bottom. Place in an oiled plastic bag or oiled bowl and turn to coat. Seal or cover and let rise until doubled. Punch down.

Roll out the dough on a floured surface into a 14- by 10-inch rectangle. Brush with the butter. In a bowl, stir together the Parmesan, olives, tomatoes, mustard, basil, and rosemary. Spread on the dough all the way to the edge.

Starting from a long side, roll up the dough, and pinch the seam to seal the roll. Slice into 10 pieces. Lay the spirals on their sides on a baking sheet and place the baking sheet over a large bowl of hot water or in a warm place for 30 minutes, until the rolls are puffy.

Preheat oven to 375 degrees. Bake the rolls 25 to 30 minutes, or until golden. Let cool slightly and serve warm.

- **To serve as appetizers, cut the rectangle in half lengthwise, roll up each piece as above, and then slice the dough ¾ inch thick.**

The rolls freeze in an airtight plastic bag. To reheat, wrap in aluminum foil and bake in a 350-degree oven for 10 to 12 minutes. Serve at once.

Quick Breads

Barbara Robinson's Cheddar Muffins

MAKES 6 DOZEN MINI MUFFINS

My friend Barbara Robinson serves these bite-sized muffins frequently for luncheons and special occasions—even parties. I often pop them out of the freezer as a light, tasty accompaniment to soups and salads as well. The muffins can be made ahead to give as gifts. They freeze beautifully; reheat in the oven.

3 cups self-rising flour (see below)
6 tablespoons cold butter, cut into bits

¾ pound extra sharp Cheddar cheese, coarsely grated
1½ cups milk

To make self-rising flour, add 1½ teaspoons baking powder and ½ teaspoon salt for each cup of flour.

Preheat oven to 425 degrees. Spray mini-muffin tins with non-stick cooking oil.

Place the flour in a bowl and cut in the butter. Stir in the Cheddar cheese and add enough milk to make a sticky dough. At this time the dough may be refrigerated, covered. Bring to room temperature. Spoon dough into the tins. Bake in the middle of the oven 10 to 15 minutes, until pale golden brown. Remove the muffins from tins and cool on a rack.

The muffins may be frozen in a plastic bag.

Pumpkin Bread

MAKES 2 LOAVES

This pumpkin combination makes for a refreshing change, especially over the holidays, when I love having it on hand as a tea bread.

3 cups sifted all-purpose flour
2 teaspoons baking powder
2 teaspoons baking soda
1½ teaspoons cinnamon
½ teaspoon ground ginger
½ teaspoon freshly grated
    nutmeg
1 teaspoon salt

½ cup vegetable oil
2 cups sugar
4 eggs
1 (14½-ounce) canned pumpkin
    (do not use pumpkin pie
    filling)
1 cup raisins

Preheat oven to 350 degrees. Grease two 8½- × 4½- × 2½-inch loaf pans. Line the bottoms with wax paper and grease it.

Into a bowl, sift together the flour, baking powder, soda, cinnamon, ginger, nutmeg, and salt, and set aside. In a large bowl or food processor, mix together the oil and sugar. Add the eggs, one at a time, beating well after each addition. Add the flour alternately with the pumpkin, beating well or processing after each addition. Stir in the raisins. Do not overmix. Divide between pans. Place pans in the middle of the oven and bake 1 hour, or until a toothpick inserted in the centers comes out clean.

Remove from the pans and let cool on wire rack.

The bread freezes, wrapped in plastic wrap and foil.

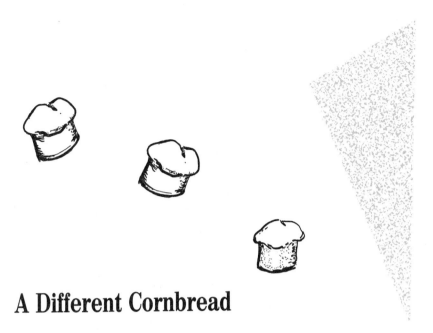

A Different Cornbread

Just about anything can be added to vary cornbread—one of the easiest quick breads to fix. These spices give it a very exciting flavor. It goes very well with hearty meats and stews.

¼ cup melted shortening or
    vegetable oil
2 cups self-rising cornmeal or
    cornmeal mix
1¼ cups milk

1 egg, beaten
1½ teaspoons cracked fennel
    seed or cumin seed
1½ teaspoons cracked black
    pepper

Preheat oven to 450 degrees.

Pour the shortening into a 10-inch cast-iron skillet. Place the skillet in the hot oven.

Place the self-rising cornmeal or mix in a bowl and whisk in the milk and egg. Add the fennel and pepper and stir until thoroughly blended. Stir the hot shortening into the batter, then pour the batter into the hot skillet. Bake 15 to 20 minutes, until done. Serve piping hot with butter.

Cornbread with Red Peppers
- **Omit the fennel and cracked pepper from the cornmeal mixture and stir in 2 red bell peppers, roasted (page 99), seeded, and cut into strips.**

Cheese Sablés

MAKES 15 TO 20

Sablé—pronounced sa-blay—is a French short crust pastry. Made with cheese, these are golden, munchy treats. It's no wonder they are so popular! They are buttery, cheese-flavored, and crisp. Use them as a snack, as a garnish for soups, or an accompaniment to dips.

¾ cup flour
4 tablespoons butter
2 ounces freshly grated
    imported Parmesan or dry-
    aged Cheddar cheese

Salt
Freshly ground black pepper
1 egg, lightly beaten

Preheat oven to 375 degrees.

Sift the flour into a bowl. With a food processor, spatula, or your hands, cut in the butter until it resembles fine bread crumbs. Add the cheese and season to taste. Press the mixture together and make a dough. Sprinkle the surface lightly with flour and wrap it in plastic wrap. Chill at least 30 minutes.

Roll out the dough on a lightly floured surface or between sheets of plastic wrap into a fairly long oblong about ¼ inch thick. If the dough sticks, ease it free from the board with a spatula. Cut 2-inch wide strips, brush them with the beaten egg, and cut them again on the diagonal to form small diamonds, or cut into small rounds. Place on a non-stick baking sheet or one that has been lined with parchment paper. Bake 12 to 15 minutes until light brown. Cool slightly, then remove to a rack.

The pastries freeze in an airtight plastic bag. Recrisp if necessary in an oven set on low.

Cinnatoast

SERVES 2

There is nothing like oven-cooked toast, a forgotten treat from the days before toasters. The buttery center of the toast is soft and the rest crisp. Accompany with hot chocolate made with hot milk. I like this as a special mid-day treat or late at night when I can't sleep.

2 slices white loaf bread
2 to 4 tablespoons butter, at
   room temperature

Sugar
Cinnamon

Preheat oven to 400 degrees or preheat broiler.

Place the bread on a cookie sheet and brown on one side. Turn. Spread butter on the untoasted side. Mix sugar with cinnamon to taste and sprinkle on the butter. Place the toast back in oven until bubbly and soft in the center and brown around the edges. Cut each slice on a diagonal into 2 or 3 pieces.

Melba Toast

MAKES 30 TOASTS

Melba toast is a handy way to use up stale or old bread and rolls.

3 dinner rolls

Preheat oven to 225 degrees.

Cut the rolls into thin slices and place in one layer on a baking sheet. Bake until crisp and the edges curl up. Cool.

The toasts freeze in an airtight plastic bag. Reheat in a 350-oven for 10 minutes.

Dried Tomato/Garlic Bread

MAKES 40 PIECES

By itself this is a good snack. Or, serve it as an hors d'oeuvre or as an accompaniment to soup or salad.

10 slices thin sandwich bread, crusts removed and cut into quarters, eighths, or rounds
5 tablespoons butter or olive oil, or a combination of both
5 tablespoons chopped dried tomatoes
2 garlic cloves, chopped
1 teaspoon chopped fresh basil or thyme
3 tablespoons freshly grated imported Parmesan cheese
Salt
Freshly ground black pepper

Preheat oven to 350 degrees.

Toast bread very lightly on both sides. Purée the butter, tomatoes, garlic, herb, and cheese in a blender or food processor. Add salt and pepper to taste. Spread on toasts. Bake for about 5 minutes.

Herb Butter

MAKES 2¹/₂ CUPS

When I had a large herb garden at my restaurant in Social Circle, I used to pick fresh herbs, chop them, then mix them with butter. I never had a set amount of how much to use, except for sage, which I don't normally combine with butter because of its overpowering flavor. Try thyme, oregano, rosemary, tarragon, and/or parsley. Reduce the recipe considerably to experiment. This is a good way to see which herbs you like.

2 cups butter
½ cup chopped fresh mixed
    herbs

Combine butter and herbs in food processor. Turn off and on to mix. Using a pastry bag, pipe into rosettes, or place in little pots to serve. Or shape into logs, wrap in plastic wrap, and refrigerate. Slice off amount desired.

    The butter freezes.

Bibliography

BERANBAUM, ROSE LEVY. *The Cake Bible.* New York: William Morrow and Company, Inc., 1988.

BUGIALLI, GIULIANO. *Bugialli on Pasta.* New York: Simon and Schuster, 1988.

————.*Classic Techniques of Italian Cooking.* New York: Simon and Schuster, 1982.

CALIFORNIA OLIVE INDUSTRY. *Quick and Easy Meals with California Ripe Olives.* Vol. 3. Fresno, CA.

CARRIER, ROBERT. *A Taste of Morocco.* New York: Clarkson N. Potter, 1985.

CHILD, JULIA. *Julia Child & More Company.* New York: Alfred A. Knopf, 1979.

CHILD, JULIA. *The Way to Cook.* New York: Alfred A. Knopf, 1989.

CLAYTON, BERNARD. *Bernard Clayton's New Book of Breads.* New York: Simon and Schuster, 1987.

CULTURED COOK THE. *Yes! You Can Cook with Yogurt.* White Plains, NY: The Dannon Information Center, 1989.

DAIR, HUGUETTE. "From Huguette Dair's Kitchen," MA: Yankee, 1990.

DIXIE CRYSTALS SUGAR. *Homemade Good News.* Vols. IX and X. 1989.

DAVIDSON, ALAN. *Seafood: A Connoisseur's Guide and Cookbook.* New York: Simon and Schuster, 1989.

HARRIS, VALENTINA. *An Italian Farmhouse.* New York: Simon and Schuster, 1990.

HEATTER, MAIDA. *Book of Great Desserts.* New York: Alfred A. Knopf, 1974.

HOFFMAN, MABLE, and GAR. *Frozen Yogurt.* Tucson: Fisher Books, 1990.

JUNIOR LEAGUE OF JACKSON, MISSISSIPPI. *Southern Sideboards.* Jackson, MS: 1977.

KAFKA, BARBARA. *Microwave Gourmet.* New York: William Morrow and Company, Inc., 1987.

LIONGO, PINO. *A Tuscan in the Kitchen.* New York: Clarkson N. Potter, 1988.

MANDEL, ABBEY. *More Taste Than Time.* New York: Simon and Schuster, 1988.

McCUNE, KELLY. *The Art of Grilling.* New York: Harper and Row, 1990.

McGEE, HAROLD. *On Food and Cooking.* New York: Macmillan Publishing, 1984.

McMILLAN, CECIL. *The Once in a Blue Moon Cookbook.*

MONTAGUE, PROSPER. *New Larousse Gastronomique.* Twickenham, England: Hamlyn, 1960.

MORGAN, JINX, and JEFF. *The Sugar Mill Hotel Cookbook.* Tortola, British Virgin Islands: The Morgan Corporation, Ltd., 1987.

NATHAN, JOAN. *The Jewish Holiday Kitchen.* New York: Schocken Books, 1988.

PELLAPRAT, HENRI PAUL. *The Great Book of French Cuisine.* Edited by Rene Kramer and David White. New York: Thomas Y. Crowell Co., 1971.

PÉPIN, JACQUES. *The Art of Cooking.* 2 Vols. New York: Alfred A. Knopf, 1988.

PRUDHOMME, PAUL. *Chef Paul Prudhomme's Louisiana Kitchen.* New York: William Morrow and Company, Inc., 1984.

RECIPE CLUB OF ST. PAUL'S GREEK ORTHODOX CATHEDRAL, THE. *The Complete Book of Greek Cooking.* New York: Harper and Row, 1990.

ROOT, WAVERLY. *The Best of Italian Cooking.* New York: Grosset and Dunlap, 1974.

WALDRON, MAGGIE. *Fire and Smoke.* San Francisco: 101 Productions, 1978.

WILLAN, ANNE. *Classic French Cooking.* New York: Pantheon Books, 1986.

————.*La Varenne Pratique.* New York: Crown Publishers, 1989.

YANILAN-ANEND, THERESA KARAS. *The Complete Greek Cookbook.* New York: Avenel Books, 1970.

Index